If Only I
Had Told

If Only I Had Told

The shocking true story from the girl
at the heart of Orkney's satanic sex ring

ESTHER W.

EBURY
PRESS

7 9 10 8

First published in 2013 by Ebury Press, an imprint of Ebury Publishing
A Random House Group company

The Random House Group Limited Reg. No. 954009

Addresses for companies within the Random House Group can be
found at www.randomhouse.co.uk

A CIP catalogue record for this book is available from
the British Library

The Random House Group Limited supports The Forest Stewardship
Council® (FSC®), the leading international forest-certification
organisation. Our books carrying the FSC label are printed on
FSC®-certified paper. FSC is the only forest-certification scheme
supported by the leading environmental organisations, including
Greenpeace. Our paper procurement policy can be found at
www.randomhouse.co.uk/environment

MIX
Paper from
responsible sources
FSC® C016897

Printed and bound by CPI Group (UK) Ltd, Croydon, CR0 4YY

ISBN 9780091950156

To buy books by your favourite authors and register for offers visit
www.randomhouse.co.uk

For my two boys, thank you for teaching me
how to be a mother.

And to my own mother, who realised too late
what being a mother means.

Nothing to Worry About

27 February 1991, South Ronaldsay, Orkney Islands

I'm packing my bag for work, when the rolling crunch of tyres upon the gravel outside startles me. I glance at the clock, it's just before seven – my taxi doesn't usually get here until half past.

I go to let the driver know I won't be long. But as I get to the door, ice plunges through my stomach. From the window, I see two police cars, fit to bursting. Before they are fully stopped, officers in black are swarming our house, hammering at the door, checking the handle and peering through windows. I spin round to Mum who's asleep on the couch – her temporary bed for the last three months – and forcefully shake her arm.

'What is it?' she murmurs, confused and bleary-eyed.

'It's the police!' I whisper urgently.

Her eyes stretch wide in fearful panic and she's instantly awake, scrambling to her feet. My older brother stomps downstairs, dazed and scratching at his head. 'What's going on?'

As if in answer a man's voice orders 'Open up. Police!'

The thump of my heart pounds through me and we stare

bewilderedly into one another's frightened faces. Mum looks around wildly – as if in search of an escape route. We all know that once that door is opened, everything will change – again. Silently, my brother steps forward and turns the handle. Five police officers tumble in, filling every space in our small hall – two of them armed with black plastic bin liners. Waving a piece of paper at us, a chunky red-cheeked policeman announces, 'We have a warrant to search this property for evidence!'

A couple of them immediately start looking about, while Mum, my brother and I tremble and stare at the police surrounding us. 'What's all this about?' asks my brother, his steady voice betrayed by his sheet white face. A slim police-woman with cropped dark-blond hair surveys us slowly and with a smile that doesn't reach her eyes, icily replies, 'It's nothing for you to worry about.'

'Right,' the red-faced policeman interjects, 'after my colleagues and I have searched this property, you will all be coming down to the police station for questioning. Understood?'

We nod dumbly, without understanding. Then with relief I remember. 'Oh, I'm sorry,' I hesitantly pipe up, 'I can't come to the police station today. I have to go to work.'

'Not today you won't!' he replies firmly.

'But … but I have to, my taxi will be turning up in a minute,' I stammer.

'Then cancel it!' he demands irritably, before heading for the door.

Mum, who has sunk back down to the couch, suddenly leaps up and shrieks, 'But what are you looking for? Evidence for what?'

Wheeling back round, the red-faced policeman replies darkly, 'That, Mrs W, will be revealed at the station.'

The police officers' radios beep and rasp with urgent-sounding messages. It seems we are wanted at the police station for 8 a.m exactly. A policeman is stationed outside the bathroom as my mum and brother are allowed to quickly wash and get dressed. Another stands guard in the kitchen, where I've been ordered to sit and wait. He doesn't seem much older than me, and paces about awkwardly, looking at things, trying to make conversation. 'Oh, my aunt has a table like that,' he tries, then 'Where do you work?'

I don't want to talk. The TV is on, but I don't hear a word, I stare blindly at it – attempting to tune everything out.

My mother, brother and I are ready to go, but the police officers haven't finished their search, so we sit on the sofa in silence. The programme on the TV goes to the weather, causing our police guard to cheerfully chirrup, 'It looks like it's going to be a nice day!'

My brother stares up at him incredulously, and mumbles, 'Well, not for us it isn't!'

Their plastic bin liners remain baggy and the red-cheeked policeman's face is serious as he shows us the evidence they are taking with them; a used postcard of the Standing Stones, an ancient circular stone structure, which is a famous tourist attraction in Orkney, and a video of the Clint Eastwood film, *Dirty Harry*.

By ten to eight we are speeding the 38 miles to Kirkwall Police Station, glimpsing the Standing Stones on the way. Orkney's vast early morning sky flashes by in steel blues and moody purples as she is violently shaken awake. In this endless desolate landscape there are no passers-by to scream out to for help – we might as well be alone in the world. The icy grey Atlantic Ocean furls up explosively as we cross the bridge to the Orkney mainland. In blurry dark green fields black crows squawk angrily at being disturbed before taking flight from their night-watch posts, scattering clumps of sleepy cattle from eerily empty roads.

When we arrive, cars jostle for space in the police car park. We are escorted to a reception area and ordered to wait on grey plastic chairs in front of the main desk. One of the police officers with us talks to the man behind it, who throws us an annoyed glance. 'I didn't realise there'd be three of them, we just don't have the room,' he grumbles.

My stomach lurches at the sound of distressed cries and muffled voices that bounce from echoing rooms and I feel myself flinch as countless police officers, files tucked under their arms, stride purposefully about.

Although we sit next to one another, we don't speak; we are each locked inside our own bubble of fear. But we don't have long to wait before a lanky stern policeman approaches and points at Mum. 'You, come with me!' he commands. Mum hesitates, looking around at us uncertainly. Stepping forward he impatiently grips her arm, hoisting her to her feet. 'You can wait in a cell,' he says, marching her from us.

My brother and I become even more frightened and begin whispering frantically, trying to figure out what's going on.

Minutes later the lanky policeman returns. 'And you!' he barks. I jump to my feet and follow him down a narrow darkened corridor. Ahead, he opens a door. 'Wait in there!'

4

he orders and watches me tentatively enter the tiny dark room. The door bangs shut and I am alone.

I find myself inside a small dark messy office, nothing like the interviewing rooms I've seen on TV. I strain to see through the dirty barred window that looks out to the front of the station. The desk I've been ordered to sit at is weighed down by fat green files. The room is made smaller still by tall grey metal cabinets lining the walls. My stomach churns while I wait to find out what I've done wrong. Wishing I was anywhere but here, my eyes sting and soon hot tears course freely down my cheeks.

I've only been waiting a few minutes when I jump as a tall pale policeman, with thinning sandy hair, darts into the room. He eyes me suspiciously, as if he's caught me doing something I shouldn't. I look away, wiping my eyes on my sleeve. From behind the desk he informs me in a broad Scottish accent, 'I'm PC McGrath and I'll be interviewing you today. But we'll have to wait for my colleague to join us.' He opens the file he's carried in with him and focuses intently upon it.

I'm bursting for the toilet and soon the pressure becomes too much. 'Sorry,' I say quietly. He looks up testily, as if surprised I talk. 'Can I go to the toilet please?'

'Fine,' he huffs, thudding his file shut.

He knocks and waits, making sure the Ladies is empty, before letting me go in. 'I'll be out here waiting,' he assures me, 'so don't try any funny business.'

I shake my head, confused at what funny business he thinks I might try in there.

Returning to the room, we once again wait. Me, shifting about uncomfortably on the hard chair and him becoming increasingly irritated. His jaw is clenched tight as he impatiently rifles through the file he's long stopped reading. Inhaling sharply he checks his watch, before leaping up and striding across the room, where he pokes his head into the corridor. When, once again, he finds nobody there, he slinks back and resignedly sags into his seat, before doing it again a few minutes later. We've been waiting for about 40 minutes, when he sits up decidedly. 'Right, I think we've waited long enough, we'll just have to start without her!'

PC McGrath eyes me squarely across the desk and I straighten up. This is it; I'm about to find out what I'm accused of. I confirm my full name and date of birth, which stops him. 'So what ... wait a minute ... you're only 17?'

'Yes,' I reply sullenly, desperate for him to keep going and get this over with.

He frowns and bites his lower lip, closing the file. 'Mmm,' he murmurs vaguely. 'I'll just have to check something.'

Jumping to his feet, he hurries from the room. When he returns a few minutes later, I sense a shift in the way he is with me – more gentle. 'Well, Esther,' he says, curling his lips into a forced smile, 'I'm going to be asking you some questions, do you understand? Do you know a Reverend Timothy Bracegirdle?'

'Yes,' I eagerly reply, 'I know him ... and his wife, Fran.' I look at him, surprised he would ask me that, but he's looking down.

'How long have you known Reverend Bracegirdle?'

I try working it out. We usually only call him Tim, so it seems all official-like to hear him being called Reverend Bracegirdle. I think back, wanting to be precise for him.

'Well, probably about three years. Yes, I would say three years.'

'What do you think of Reverend Bracegirdle, as a person?'

Timothy's pudgy moon face framed by fuzzy white hair, his little half-round spectacles perched on the end of his bulbous nose comes to mind. I imagine him blustering about in his friendly, distracted by bigger things, way. 'He's all right, I s'pose. He only talks to my mum or older people.'

PC McGrath nods and waits, like he's expecting more.

'Yes, he's okay,' I add, trying to sound helpful.

'Right,' he mutters, his voice trailing, before continuing. 'Well, have you – and I want you to answer this carefully, Esther – have you ever seen him with his crook?'

I think hard, asking myself, have I seen Timothy with a crook? But I can't think what a crook is. Then I realise something and feel excited. 'Do you mean have I seen him at Crook? That's where I live. Crook Farm, do you mean that?'

'No,' he frowns irritably, 'not at Crook Farm. Not anywhere. I meant, have you seen him holding his crook?'

I try to think harder. I don't want PC McGrath thinking I'm stupid, but I must ask, 'What ... what is a crook?' I stammer.

Looking back to his file, his face floods with relief, 'No, sorry, my mistake. I should have said hook. You know, a long piece of metal with a hook on the end. Have you seen Timothy holding and using his hook?'

'Oh!' I say. 'Um, no, I haven't seen him with one of those.'

His face falls and I wish I could have told him something more constructive.

'Okay, that's fine. Where's the quarry?'

'The quarry? What quarry?'

'I'll put it differently. Have you been to the quarry, with friends and family?'

'No,' I shake my head vigorously. I'm certain I would know if I'd been to a quarry.

An excruciatingly long silence follows as I watch PC McGrath sucking in his cheeks and frowning into the distance. My stomach drops and I tear at my nails; I'm trying to grow them but today doesn't count. I know I've disappointed him; I don't want him to be unhappy with me.

He studies his file, while I squirm – I must try to answer the next question better.

'Right,' he starts sternly, his full-beam focus causing my cheeks to burn. 'If there was music at the quarry, what kind of music do you think it would be?'

A prickly, panicky sensation threatens to overwhelm me, as I frantically search my mind for the kind of music people might play at a quarry.

Growing impatient, he adds, 'Well, what kind of music do you play at home?'

That's easy; we haven't played music at home for over three months. But I don't tell him that, instead I simply state, 'We don't play music at home.'

His shoulders drop and he releases a long breath.

Another agonising silence stretches out. To my relief when he speaks again, instead of asking me more questions, he reveals what today is about. 'Look, Esther, we really need your help. Some extremely serious allegations have been made against Reverend Bracegirdle.' He watches me until I become uncomfortable. 'It has been alleged that Timothy is the head of a satanic sex ring, which operates at night around a quarry in South Ronaldsay.'

He is waiting for me to say something. My mouth is open, but I don't make a sound. I'm staring back at him wide-eyed. 'Timothy?' I manage to splutter.

'Yes,' he replies grimly, 'Reverend Timothy Bracegirdle.'

'Oh,' I say and we return to silence, as no matter how hard I try, I can't imagine Timothy doing stuff like that. This just doesn't make any sense!

'Well, what I need from you is …' But PC McGrath is interrupted by a harrowing scream from outside the station.

I leap up and rush to the small window. 'If you'll give me my babies back, I'll say anything you want! Please just give me my babies back!' begs a woman between heartbroken sobs.

My blood turns icy as in numb disbelief I recognise the thin dark woman from her accent; she is probably the only American in Orkney. Fear flares up in me as I watch Susan pitifully throwing her slight frame against the giant bolted doors of the police station. I spin round to PC McGrath, my breath shallow and fast, as frightened tears burst from my eyes. 'What's happening? What does she mean?'

He returns my fearful stare and even the freckles upon his face appear to have paled. He grips my elbow and tries to guide me back to my chair. 'It's nothing for you to worry about. Come on, come away.'

But I can't take my eyes from Susan. Her pain shoots through me, as she drops to her knees, beseeching the cold silent building. 'Please,' her weakened voice cries, 'tell me what I have to say?'

What could she be talking about? I wonder frantically, before a thunderous revelation crashes in on me. There is everything for me to worry about. This is about my family.

Sobs overwhelm me and I turn away; I may as well be kicking her myself. I stare at PC McGrath, determined to discover the truth. 'This is about my brothers and sisters, isn't it?'

He looks down for a moment. 'Yes,' he quietly confesses. 'It is.'

'Well, what about them?' I demand, my voice loud and angry.

His hard policeman facade dissolves. 'Well, as you know your brothers and sisters were taken into care three months ago, on suspicion of sibling abuse.' He waits for my agreement, but I don't give it – I'm too busy fighting the anger rising up from the pit of my stomach. He nods to himself. 'Well, anyway, there haven't been any sibling abuse allegations made. But it seems we have unearthed something worse. Something much worse! Your siblings have revealed that there is a major satanic sex ring operating at a quarry in South Ronaldsay.'

I feel myself begin to shake. This is serious. It isn't a joke. This really is happening. My head swims, as PC McGrath goes on, as if recounting a story I already know. 'The satanic sex ring takes place around a quarry that is near one of your family friends' houses. As well as your own family, there are four other families involved, that we know of so far. The adults and children dance around the quarry to music and then ...' he draws in a deep breath, as if even he's having difficulty believing his words, 'well ... the minister and the adults have sex with the children,' he says, clapping his hands in a that's that, way.

'No,' I gasp, 'no, it isn't true. None of this is true!'

'Well, whether you want to believe it or not Esther, it is true. The children from the four other families were forcibly removed from their parents this morning and flown out of Orkney to Scotland. They've all been placed, like your own siblings, into care. Where they'll undergo investigation,' he concludes matter-of-factly.

I know the drill; I've been here before. The last time was only three months ago, but that was with my brothers and sisters, not with other people's children. 'So Susan was screaming for her children?' I ask tearfully.

'Yes ... yes, I suppose she was,' he replies quietly, dropping his head.

Susan's cries have stopped and I try to straighten my thoughts, but my head is too full, as though I'm drowning beneath too much information. Although the policeman has explained everything, I still don't understand a thing.

PC McGrath suddenly seems hesitant, he looks down and fiddles with his pen, and when he continues I know why. 'I have to ask you this, Esther. I know it's a very personal question, but ... but have you been sexually assaulted by Reverend Timothy Bracegirdle in a satanic ring?'

I meet his eyes. Hasn't he heard a word I've said? 'No, no I haven't,' I reply weakly.

After six exhausting hours of questioning, I'm released into the afternoon light. It has a surreal quality about it, as if the time spent in there never happened at all and I'm still waiting for the taxi that will take me to work.

When I meet with the rest of my family we compare notes. With mounting horror we piece together how huge this investigation is. Not only have Susan and John had their two children taken, but Glynnis and George – who have been very supportive friends of our family – have had two of theirs snatched. Mrs Millet from up the road, whose older daughter was a great childhood friend of mine, has had all three of her younger ones taken, and poor Mrs Hughes – with an ill husband – has had both of hers stolen. In total the police and social workers have snatched nine children from four families on South Ronaldsay. Timothy Bracegirdle remains at the police station, still being interrogated about being the master of a satanic sex ring. But by far the worst part for me and my family is that the evidence used to seize the other families' children came from allegations the police claim were made by my younger brothers and sisters.

The following day passes in a blur of phone calls to the other families, offering to help in any way we can. We spend hours trying to work out how this has happened. Can it be just coincidence that all of the families whose children have been stolen are incomers – or what in Orkney are called 'white settlers'? Most crucially, though, all were family friends of ours and played a part in trying to get our family's children returned. Whether that was sending cards and letters to our children, or signing petitions of support to those in power, these families are paying the ultimate price for their friendship and loyalty.

A public meeting is hurriedly convened. Most of my family believe we should stay away, as we don't want to intrude on the recent raw pain of the other families. But

Mum insists on going, believing she must let people know the truth.

As Mum meekly shuffles into the tightly packed community centre, she finds a seat at the back. The air is thick with angry fear and a constant crying. Mum's heart races and her stomach ripples with anxious knots. She begins to wonder if this was such a good idea, but firmly reminds herself why she must do this. Craning her neck to catch a glimpse of a familiar face, she can't – as all the parents of the newly stolen children are seated in the front row.

When everyone has settled down, the doctor's wife climbs on to the stage. She recounts in horrified gasps what happened early yesterday morning, while most people slept peacefully in their beds. She asks who Orkney Social Work Department think they are, to steal decent folks' children? And how, with the law on their side, could they concoct such an incredible story of satanic sex abuse rings in South Ronaldsay, where everyone knows everyone else's business – sometimes a little too much! 'Where has all of this come from?' she demands.

Mum realises it's now or never. Using the chair in front of her to help steady herself, she quietly interrupts. 'Uh, may I say something?' All eyes swivel to her. Mum is instantly recognisable by her golden arm bangles, olive complexion and long dark hair. There is an expectant hush, so she continues, 'I just wanted to say the allegations of a satanic sex ring are alleged to have come from my children.' There is an audible gasp. 'But,' Mum goes on, her voice rising, 'they aren't true, none of them. It's the Orkney Social Work Department, they want to take my children off me and they'll use anything to get their way. At first they said there was older sibling abuse, but they couldn't find any evidence. So now they are making up lies about a satanic sex ring.' Mum looks around, and a sea of horrified accusing faces glare back. The atmosphere has become darker and pulsates with barely concealed hostility. 'I ... I just ...' Mum struggles on '... wanted to say I'm sorry,' she finishes, before collapsing into her chair, regretting every word.

The doctor's wife surveys the room for a moment. 'Well,' she breathes, 'it has become apparent this evening that there are two very different cases here. But thank you all the same for your input.'

Mum suddenly feels isolated in this crowded room. She had been hoping, like the rest of our family, that people would realise we are fighting a common enemy. But it's common knowledge that three short years ago my father was imprisoned for physical and sexual abuse. Now, to everybody on the outside of our family, it seems that his disturbed and abused children are making up satanic sex ring allegations, ruining poor innocent people's lives. And whether we like it or not, we are being aligned with our enemy – the Orkney Social Work Department.

So Mum stays silent and listens as the parents of the recently snatched children recount the traumatic events of yesterday morning. One mum recalls how she was woken by the sound of screeching cars outside her house, which was immediately surrounded by social workers and police. She was watched as she got her children dressed. She tried to ask the social workers why they were doing this, but they just said they had reason to believe her children were being abused. They explained they were being immediately removed and taken to a place of safety. Welling up, she looks around the room and cries out, 'We were beside ourselves, me and my children!' She was then taken to the police station and questioned about a quarry, music and other strange things before being dumped back home, many hours later, childless. Others speak of their houses being turned upside down by police – as ours was – without knowing what the police were looking for. All the parents recall not being allowed to phone anyone about what was happening to them. They relate the heartbreaking torture of their children being forcibly ripped from their arms and taken from them, their little ones allowed none of their personal possessions and nothing to remind them of home.

Mum listens in agonised silence, swallowing hard and biting her lip, her arms folded tightly, not daring to share her own heart-wrenching memories. She doesn't say how her own children have been torn from her *twice*. Mum has heard the message loud and clear: your children are Orkney's devil children; we are speaking about our innocent children – children who *deserve* justice. So Mum stays mute, her heart aching beneath the weight of her own recent tragedy.

The following day I see John – one of the parents whose children were snatched – walking his dog along the beach. He and Susan have always been good family friends of ours. I call his name and run over to join him. He wheels round on me, his face crumpled and freshly tear-stained. 'I just wanted to say …' I stammer, momentarily distracted by how upset he is, 'I'm really sorry about what's happened and if I can do anything to help—'

'Help?' John spits. 'Don't you think your family have done enough?' Startled, I step back and he leans in. 'This is all your brothers' and sisters' fault. It's your family's fault! In fact, all the trouble started when your family came to Orkney!' he spews, his face twisted in bitter rage. 'You're different – you and your family. Different in a bad way!'

I turn away, mortified. My head is dizzy from his venomous words. Tears of self-hatred stream unchecked down my cheeks and my body aches as if beaten. I turn and run from him, but I can never get away from his words. Worse still, I know he is right: me and my family *are* different and it is in a bad way!

Part One

1980–1987

Part One

CHAPTER ONE

Different in a bad way

It's a clear spring day. Bunches of yolk-yellow daffodils sprout from thick grassy verges. Squeals of laughter erupt from the flood of six-year-olds let loose into the playground. But I'm to sit in the dark cold classroom and copy out big words. Teacher said, 'If you don't want to do as you're told and take your tights off for gym, you can stay inside!' But she's wrong: I do want to take them off, my legs are hot and stick to the chair. I thought teacher would understand why I couldn't.

I watch the other children playing with their hoops and balls. All of them seem carefree and happy. The girls' bare legs flash as they hop and jump. Some of the girls wear long white socks with diamond and flower patterns on them. But my favourite are the really short ankle socks, the ones with a coloured frill round the top; they're the prettiest.

I watch the girls' legs for a while before I realise something is different from mine. Their legs look whiter and I count; there are only one or two little round purplish bruises on each of their legs – *that's all*! I glance down at my own, hidden inside their thick navy tights on this hot spring day. The tights Dad says I must wear and now I know why – it's because I'm different. There aren't little round purplish bruises on my legs, there are big dark bloody cuts. Dad got angry with me this morning and held my shoulders while he kicked my shins with his steel-capped boots on. I wouldn't be able to get the tights off now anyway, cos when I do they catch the cuts and new little blood trickles out, sticking the tights harder to my legs. The cuts flick little ticks of pain at me, like they each have their own heartbeat. Now I know, even when the teacher tells me off in front of the class, saying I must take my tights off, I must never take them off. Hot tears fall from my eyes, not from my legs hurting, but because I want to play outside like a normal little girl – without tights on, without caring.

But my mum and dad are different from other mums and dads. Secretly I know they aren't my real ones, because I heard someone call them gyppos. They must have stolen me in the night, from my real mum and dad, the ones who love me. My real mum cries because she misses me so much, and my dad looks worried. They are out there now, searching everywhere for me. My real mum has pretty golden hair, big blue eyes and her soft caring voice speaks from bright red lips. She wears flowery dresses and her shiny heels clack clack clack wherever she goes. My real dad is very handsome. He is tall with dark shiny smooth hair and he wears a suit and keeps his hands in his pockets. On the best day of my life I hear their car pull up outside. We live well away from other people, so it's always exciting when you hear cars outside! I run to the window and straight away I know. I stand close while the door is answered. My heart is jumping and my feet are hopping: this is it, they've finally found me. I hear my real mum's silver bell-like voice, 'Have you seen our little girl?

She was stolen from us when she was a baby.' I can't wait any longer and I break through my pretend mum and dad's legs and grab hold of my real mum's hands. Instantly she knows me and pulls me inside the safety of her arms! The horrible mum snatches at me, but dust from the car gets all in her face. Then me and my real family disappear from here and live happily ever after.

But we move too often for them to ever find me. Mum's empty face looks down at me, without love, without affection, without anything at all, only to tell me to do things. 'Go and get me a toilet roll!' her sharp, witchy face orders, so she can wipe her red leaky nose. Or, 'Fetch me my scarf!' to tie back her long straggly black hair. She walks tired all the time, hunched over her round baby belly – she got so tired once, she fell asleep leaning on the byre wall.

But sometimes I watch her when she's looking after an animal and I think if she could love me the way she loves that animal, then everything would be all right. But what do I have to do to make her love me? In the morning I wait behind the bathroom door for her to finish. Then I go in and get swallowed inside a wet, warm perfume world, so thick with misty steam everything is soft shadows. Lemony sunlight strains through the frosty window full of glassy water worms, which race to the edge before they plop and disappear. I reach out and touch the sink, dusted like everything in her sweet honeysuckle talc. I look at the floor where her powdery footprints magically appear to my waiting eyes. My seven-year-old feet, baggy inside hers, mark out her journey, this is where she stood and this is where she walked. On the back of the door hangs her still warm blue dressing gown and I push my head into its body and cross the limp arms around my neck. My mummy hugs me before the lemony sun takes her away. Before the water worms disappear and the fluffy talc turns to grey sludge. Why doesn't she love me? Why doesn't she see me? But Dad sees me, he sees me all the time.

From morning to night I watch his hands. They scratch and scrunch his wire-wool beard and he says, 'Aaah,' and his gold tooth peeps out. His hands try to flatten the beard, but it springs back up. He pinches the loose red skin on his neck, stretching it so far, you think it will tear and blood will come out. Then both hands catch his hanging red braces and hook them over his shoulders. His hand points at one of us. 'Get me socks on,' he gruffly orders and leans back – for now his hands hidden behind his head. But the time I must watch his hands the most is when his finger curls and his angry voice says, 'C'mere.' Then my mind starts asking over and over, 'WhathaveIdone? WhathaveIdone? WhathaveIdone?'

You must always be doing something, because Dad hates seeing us kids playing or not doing work. But it's best if you can stay away from him. That's what me and my sister Bella do. She is only one year younger than me, so we are called EstherandBella. We do everything together, waking up and going to sleep and everything in the middle. But mainly we hide from Dad together, under beds, behind bales, anywhere he can't find us; our whole lives are about trying to escape him.

'Get up, EstherandBella, go to the toilet.' Our older brother wakes us from our hiding place behind the sofa. We must have fallen asleep. I try to open my eyes, but a stinging pull at my lashes reminds me they are full of crusty gunk.

Bella's head lolls on my shoulder as I pee. 'Is it sleep time yet?' she asks.

I look up at the shiny black window. 'I think so,' I mumble sleepily.

With barely open eyes we stagger through to the bedroom where we fall straight back into sleep.

But from inside the deep darkness, someone is grabbing hold of the front and back of me in hard handfuls, squeezing all the air from me. Picking me up and moving me. Bang! A short sharp scream comes from inside me. A deep pain shoots through my head, back and tummy. All breath gone out! Sharp hurting chest! I drag air in, while scratching at my eyes. I need to see, I need to see! In the little light from the doorway, I see Dad picking up Bella. She screams as he throws her at the wall next to me. I look down at my heels, frantically kicking at the wall. I dare to glance at the open door – if only I could escape.

'Whathavewedone? Whathavewedone? Whathavewe-done?'

My brain won't answer, but Dad's voice does, 'EstherandBella thought they'd go for a little snooze, didn't you girls? Thought you'd keep the rest of us waiting?'

My stomach drops as I realise we went to bed without Dad's permission! Dad's angry scrunched-up black-socked feet are planted in front of us and my tears won't stop falling and dripping from my chin. There are two other sets of feet – naked – that belong to my brothers or sisters. Then Dad's deep angry voice again: 'Who do you think you are?'

I hear Bella quietly crying beside me and I know she feels the same like me, all shaking scared, trying to think what will happen to us. Dad's feet turn to the bare ones. 'Go and collect some nettles for our lazy layabouts, they deserve a treat!'

I can nearly count my toes. No I can't, just fuzzy shapes. Breathing sharp painful gulps, up down, up down. Waiting for nettles. They are here, big green leafy armful after big leafy armful, laid in front of our feet. Dad is laughing, his quiet happy laugh. 'Get my glove,' he orders. 'This'll make you think twice about sleeping, while the rest of us wait.'

My mind is full of buzzing noise, I can't think straight. I just wish I knew why we went to bed without Dad's permission, but I don't.

Dad pulls on his blurry orange nettle glove and picks up a big bunch of nettles. 'Bend over, Esther,' he orders. My stomach twists with spiky wire knots. Dad chuckles as he slowly rolls up my jumper. He trickles a handful of nettles across my naked back, releasing a sharp stinging attack and my body jerks involuntarily. Then suddenly he goes red angry, and grabs big handfuls and starts shoving them all over me. My breath sharply catches at the back of my throat as the itchy pinching attacks me over and over again. My stomach lifts, trying to get the sour ground smell out, but nothing comes, it's too late, it's gone through my skin, it's inside me. The prickling nettle heat spreads from my back to my tummy, then rushes up my shoulders to my face, it's in my hair and I'm on fire.

'Stand up!' Dad orders. 'We don't want the rest of you feeling left out, do we?'

He spins me towards him. I glimpse his blurry red hairy face, all gold-tooth smiley, before my chin clamps back to my chest. He pushes nettles up the front and sides of my jumper, until they poke out from the top. He steps back for a moment and I pray he's finished. But then he's grabbing more nettles and squeezing them up my sleeves until I can feel almost nothing. Eventually his feet move back and again I pray, please God, please make him finish. But he's coming back at me with a big handful and he's opening my pants and shoving them down there, and then down the back, until I'm packed with nettles. My voice breaks from my body and I hear it releasing long painful screams.

I'm vaguely aware of Bella having her turn and she cries more than me. I wish she wouldn't, it just makes Dad even more mad. When he's finished with her, we wait for his orders, wishing hard he would leave us alone. But then he leans in to us, pressing his hands on our tummies, pushing us up against the wall, causing us both to cry out. 'What's all the fuss about?' he asks in a happy voice. 'It's only a few nettles!' He stops abruptly and leaves the bedroom, before calling from the living room, 'Come on, girls, prayer time!'

Me and Bella stand in the prayer circle with Dad, Mum and the rest of our brothers and sisters. My breath comes in short aching huffs as my tears roll into the nettles, making my chest hot and wet. When I put my hands together to pray, I press the nettles closer to my sides, releasing a surge of painful new stings. I look up and catch Dad watching me and Bella. He flashes a gold-tooth smile from inside his fuzzy grey beard. 'Heads down, girls, and close your eyes!' he orders cheerfully. The nettle tips poke out from the top of my jumper and tickle my lips before stinging them. Dad starts with his prayer and we all join in. 'Our Father, who art in heaven, hallowed be thy name. Thy kingdom come. Thy will be done ...' I don't want to pray, I just want to cry.

It stops me feeling so much, '...on Earth as it is in Heaven. Give us this day our daily bread, and forgive us our trespasses, as we forgive those who have trespassed against us. Lead us not into temptation, but deliver us from evil, for thine is the Kingdom, the power and glory, for ever and ever, amen.' I offer up a prayer of my own – please, God, stop the stings, please help me – but I know he won't; he never does.

Then we say Mum's prayer: 'Hail Mary full of grace, the Lord is with thee, blessed art thou amongst women and blessed is the fruit of thy womb. Holy Mary, mother of God, pray for us sinners now and in the hour of our death, amen!'

I open my eyes and quickly check if Dad is watching me. His head is down so I dare to lift my arms slightly away from my sides. 'Glory be to the Father, the Son and the Holy Spirit, as it was in the beginning, is now and for ever shall be, world without end, amen!'

After prayers, Dad pushes me and Bella outside. It's freezing cold in the porch where we wait out our punishment. I hum to myself as I wrap one foot over the other for a while, before swapping, trying to keep at least one foot off the icy concrete floor. My stings don't hurt and itch as much out here, not like inside where nettles grow hotter and hotter. 'Esther, Esther!' Bella whispers at me. I don't look at her; I don't want to see her ugly, crying face. And I know Dad will be listening out, so I keep humming. Her voice whispers louder. 'It's your fault, you said it was sleeping time!' I know I did, but that doesn't make it my fault. Without looking at her, I whisper, 'It's not up to me, stupid head.'

She turns towards me. 'But you're older, you're s'posed to know!'

She always wants to think everything's my fault because I'm eight and she's seven, but that's not true. How could I know we would fall asleep and Dad would find us? I turn away, but then I'm thinking Dad might have heard her say it was my fault and I'll get punished again. So I loudly tell her, 'We shouldn't have gone to bed without Dad telling us. We aren't ever s'posed to do nothing without Dad telling us!'

And we both know that's true, so we go back to quiet humming and crying. Wait, I hear something. Is Dad coming to the outhouse? Is he spying on us? Dad is everywhere; he sees everything. No, it isn't him. Not this time, my body doesn't feel him near yet.

A while later the hairs on the back of my neck rise at the sound of his light footsteps approaching the porch. Stopping behind the door, he listens and we freeze like scared baby rabbits in a field. He waits a moment, wanting us to do something bad, before he yanks the door open. My body jumps. Is he still angry? Does he think we've been punished enough? I stare at the floor, watching his black-stockinged feet walk in front of us. I flinch when he talks but I don't feel anger in his words. 'Get your nettles out and get yourselves to bed!' he snaps, before he's gone.

My stomach twists and turns as I know what's coming. When nettles stay in the same place they stop stinging, but when you move they start painful new stings. I waddle slowly outside, where tensing, I stare hard at the black sky and hum loudly. I carefully open my pants, revealing a nettle clump, which thuds at my feet. I lean forward and slowly pull the bottom of my jumper outwards, to try to get it to drop as a clump too. I do the same with my back and my sleeves, before peeling the soaking wet jumper off my body and turning it inside out. The cold night air soothes my painful zinging skin. I momentarily let myself stand here, with my arms stretched out being soothed by the cold, before remembering in panic that Dad didn't say I could do that.

With my head down, I creep back into the house and sneak through to the bathroom for a wee. In the light of the naked bulb, I look at my zizzing, pain-filled body. Every inch is mottled in sprawling purple patches, which have become a continuous buzzing ache all over me. I listen out for where Dad is before I dare go back through to the bedroom, where it happened. I gingerly lower my painful body to the mattress, where me and Bella lie still side by side and whimper. My eyes won't close; whenever I nearly fall asleep, they click back open – I must watch out. I must always watch out. So in my head I play my favourite fantasy, after being found by my real parents: being saved by a social worker.

Once, my older brothers and sisters whispered to me, 'Dad isn't supposed to hurt us like this. If a social worker found out, he'd go to jail!'

'Wow!' I gasped amazed. 'Could they really stop him?'

My older brother nodded knowingly. 'A social worker,' he explained authoritatively, 'is a big person who cares about children.' I looked up at him, my eyes full of wonder at the sound of this incredible superhero. 'Yes,' my brother continued, 'they only listen to children. Dad would one hundred per cent be put in jail.'

It sounded so wonderfully simple. We just needed to get one of those, then everything would be all right.

But Dad had always abused and tortured us and got away with it, so with the best imagination in the world, how could a social worker really save us? But the only thing that keeps our day-to-day life bearable are our dreams and the hope that somehow, in some way, our lives will get better.

CHAPTER TWO

My brother Alfie — the dog

Mum has a baby every year, so eventually there will be 15 of us kids.

Alfie was born the year before me. But he is treated differently from the rest of us. Dad abuses us all, but he abuses Alfie more. I don't know why, but Alfie isn't allowed inside the house. Instead, whenever we move, Alfie is put in the porch or in one of the outbuildings. If Alfie needs the toilet he has to go out to a field or a ditch and bury what he's done. Dad won't even let him wear clothes, so most of the time he is naked. A potato sack or a thin layer of cardboard is the only thing between Alfie and the hard cold concrete floor. As you walk past him, his deep brown eyes glance fearfully up at you before he shrinks further down. With his knees pulled up tight under his chin, his body is made as small as possible and his patchy shaved head rocks forwards and back, forwards and back. This is where Alfie lives and you wouldn't know he was here, because he rarely makes a sound. Except at night, when there is a low sad crying that goes on the whole night through.

If Alfie accidentally goes to the toilet inside, Dad forces the poo into his mouth and Alfie just lets him, not fighting back. There is a stomach churning stench and a wet slopping sound, as Dad grins and grunts over him, happy to have an excuse to hurt him. Or Dad might order Alfie to sit in the large green water bin that's usually used for nettling, making him sit in his own poo and wee all day. When he lets him get out, no matter how cold it is, Dad hoses him down with icy water and Alfie crumples to the ground like wet paper, the water too strong for his frail body.

In the morning, Alfie only gets to scrape out the porridge bowl after we've all had ours– not with a spoon, but with his fingers or something he's found. Alfie throws his food straight into his throat, without chewing, like a dog. Once, he showed me how he makes his food come back up so he can eat it again, like a cow chewing its cud. I tried to do it, but it made me feel sick. Sometimes I look at him and a pain goes through me like sharp smack, but then Dad hurts me too and I can't think too much. That's just the way it is and it's the way it's always been.

When we moved to an island in Orkney called Rousay, a man came to the house and said Alfie had to go to school. But Dad wouldn't let Alfie take the bus with us, and made him walk. It was a long bus journey, but Alfie wanted to go, and he would start walking before we had breakfast. He was in the slow classes, but sometimes I'd see him in the school playground. He'd always be staring at the floor and wearing any clothes he could find, a holey girl's jumper, odd shoes without socks and too-big trousers, held up with a piece of dirty old rope.

Alfie quickly got a reputation for stealing food at school. The headmistress, Mrs Danvers, kept a bag of fun-sized Mars bars in her desk to hand out as treats for good behaviour or bingo prizes. One day in assembly, she announced the bag of treat Mars bars had been stolen, adding that, 'If the person or persons responsible come forward and admit their crime, no further action will be taken!' Everyone, myself included, turned to stare at my brother Alfie, the shabby little figure at the back of the hall. As we watched, he slowly and unsteadily rose to his feet, his head still bowed. A hushed silence fell over us as a visibly trembling Alfie made his way to the front of the assembly. He looked so small, so scared and unloved, a rush of tears rose up in me and I wanted to shout 'That's my brother! Why doesn't someone protect him? He is hurt all the time at home, why should he be hurt here as well?' As if my wish was coming true before my very eyes, Mrs Danvers walked up to him and instead of telling him off, like I thought she would, she put her hands out. He grasped hold of them, stumbling forward. Her face was full of sadness as she said something to another teacher and quietly led him from the hall.

After that, Mrs Danvers looks after Alfie. He is at school early and goes to her house. He seems to be coming to life – like a sepia photograph changing to colour. One day he is even allowed to go on the swimming trip from school, on the bus, where he sat up front with Mrs Danvers.

My favourite thing at school is swimming and if I haven't got new bruises I'm allowed to go. Alfie sits wrapped in a towel, sitting on the side while the rest of us race the length of the pool – as I don't think Alfie has swum before. At the end of the lesson we are allowed to play and that's when Alfie takes his towel off and carefully climbs down into the shallow end. I join him and for a moment we play like a real brother and sister, splashing and laughing in the water. Looking up, I catch the worried eyes of Mrs Danvers and Mrs Brown. I follow their gaze to Alfie's back and, with horror, I recognise tell-tale long red welts across it. I look at Alfie, still splashing unaware. I feel scared for him and for me – we aren't supposed to let anyone see our hurts, *we're in big trouble*. I must get out!

I hurriedly make my way to the steps and start climbing out. But Mrs Danvers and Mrs Brown are at my side. I look up at them fearfully. 'You're not in trouble, Esther,' Mrs Danvers says in her soft cigarette-perfumed voice as she takes hold of my hand, 'but I do need to ask you a question.'

I look at her, then at Mrs Brown and they look, frowning down at me. Mrs Brown joins in. 'We were just wondering what those big horrid marks on Alfie's back are?'

I can't think what to say. I'm not supposed to lie to teachers, but more than that, I'm not supposed to tell anyone anything. 'Don't know,' I mumble, looking back to Alfie.

'Esther, I think you do. Now just take a minute and think. It's very important!' adds Mrs Danvers.

Suddenly I feel a never-ending hurting for Alfie: he's my brother, my poor hurting brother. 'Dad did it, he hit him with a chain!' I blurt out hard and fast.

Their faces are shocked, but so am I! First that I even said it, then with surprise that hurt can be put in words. I yank my hand from Mrs Danvers' and make a run for the changing room. Sitting down to catch my breath, my head spins at the enormity of what I've done. I've ruined everything. I can never go home. I'll have to run away. But where can I go? Would Mrs Danvers let me live with her? That would be the perfect answer to everything.

I hoped there would be an accident on the way home. Or something bad would happen so I would never have to go back there again. But the bus drops me off at the same time, at the end of our gravel drive as usual. I keep thinking I might faint as I'm sure Mrs Danvers will have phoned Dad and told him everything. He isn't home and for a moment it all lifts from me and I could skip and jump. But then I realise that it means I have to wait longer for my punishment, and the black dread covers me again. When he gets home, I keep my head down and stay away from him, thinking he'll call me to him any minute. But he doesn't. Not even the next morning.

The following day at school Mrs Danvers and Mrs Brown treat me like normal. I'm not made to stand on my seat for punishment and I'm not put out in the corridor to wait. They say nothing – like it never happened, and it's the same the day after that. Sometimes Dad calls me to him or he'll be staring at me and I'll think it's because I told and now he's going to beat me. But it's always something else. I start thinking this must be one of the games he likes playing, not telling me he knows, until I admit it. Guilt-filled days creep slowly by, punctured by heart-stopping scares. Days become weeks of it not being mentioned. Until a day comes when even I forget to remember it.

But a couple of months later Dad's face is purple thunder as he orders us to gather round him in the sitting room – even Alfie! He paces about, all agitated and jumpy, his odd eyes – one pale grey and one dark brown – glowering wildly at us. 'A person called a social worker will be visiting us!' he announces angrily. Staring accusingly at us, he adds, 'Because of one of you!'

My belly flops as all at once I know – it's because I told about the chain marks on Alfie's back. Despite Dad's volcanic anger, a flicker of light-filled hope shoots up from my toes. A social worker, a true-to-life one, they are real and they will be coming to save us!

For a moment I am lost inside my head as the superhero social worker, on his great big white horse, charges through the doors and gallops into the house. 'Take my hand, Esther,' he gently urges. I reach up and I'm rescued and we are out of here, faster than the speed of light.

I don't know what my brothers and sisters are thinking, but outwardly nobody reacts. We continue waiting silently, like his dutiful slave children, rooted to the spot. When Dad is angry you never do anything to attract his attention.

But he isn't finished yet. His face is twisted with hate, as he spits, 'These pieces of filth are not to be trusted. They are evil interfering baskets!' Stopping to focus on an older sister who is trembling and bent over, Dad's voice drips with revulsion: 'They take nasty, lying children and lock them away in children's prison where they torture them so much, they wish they could die!' Some of the younger ones are whimpering and scared tears fall from my eyes as I struggle to catch my breath – it's me that told and Dad knows it. Seemingly pleased with the impact of his lecture, Dad's voice becomes lighter, adding, 'I just don't want any of you kids taken and put in prison, that's all. So you mustn't trust them –. at any cost!' He looks around at us again, as if searching for somebody to vent his anger on, but instead of attacking us, he scowls. As if using superhuman strength to restrain himself, he hisses through clenched jaws, 'Now, get out of my sight, the lot of you!'

*

Since Dad told us about the social worker coming, he's been pretending to be nicer.

I thought he might have truly changed when he let me keep the lamb a neighbour gave me. I don't care that she has broken back legs, she is my pet and I name her Polly. I love feeding her bottles of milk while I stroke her bobbly porridge coat and share my secrets. I'd had her for two weeks, when as usual I rush home to feed her. Running towards the garage, it seems strange that she isn't bleating. Opening the door, I find her straw pen has gone, and there is no sign she was ever here. The sound of grinding metal startles me and I look up. There she is. She's been hung up alive from a metal hook. Her eyes stretch wide, as she twists about, stopping every now and then to catch her breath. I am confused for a moment; she shouldn't be up there. I am overwhelmed by sobs before I remember something I have known all along: Dad was always going to kill her. It had been a surprise he'd let her live at all! Because of the social worker coming, a tiny part of me had dared to believe he might have let her live – what a stupid little girl. Of course, he was only ever pretending, to put on a show of a loving, caring father in front of the neighbour who'd given her to me. Finally Polly stops the twitching that's making me jump. A cold numbness creeps over me as I watch her deep red life splash to the floor.

If the social worker had arrived earlier he would have entered a house of child abuse nightmares. He would have discovered ten neglected children fighting for survival under the abusive dictatorship of a psychopath. There would have been unfed, unclothed, unwashed and unloved children, everywhere.

But instead when the social worker does arrive, us kids have scrubbed the house cleaner than it's been since we first came here. We've been ordered to get dressed and warned to stay out of the way while the social worker visits.

I'm not sure how I feel about the social worker coming any more. As desperate as I am to get away, I don't want to go to a place that's even worse.

Rousay is surrounded by water, so the only way to get to it is by boat, and the social worker is arriving on the lunchtime one. Dad watches through binoculars and eventually a shiny green unfamiliar car rolls up our drive. I watch from a hidey-hole in the straw bales, curious to see what a social worker looks like – is he the shining saviour of my imagination or the slimy evil creature that Dad has told us about? I am surprised to see he looks just like an ordinary man. He stumbles slightly as he climbs from his car, a large important-looking folder clamped beneath his arm. Strong winds tussle his mousy brown hair over his flabby pink face, revealing a mottled red scalp, as he battles to close his car door. Once his pointed chubby hand has flattened down his hair, he juts out his chin and shambles over to our house. He definitely isn't the superhero social worker of my dreams!

Dad is ready and swings the front door open, but not before he spies one of my brothers and glowers threateningly at him. Then, like it always does when he meets someone new, Dad's face changes into that of a happy stranger. His eyes crinkle and his mouth stretches wide, revealing the whole of his gold tooth, and in his other voice he says, 'Ah, Sid Limey, so pleased to meet you!'

I thought he would only come once, but the social worker comes every week. I found out he was Scottish from the one time he spoke to me. He reminded me of a fat fish, gasping for air. I didn't care if he didn't speak to me again. He didn't anyway – he doesn't come to see us children, he comes to see Dad. He's the opposite of what we thought a social worker was, so I told my older brother, 'You was wrong!' and I knew he knew it too, because he didn't say anything.

Every week Sid comes into our house, rubbing his hands together. 'It's bitter, my gawd it's bitter,' he says, going over to the fire. He holds his fleshy hands to the flames. 'You've a good fire here, a hot fire,' he adds. He talks about everything, everything that doesn't matter, that is. He always mentions to no one in particular, 'that boat was a long time getting in', and I imagine the boat climbing inside Rousay island, and I think, Sid Limey is a silly man!

Having a social worker changes nothing in our lives, apart from Alfie being sent away to a place across the water. A teacher at school took me out of lessons a couple of times and asked me questions about my life at home. I kept wanting to tell her everything, but the words got stuck in my throat. I didn't want to go to the child prison.

Soon after Sid Limey started coming, Dad said he was sick of interfering busybodies, buzzing around all the time and we'd have to move. I didn't want to go, I'd become used to Rousay.

It is a dark hail-stoning day, when we arrive at Crook Farm on South Ronaldsay. It's not really a farm at all, more a big old run-down house, with ruins for outbuildings. Rats poke out from every hole, glaring at me, like it's their house really, and we're the unwanted visitors.

I don't know why but since Alfie was sent away, Dad has changed a little bit. He doesn't beat us as much. Instead the hurting he does now is more hidden. When he gets angry he'll throw us across the room by picking us up by our ears, making chilblain-like tears at the top of them, that sting and itch. Or he pinches and twists the skin in our armpits until it splits and bleeds. He mostly hits us on the pads of our feet now or the palms of our hands – all places that can't be seen. I'm 12 now and I have made friends with some of the girls from my class; they don't live far from us, and sometimes, Dad even lets me go to their houses.

He's behaving strangely in other ways too. He never gives us money to buy food at school, so every now and then, taking my life in my hands, I take 20p from his trousers to buy something to eat. One day I'd taken 20p, and when I came home I was met by one of my brothers. His face chalk white, he warned, 'You're in big trouble, Esther, you're to go straight to Dad. He knows you've stolen money!' My stomach twists as I make the dreaded journey to where he sits on the couch in the kitchen. Something is different, the air isn't as crackly as usual and my skin doesn't prickle. He glares up at me. 'I know what you've done,' he growls. My chin drops instantly to my chest and I start to tremble. 'Don't you dare let me catch you ever doing something like that again, or your life won't be worth living!' he warns. I wait, weak-kneed, wondering what weapon he'll order me to bring him. Will it be the stick, the pipe, the orange glove or will he take off his belt? 'Now get out of here!' I stay statue-still, knowing this is a game he's playing and he'll grab me when I try to go. 'I said, get out of here before I change my mind!' he adds. This time I shoot out of the kitchen and run for my life. It's only once I'm far from the house and safely hidden in the barn and my breathing has slowed down, that I dare thank my lucky stars; for once I've got off lightly.

Dad hasn't changed really, it's only pretend, he still has to hurt something. One of his favourite pastimes, when he's not abusing us kids, is abusing animals. Soon after a goat has given birth to a baby kid, he checks to see if it's a male. If it is, he takes great pleasure in killing it, saying, 'It's of no use anyway.' The newly born baby kid, still covered in afterbirth, is unsteady on its legs, as Dad gives chase. It stumbles, bleating to its mother and she goes demented, trying to protect it. Dad lets the baby goat get away before catching it again and wrestling it to the ground. The mother goat tries to butt Dad and save her baby but it's no use, if anything it makes Dad smile more. The kid's high-pitched cries ring through the air as Dad holds it to the ground and presses on its windpipe, making its voice rattle as it gasps for air. When he's had enough, he holds its back legs together and swings it through the air, its sharp cries dying on the wind. Then with a wet crack, he smacks its head off the wall. Blood roars from its eyes, nose and mouth and its tongue stretches out – as if even in death it hurts. Having finished with it, Dad slaps its little broken body to the ground, where the mother goat mourns over her new baby's corpse.

Dad can't pick on bigger animals the way he does with smaller ones, but he devises other torturous methods of dealing with them. He took a dislike to a Billy goat, so he chained him to a metal pin at the top of a hill and put food and water just out of the Billy goat's reach. He then left him there to starve to death in the cruel bitter Orkney winter. Thankfully for the Billy goat he didn't take long to kill himself. He wrapped himself tightly around the pin until he fell to his knees, strangling himself so tight on his collar, his bloody eyeballs burst from their sockets.

But none hurts me as deeply as the little red horse. His name is Ferdinand, and I wish he is my very own. With his burnt orange coat and coal-coloured mane and tail, he's the most beautiful horse I'd ever seen. His great big gentle brown eyes with sweeping long black lashes look at me with a steady, trusting gaze. I don't know why Dad put him in an old ruin with its hard mud ground and broken stony walls, and I would never ask him. Dad instructs everyone, 'Ferdinand is not to be given food or water. He is to be left alone to die.' I know the dangers, but I still go to him – I can't help it. I must try to get him food. I pull fistfuls of grass from the fields surrounding his prison and stretch my hand through a stony hole. He greedily snaffles the lush green shafts, his soft velvet muzzle steaming hot puffs against my palm. Soon when he sees me coming, he whinnies a greeting and presses his soft body up to the gaps, to be stroked. But I can never get him enough grass and I'm always in a rush. If I'm caught disobeying Dad's orders, I'll get the thrashing of my life, so I'm always on my guard.

Every day Ferdinand grows thinner and blobs of hard mud attach to his coat, dragging him further to the ground. He could hold his head up at first and would look at me, as if to ask why he's been put in here. But I'm no good, because I don't know why Dad does these things – so I just cry at the sight of him. But soon his head got too heavy for his thin neck and he dropped it into the mud. So now I throw the grass to the ground, trying to get it near to his mouth because he finds it too hard to walk. And when his square behind is pointing at me, with the little black tufts left behind from his tail, I know he will probably not get any food today. After a couple of weeks he is still alive, but only because his ribs force loud crackling gasps through his bony frame.

When I get home from school one day, I go straight to him, I don't usually dare but something tells me I must. His legs have become too stick-like to hold him up any longer and he's fallen to his side. I call out to him and he tries to lift his head, murmuring a little burr to me. 'It's okay, Ferdinand, don't worry, it's all right,' I tell him, but I know it isn't and it won't ever be. Tears blind me as I rip up as much grass as I can and throw it at him. Most catches on the air and cruelly lands just beyond his reach. He half-heartedly nibbles the strands closest to his mouth. I stay as long as I dare; I don't want to leave him, but I must.

The next morning before I leave for school, I go to see him. His legs and neck are splayed out rigidly from his body and his head seems to have sunken further into the muddy ground. It is difficult to make out where his coal mane ends and the earth begins. But his orange coat dazzles like never before as the early morning sun bathes him in a protective luminous mist. His long black eyelashes sweep down peacefully. I am happy for him. He has at last escaped the ruin my father imprisoned him within.

But Dad struggles most when he's pretending to be nice to Alfie when he's home from his special school at the weekends. Even though Alfie is like a real boy now, Dad still hates him and treats him badly. Alfie comes back dressed in clean clothes that smell like flowers. He speaks in a soft voice, trying to be nice, while the rest of us are still fighting to survive. He doesn't look at Dad, but talks to us kids. My younger siblings and I love getting him to tell us about the place where he lives now. We crowd around him and listen with a mixture of awe and envy, wishing we could all get sent there. For the umpteenth time, Alfie recounts how wonderful it is there. How it's full of lovely caring big people. Children aren't hurt there, but are loved, like in storybooks. I especially like hearing about the delicious food he gets to eat: pies, sausages and fish fingers, as well as puddings afterwards, like strawberry jelly, chocolate cake and ice cream, every day! They are even teaching him to read and write. But when he's at Crook Farm, Dad still makes him live in the outside loo – which is just three grey concrete walls around a toilet.

Going to his new school has made Alfie brave, as when Dad isn't around he will sometimes come in the house. But one day Dad catches him. 'What are you doing in here, you filthy runt,' he growls.

Alfie's head drops and he brings his arms up over his chest, trying to make himself small. The air is thick and prickly as Dad reaches across the room, lifts him up by his jumper and throws him down on the gravel outside. No sound comes from Alfie as he thuds to his back, but his face is etched with terror as he attempts to crawl away.

Dad stands over him. 'C'mere, you piece of filth,' he commands.

Alfie slowly climbs to his feet. We all know what is coming and look away, trying to block out Dad's groans of satisfaction as he beats Alfie up – for what will be the last time.

CHAPTER THREE

Dad goes to jail

I wake up shivering and desperate for a wee. It must be very late as no light comes from outside and, apart from the sleeping sounds of my brothers and sisters, the house is quiet. Trying to block out the scared hollow feeling in the pit of my stomach, I force myself out of bed to make the dreaded journey to the toilet downstairs. I carefully place my feet on the outer edges of the landing where it doesn't creak. My heart sinks when I get to the top of the stairs and hear Mum and Dad talking in the kitchen below. Supporting my weight on the banister, I cautiously step over the noisiest stairs. When I finally make it to the kitchen door, I know I've reached the most difficult part. Gently pulling the kitchen door handle towards me, I slowly press it down, pushing the door until it releases a squeak. Inhaling, I press my back into the wall and squeeze through the gap sideways. Imagining myself invisible, I stare down and tiptoe past Mum and Dad, who sit cuddled up on the sofa – oblivious to me.

Pulling my feet up, so they don't touch the icy cement floor, I wee as fast as I can. Suddenly the black window in the bathroom becomes a dazzling rectangle of light. I can't work out where the lights are coming from, it's so quiet.

Then I hear the rolling crunch of tyres on the gravel outside – they must be car beams! But it doesn't make sense. Isn't it too late for anyone to be coming to the house? Within seconds there's an urgent banging on the front door. I jump from the toilet, pulling my knickers up at the same time, and tiptoe back through to the kitchen.

My head is spinning. I look up at Mum and Dad, who sit frozen, staring at each other. Fear crawls all over me, like when Dad is coming for me. But Dad is hiding in here too – while they are out there trying to get in. It's only once I hear a man's voice, I realise, it isn't all of us they want – they just want Dad! 'Mr Black, this is the police. We need to speak to you!' a man's voice gruffly demands.

'Bed!' Dad hisses at me, on the way to the front door. I scurry upstairs and out of sight. I listen from the landing, hardly daring to breathe with excitement. An important-sounding man is explaining why they are here, 'To discuss very serious allegations of child abuse. Can we come in?'

Dad mumbles something and they troop through to the kitchen. I creep over to the crack in the landing floorboards above the kitchen. I've fantasised about the police catching Dad ever since I can remember and now it's happening, I don't want to miss a second. I press my eye into the crack. The blood rushes around my head, while my heart thuds so loud, I'm scared they could hear it below. Clenching my chattering teeth, I strain to make out what the police are saying.

I count four police officers. They are being quite forceful with Dad, making him sit down, while they explain why they are here. It's better than all my dreams combined At first Dad says he doesn't know what they're talking about and tries to act innocent, but they seem convinced that what they've been told is true. While all of this goes on around her, Mum remains glued to the sofa, bent forward and hiding her face in her hands.

Two policemen continue talking to Dad while the others search about, looking through cupboards and up on shelves. One policeman explains the charges that have been made against him, saying he'll need to accompany them to Kirkwall Police Station to make a statement. Another policeman looks around the room before he comes over to the tall yellow cupboard, directly below my eyes. He reaches to the top of it and I watch his fingers feeling about in the dust. He is obviously looking for something in particular and I will his fingers nearer to Dad's abuse weapons. He looks towards the ceiling and I'm convinced his eyes flit over mine, meeting for a flicker. I reel back, shaking and breathing fast. But I calm down when I remember that today is not my day for being in trouble – it's Dad's turn. Excitement and curiosity take over again and I cautiously press my eye back to the crack and focus on the policeman's fingers. He has finally managed to grip the end of Dad's black rubber pipe and pulls it down. Two other officers join him and they all examine it as if it's a thing of great interest.

My stomach churns nervously at something as private as an abuse weapon being looked at so publicly. For the whole of my life I can only ever remember there being three black pipes. One was replaced because it got lost – suspected stolen – and Dad managed to crack another through a particularly hard beating on one of my siblings. This one is about the width of my wrist and strong, with ridges down its length. When hit with it, it gives a dull thud of pain at first before going in deep to your bone, leaving dark purple bruises.

The policeman carefully places the pipe inside a clear plastic bag. Then his hand returns to the top of the cupboard and my heart threatens to stop as he brings down the much-hated stick. Light brown wood, flat and thin, it inflicts breath-takingly sharp stings. When Dad uses it side on, it becomes whip-like, leaving tiny slice wounds on the skin. These wounds look deceptively small, but are actually quite deep and take a while to heal, sometimes becoming infected. Because it's thin, it often breaks and Dad takes great pleasure in searching out a new one. Showing us kids his specially selected stick like a new toy, delighting in how much better this one will be than the last one, triumphantly exclaiming, 'Just the job. This'll sting some!'

Then the policeman brings down Dad's nettle glove. This is deep orange and made of a very thick rubber with a long sleeve to protect Dad's hand and arm when he's nettling us kids. Dad is left standing in his steel-capped boots that split the skin painfully anywhere he wants to kick a child, especially the shins.

Once the policeman has put Dad's weapons into clear plastic bags and sealed them, I know this is real. This is serious for Dad, for Mum, for me, for all of us. Then, for the first time since the police arrived, I hear Dad's voice – it's distant and weak, 'Please can I change out of these trousers?' I've never heard him say please before and I never realised how small he was, as he is dwarfed by the four police officers. A policeman accompanies him to the bathroom, while the others wait in the kitchen and speak among themselves, ignoring Mum, still motionless on the couch.

When Dad returns a policeman holds open handcuffs out to him and he meekly places his wrists in them. Then a policeman tells him, 'Mr Eric Nicholas Black, I am arresting you on suspicion of child abuse. You have the right to remain silent, but anything you do say may be taken down and used as evidence against you, in a court of law.'

They lead Dad from Crook Farm and out of my and my family's lives for ever. I will never see him again.

The police and Dad are long gone. I wonder how it can possibly be the same night it was half an hour ago? But it did happen, because I feel it in my chest – I can breathe. I never had to be told when Dad wasn't home, my body felt it and everything was lighter. When he was home, a heavy blackness polluted everything and I struggled to inhale. But the police taking him away feels more than lightness. The walls have tumbled down and winter has ended. Now the sweetest summer air is breezing through the house, dazzling everything in bright yellow light.

But Mum continues to sit frozen in a darker time, unwilling to feel the sunshine. Her body is pushed up against the arm of the sofa. Her hand is still clutching the material at her chest. The empty half of the sofa, where until recently Dad sat, stretches out beside her. She looks all wrong as one, small and halved.

I creep downstairs, like I always do during the night, and I go to the kitchen. But for the first time, I don't gently press the handle down, instead I bounce the door open.

Still she doesn't move, so I step further into the room. 'What's happened?' I ask, my rusty voice startling her. She springs from the sofa and turns towards the kettle. With her back to me, she raises her face skyward and in a small tight voice replies, 'The police have arrested your father, that's what's happened!'

'Oh,' I say. 'Do you want me to make your coffee?' I ask softly, like she's the child.

Taking the cup in trembling hands, she looks through me. We don't talk. It feels strange – is it because we've never sat together like this before? Even though I know I'm not the person she wants here, I'm still glad I am. All my life I've yearned to be near her. I've longed to breathe the same air as her and for the first time in my 13 years of life, I am. But I don't know what to say. In my fantasy of what this night would be, she did the talking, she was the one who reassured me, and told me that everything would be okay. She would cuddle me and tell me over and over how much she loved me. But she says nothing, so I keep quiet too. I don't want anything to spoil this time with my mum.

Into the night she sits motionless, staring blankly ahead. I need the toilet and I wonder if I should ask if she wants to go too – like I do with my younger siblings. But suddenly I can't sit still. My body is buzzing and tingling, I must get up, before I explode with happiness. I want to shout and tell everybody. The twitching in my cheeks is getting harder to control; I need to laugh out loud. He's gone, they've really truly taken Dad. At long last we are free. YES!

I quietly pad through to the bathroom. Firmly pushing the door closed behind me, I allow myself to feel the flood of relief that's been threatening to overwhelm me. Then I'm startled by a horribly familiar sight. There, newly stepped from, are Dad's dirty jeans that are held together by his thick brown leather belt; another abuse weapon. Flat and wide, stiff and cracked, which end of the belt, buckle or tip, would be used on you, depended on Dad's mood. He would alter the length to change the pain and effect. Thankfully the belt wasn't used as often as the other weapons as I don't think Dad liked taking it off.

I automatically pick up the jeans and they jangle heavily. With mounting excitement it dawns on me – now the police have taken him, I can have a few 20ps to buy some food at school. Gingerly sliding my hand into the pocket, I slide some change out and wrap it inside a towel, for collection later.

On the way back through to the kitchen, I glimpse a girl's face in the little mirror. She's got a happy look about her. Her hazel eyes shine and her lips are turned up, as if she's holding back a laugh. I smile at her, creating a dimple in my left cheek that I never knew I had. But before I leave the bathroom I change my face to sad for Mum's benefit. I lower my eyebrows and turn my lips down and make sure to carry some crumpled toilet tissue.

I return to sitting with her. Her all sad and shocked and me happy beyond anything I've ever known. My brain is firing off questions that I'm desperate to ask someone. Like, how did they find out about Dad? Will they put him straight in jail now? Or will he be coming back home?

Mum eventually falls into a restless slumber. But I daren't go to sleep in case this is all just a wonderful dream. As soon as there's a little light, I escape outside and sit in a nearby field. I watch the morning sun peep up from behind the Atlantic Ocean, painting the sky in soft pink and candy orange streaks. Now that Dad has gone, I realise how beautiful everything suddenly looks.

When I return, Mum is awake and on the phone to the

local doctor, then on to a solicitor, urgently begging them, 'My husband has been taken to the police station for questioning, what am I supposed to do?' But by half nine the decision is taken out of her hands. The house is buzzing with police officers who have come to question me and my siblings about how Dad abused us.

Among them is a pretty, young, softly spoken policewoman with long brown hair and clear pale-brown eyes. Introducing herself as Kelly, she explains she's travelled all the way from Inverness, especially to speak to me. She drives me to Kirkwall Police Station to take a written statement and for a while we travel in silence.

After a few miles, my curiosity gets the better of me and I ask the question I've been asking myself since last night, 'How did you find out about my dad?'

Glancing at me, she replies, 'I'd prefer to tell you that at the station, if you don't mind.'

There's a while to go before we get there and now I'm even more desperate to know. Why won't she tell me now? So I try asking a different way: 'But who told? Was it someone from my family?'

'As I've said, Esther,' she replies patiently, 'I really think it's best that we discuss it at the station.'

I look away, knowing she won't be pressed.

I wonder if this has anything to do with my oldest sister. I haven't seen her since she got pregnant at 16 to a local farmer on the island of Rousay where we used to live. Dad went ballistic when he heard about the baby. He rained down on her with kicks and thumps, yanking out great clumps of her hair until she was a cowering ball in the corner. Then he threw her out into the night. As far as I know she went to live with the farmer – she had nowhere else to go. But last year she reported Dad to the police for abusing us. The police came to speak to him and I prayed he had finally been found out. But they just talked to him outside the house for a few minutes – then went away. Everything went back to the way it was and it was as if they had never come. But, I reason, maybe they've had a chance to think about it?

Once Kelly and I are in an interview room at the police station, she looks at me compassionately. 'Okay, Esther, are you sure you want to know how we found out about your father? You might find it upsetting.'

'Yes,' I reply urgently, 'I'm sure.'

'Right, well, as we speak your brother Alfie is recovering in a hospital in Inverness, after he tried to take his own life.'

I gasp and she waits, letting the information sink in. I sit in stunned silence, as she continues. 'He was so frightened of returning home to your father's abuse, he tried to kill himself. When the staff asked him why he'd done it, he eventually told them everything about your dad.'

Tears burst from my eyes, not just at Alfie's bravery, but in relief that it's all out in the open and important people, like the police, are finally taking it seriously.

I can't help recalling the whispered conversations between my older siblings and it suddenly hits me that what they said all along was true. Dad abusing us was wrong. He had been committing crimes against us our whole lives, and we did matter – we just got the wrong social worker!

'Now I need you to tell us what your dad did to you, Esther. Everything you can think of.'

But after all the years of wishing for this moment, the

words won't come out. I'd always imagined the police would somehow know and they wouldn't need me to explain. I cry in frustration that I can't put my pain into words.

Kelly looks at me worriedly. 'You must tell us, Esther. It's the only way we can put your dad away for what he's done.' But even in the next few interviews with her, I still can't.

The abuse secrets have been locked inside me so long, I'm unable to let them out. No matter how many times Kelly reassures me it's okay to tell her, I don't believe it. Telling doesn't come naturally, it feels wrong, every part of it. I'm going against my father. I'm telling an outsider his secrets and I am certain he will hunt me down and kill me. They can't lock that powerful man away, not he who can take me down with one swipe. Not the man who can hurt me so badly I wish I could die. They don't have the power, they have to work within rules, while Dad can do anything.

A couple of weeks into questioning, I still haven't managed to complete my statement. Kelly has been calm and understanding up until now, but I can tell she's losing her patience. One day she gives me an ultimatum: 'Esther, if you don't tell us what your father did to you, we will be forced to release him. He will come home and terrorise you all again. It isn't only you you have to think of, but your younger siblings. Think of your little sister Holly! You can help us stop him!'

At the mention of Holly, everything becomes clear. Even if they don't manage to hold him and he comes and gets me – like he does in my nightmares – I have to tell. I can't go back to living in constant fear. I don't ever want to be hit, kicked or used as a punchbag again. And I know I can't bear to watch my little sister being abused again. If telling Kelly will help make that stop, then I must tell.

I try to explain that every day in our house was a living nightmare, revolving around Dad's moods. Each morning he would whack us awake with the stick. He'd beat us for the simplest of things, for infractions against his orders that only existed in his head. He only ever seemed to get pleasure from hurting us kids. Every day was filled with his mind games and traps that we always fell into so Dad could justify abusing us.

As I speak, I sense Kelly is finding it difficult to comprehend what I'm telling her. But this was my everyday life – the way I had been brought up. This was my normality. She asks me about my earliest memory and I recall being beaten for wetting my nappy. Then I remember my first toy – a pop-up clown. I must have been around two years of age and that toy – given to me by one of my older siblings' teachers – brought me so much joy. It never failed to surprise me how the clown appeared to pop up from nowhere – making me giggle. I was playing with it one day and suddenly it was wrenched from my hands by Dad. He sneered at me, before snapping it like a twig and throwing it at me. Looking down at the broken toy, I experienced the hitching at the back of my throat and sharp hollow pangs of anxious bewilderment in the pit of my stomach that would become a constant feature of my life.

But Dad's speciality was sadistic abuse. I was three years old when he pointed at shoes and told me to put boots on. He watched me struggle to get the shoes on, then beat me because they weren't boots. I cry as I relive my confusion at never understanding what I was doing wrong.

But I still can't tell her about the sexual abuse. So instead I, along with my sisters, are sent for a physical, which proves I've been sexually abused.

Meanwhile, life at Crook Farm is turned upside down. Having lived our whole lives under Dad's abusive regime, my siblings and I have never known such freedom. So we let off steam. We swear and shout for the first time and inevitably fights break out among us as we struggle to understand our new boundaries.

But the biggest change is in Mum. It began soon after Dad was taken. It's almost as if she is waking up a different person. She is much friendlier and nicer and talks to us kids like we are real people. I think it might have something to do with the tablets the doctor put her on. I notice it most in her face; it's gone from an empty expressionless mask to a face that alters with her feelings. She has promised us Dad won't be coming home and has even changed our surname to her maiden name of W. Mum has never disciplined us – that was left to Dad. But now she tells us off when we've done something naughty and gives us comfort if we've been hurt. She has been asking Keith Pratt, the director of social work, for help, as she's struggling to cope. Lots of neighbours are helping us too, making food and watching us kids, while Mum tries to sort things out: nobody wants our Dad to come home.

Because ours is such an unusual case, especially with us being a large family of 15 children and the abuse being of such a sadistic nature, Dad's case is given almost daily news coverage as it goes through court. One article in a national newspaper is written beneath a cartoon that, at the age of 13, I find excruciatingly painful. It is an illustration of the old woman in a shoe who had so many children she didn't know what to do. When I see the cartoon, I realise that as well as my dad, there are other horrible adults in the world. But I had already been experiencing this at school from one of my teachers. She lets her son bring in all the latest press cuttings about my family's case and he reads them out to the class of 20 other kids. At first I protest, but she threatens I'll be punished for my insolence. So I sit there, feeling like I want to curl up and die with humiliation, as her son reads out the graphic personal details of my abusive past, as if my life is one big joke.

With the court case looming and the teacher's incomprehensible cruelty to contend with, I struggle to continue in normal mainstream education. Our family social worker, Mona Drone, gets an educational psychologist to assess me and it is realised how badly my education is suffering. I am given the choice of extra tuition or leaving Orkney for a special school in Inverness. I jump at the chance of getting away from everything I have ever known. I am finally looking forward to my future – my wonderful life seems about to begin.

But my suffering isn't over yet, not by a long shot. A chain of events has been set in motion that will have far-reaching consequences, for me and many others.

Part Two

1988–1990

CHAPTER FOUR

Oakhill: a place of safety?

I t's great to be spending time with my mum on the way to my new school. We chatted non-stop on the early morning plane ride from Orkney to Inverness. It's as if we are getting to know one another, which seems a bit strange – as I am 14! But I don't care – I am just happy to finally have a mother.

We are met at the airport by a man in a pastel-coloured outfit who introduces himself as, 'Neville, the Van Man from Oakhill House.' We climb inside the deep blue minibus with Oakhill House scrolled upon its side in decorative gold lettering.

Leaving Inverness, we both feel instantly queasy as Neville enters miles of deep countryside. Twisting down lanes, racing up over hillocks and speeding around bends, he abruptly turns off left to sweep through tall decorative iron gates. Down along a tree-lined lane he drives, and further still, up a little hill, until he finally comes to a stop, outside Oakhill House. Hidden within its own secret wood it's an imposing, grey stone building, with numerous chimneys, striking upwards, while its large, rectangular windows reflect clear Scottish skies. Mum and I unsteadily clamber from Neville's minibus. We exchange nervous glances before

I step forward and press a button set inside a stone carving of a lion's head, releasing commanding bells.

Alexander Burberry, the headmaster, fills the double doors. 'Ah, I'm so pleased you made it!' he says, his upper-class English accent sounding genuinely delighted. His plump red face is animated and his brown eyes crease and twinkle, as if he's been looking forward to my coming to Oakhill House for ages.

Without me realising, Neville has taken my bags and disappeared inside. Alexander Burberry continues to talk warmly as if we are long-lost friends. 'Esther, I'm so sorry but I will have to desert you, as there are a couple of things I must see to. But all of us at Oakhill House are looking forward to getting to know you and we'll see you shortly, up at the meeting room.'

'Yeah, see ya later,' I bluster embarrassedly, unused to such nice treatment.

Looking up at Oakhill House's grand facade, I suddenly feel overwhelmed. Should someone like me really be coming to a place like this? Mum's no help, as she conspiratorially whispers, 'Do you think we could find somewhere to have a quick fag, before going to that meeting?' Both our trains of thought are cut short, however, by the arrival of a reed-thin grey-haired man, warmly calling out 'Hello', as he approaches. 'I'm Mike, a teacher here at Oakhill. Would you like me to show you to the meeting room?'

After a short uphill walk, we arrive outside a barn which is separate from Oakhill. Melodic pipe music lingers in the air as we follow Mike up a dark wooden staircase. The small room at the top is packed with children and adults sitting on wooden benches that line the walls. Feeling self-conscious from eyes watching in every direction, I'm relieved when I'm seated in the spaces that have been saved for us. Light from open windows bounces off the white-washed walls until the room seems plunged in neon sunshine. Small rugs and bean bags litter the wooden floor and the air is delicately perfumed from numerous thick white candles dotted about. Yet more smaller candles flicker inside a huge low-slung black metal chandelier at the centre of the room, above Alexander Burberry who reclines in a chair much larger than everyone else's. His eyes are closed as if lost in meditation, and there is a calm within the room as all eyes are fixed upon him.

The feeling of expectation mounts as the music track playing nears its end. Alexander slowly lifts his head and opens his eyes. He nods at the person next to the tape player and looks around at everyone, as if seeing us anew. 'Good morning,' he says in his gentle yet booming voice, 'and welcome to one and all!'

Alexander Burberry starts by introducing me to the whole school. 'Please give an extra special Oakhill House welcome to Esther who, we are hoping, will be staying with us for a while.'

'Welcome, Esther,' the room choruses back.

Heat rushes to my cheeks and I struggle to meet their eyes while suppressing an urge to giggle.

Special mention is given to pupils who have performed good deeds that they are told they should be proud of, and everyone applauds them. Then Christopher, a member of staff, tells a story about a boy who wandered off one day from where he was supposed to be, and got lost. He met some boys, who were intent on stealing. But the boy knew he was doing wrong, so he made a very difficult choice and said he wouldn't join them. The boy then managed to find his way home by remembering what was right and true. I love hearing stories but I can't really take it in, this room is too quiet – so my thoughts get extra loud.

Alexander Burberry nods to a slim woman with straggly brown hair. 'Karen, some songs please!'

Karen picks up her guitar, and in her happy, bright voice says, 'Right, everyone, open your yellow books and let's hear those wonderful singing voices.'

In shuffling unison everyone reaches beneath their seats and we sing a mixture of songs. My favourites later become 'Little Boxes', 'Streets of London' and 'Last Night I had the Strangest Dream'.

What sounds like a prayer is read out by one of the pupils. Then Alexander Burberry asks us all to take a few minutes and think about the people we love or those who aren't as fortunate as us and everyone bows their heads. Mum and I follow suit and apart from the occasional cough there is silence. I become aware of delicate distant bird song before my stomach gives an uneasy jolt and my eyes flick open – I must always watch out!

With their eyes closed, I take my chance to look around at the other pupils. They all wear a uniform of smart black trousers and bottle-green sweatshirts, with a scrolled golden OH stitched on them. They look between 11 and 17 years of age and I'm surprised to see they all look normal. As Oakhill House is a school for children with special needs, I'd been expecting some pupils to have physical disabilities. There is one face I'm drawn to. I caught his smiley blue eyes as I came in and felt my face flush and stomach flip, so I quickly looked away. Now his head is bent to his chest, as if deep in thought. A thick curtain of white-blond hair flops over his forehead and his dark lashes brush his cheeks, and his generous lips are firmly pressed together. His arms are folded high across his chest, while his legs are slung wide open, pushing into his neighbours. Suddenly, feeling uneasy, I turn around and catch the staring eyes of a small, dark bearded man on the opposite side of the room. I hurriedly shut my eyes, feeling as if I've been caught out.

Alexander Burberry's voice interrupts my thoughts. 'Now, all to your classes and no dawdling,' he calmly instructs.

The gentle, melodic music bursts into the air once more, as everyone seems to glide from the room. Morning meetings will become part of my life here, but today I look in from the outside and see many people living together harmoniously. I've lived in a large family my whole life, but under Dad's rule, it was an existence of fighting, survival, loss and pain. But here it feels right, like I'm finally being welcomed back to my real family and my true home.

Mum and I are introduced to an older girl called Claire, who is to show us round Oakhill House. She proudly informs us she knows it like the back of her hand as she's been here for four years. We follow her bright eyes into every corner of Oakhill, having a job keeping up with her eager energy.

I can't believe this is a place I'm visiting, let alone somewhere I'll be staying. Where I'd been expecting small and bare, Oakhill House is huge and grand. Claire takes us back to where we first arrived, the front main porch. With its own seating and double aspect windows, Claire confides in lowered tones that it's where pupils are sent to sit and think if they've been naughty during mealtimes, as Mr Burberry can keep an eye on them through the windows of the neighbouring dining room. Coming in through the front door, we arrive at the bottom of a majestic staircase with a highly polished dark wood bannister balanced on long decorative metal stems. It's the kind of staircase that Cinderella would float down when she arrives to the ball. The stairway runs all the way up to the boys' wing. But, Claire explains, she can't show us up there as we are not allowed, adding, 'The boys' wing is about three times bigger than the girls'.' We turn right and down a long cavernous corridor. One side is a wall of large rectangular windows that look out on to the leafy trees at the front of Oakhill. On the other side, numerous doors lead off to a staffroom, and then a quiet room decorated in pale colours and filled with bean bags and soft chairs. The last three, Claire explains, are just random storage rooms. At the end of the corridor, we enter a huge main sitting room. The room sweeps around from a half-circle window seat to a decorative walk-in stone fireplace. Further windows over-look Oakhill's little farm made up of chicken, ducks and a couple of goats. Tucked away in the far left corner is sick bay, where Edith, the nurse, takes care of the pupils' coughs and colds, bumps and bruises. The room surrounds three very large, comfortable-looking couches, two facing one another and another facing the fireplace.

Awestruck, we follow Claire back down the corridor and past the front porch, where she shows us into the main dining room. Like the sitting room, it is oval with its own fireplace, but on a smaller scale. Windows on every available side bathe the room in morning sunshine, and the ready-laid tables twinkle a welcome to the pupils. We tour on to a huge stainless steel kitchen, where I'm introduced to the two cheerful cooks, Sam and Beth.

At the other end of the main corridor is a small plain white door. 'This goes up to the girls' wing,' Claire explains, before disappearing up the staircase, while we struggle behind her. 'There will be eight of us girls, now you're here!' she calls back. Four bedrooms lead off from a communal corridor, toilet and bathroom. Claire shows me to the room I'll be staying in. A rectangular sash window and a wooden chest of drawers separates two beds. One side of the room is surrounded by personal possessions. Clothes, hair scrunchies and numerous shoes peek out from beneath the bed, and posters of James Dean and Marilyn Monroe are on two of the walls. The other side is bare and empty, except for my two bags on the bed, waiting to be unpacked.

While Mum goes to the bathroom, I begin to unpack my bags. 'You're sharing with Tracey,' Claire warns, 'so maybe you'd better wait until she tells you which drawers and space you can have!'

My stomach ripples nervously. 'Why, what's Tracey like?' I ask tentatively.

Claire checks behind her before answering, 'Well, I don't think she wants to share with anybody as she's had this room to herself for so long.' Seeing my face fall, she adds, 'Don't worry, you might get lucky, she's supposed to be leaving, as she's over 16. But she doesn't want to go. She's all right, really, it's just she likes things her own way!'

Mum and I are sent off for a wander by ourselves. Mum's

been gagging for a fag since this morning, so under the pretence of looking around, we disappear into the woods. Concealed within the furthest leafy corner, Mum lights up and drags greedily on a cigarette. There's a tense silence as we both seem unsure what to say, so instead we admire a huge decorative tree house. After a few awkward minutes Mum looks at me through a smoky haze, her eyes filled with concern. 'Are you sure you want to come here?'

If it's a choice between going back to a world where I'm the abused girl or coming to a place where I can be someone new, there's no contest. 'Yes,' I quickly reply, scared that if I hesitate I might wake up from this magical dream.

At lunch we sit on the main table with Alexander Burberry. As the meal comes to an end, I spy the dark blue minibus, parked outside the porch. It's almost time for Mum to leave. Before she climbs in, Mum hugs me and whispers, 'You can come home any time you like, you know that don't you?'

'Yes, Mum,' I reply impatiently, desperate to get on with my new life at Oakhill.

Karen, the woman who played guitar and sang in morning meeting, waits with me, while I wave Mum off. The bus disappears through the iron gates and Karen puts an arm around my shoulder. 'Let's go and find your roomie.'

Tracey has been having a lie down, but sits up when we come in and shoots me a little smile. She's plump with pretty, delicate features framed by long poker-straight black hair, a small freckly snub nose, and pale-green almond-shaped eyes. With a long-nailed finger she point to the main chest, 'I've cleared the bottom two drawers out for you and the other three are mine!' Opening the wardrobe, she shows me the little space she's made for me, by shoving her stuff over, explaining, 'I need more space than you, because I've got more stuff.' She's right there: the two drawers will be plenty for my couple of pairs of trousers and tops, which look shabby and dull next to Tracey's fashionable colourful clothes.

I soon learn there's a strict routine at Oakhill House. We must be washed, dressed and downstairs in a clean uniform by 8 a.m., ready to go about our morning jobs. The most popular jobs are working with the animals on the little farm, but those rarely come up. I'm put on cleaning the art room, which I enjoy as I get to chat to Meredith, the art therapist. At half eight, a loud gong announces a breakfast of granola cereal and thick slices of brown toast laden with butter and home-made jam, and washed down with fresh fruit juice. Then we all traipse back upstairs to wash our teeth and tidy ourselves up for inspection in the hall at nine.

Inspection is carried out by a couple of members of staff. They walk up and down, checking our faces, hands, uniform and shoes, before we're allowed to make our way up to morning meeting. Everyone does their best to pass, as being sent to clean this or change that means that not only are you late going in to the meeting room, so everyone watches you come in, but also you don't get to sit next to your friends.

From morning meeting, we make our way to classes of English, maths, science and art. We break only for a mid-morning snack and lunch before the school day finishes at four-thirty. There's a half-hour break before teatime at five o'clock, after which is free time. In free time, you can join an organised activity, such as a sport or woodwork, or, if given permission, you can have social time to spend with other pupils. Social time is done in the main sitting room or in the grounds. As a rule, we're not supposed to go to our rooms until bedtime. Mine is 9 p.m., by which time I'm supposed to be washed and in bed.

Mike Fraser, the thin grey man who showed me and Mum to the meeting room on my first day, is the English teacher. Maths is taken by Archie Miles. A big, burly, dark-haired Scottish man with intense green eyes, Mr Miles is also a red-faced ticking time bomb, guaranteed to blow up at least once every lesson. Although it's scary, it's funny to watch if you're not on the receiving end. One day before Mr Miles arrived in the classroom, a pupil called Daniel, who loves playing jokes on people, had been messing about. He was making us all laugh by writing things on the white board, like 'Mr Miles takes it up the arse' and 'Mr Miles loves cock'. As Mr Miles entered the classroom he caught sight of the last comment and turned a very scary purple colour. 'Who did this?' he bellowed, spinning around on the class. Nobody spoke up. Leaving it on the board, Mr Miles went on, 'I'll give the culprit of this handiwork ten minutes to own up. If they choose not to, the whole class will be punished and stay in over break. So I suggest you urge your friend to own up!' Nobody likes a grass, but we like staying in over break less, so when Mr Miles goes back to the board, we are all turning to Daniel to see if he'll own up. But instead he decides to take an even cheekier risk. He attempts to add something to the board while he thinks Mr Miles isn't looking. He quietly gets up and starts creeping towards it, but Mr Miles turns so fast, Daniel looks as if he might jump out of his skin. 'Boy! What is the meaning of this?' he roars, before leaping at Daniel and marching him from the classroom.

I take to life at Oakhill House like a duck to water, and I soon love living there. I have a good group of friends, Eliza, Gordon and James, who I spend most of my time with. I've been nervous around Luke since my first day when I saw him in the morning meeting, so it becomes obvious that I fancy him. I've been told he fancies me too, which only makes it worse. Luke is known for being very shy, so it seems he'll never ask me out. Until one day Luke's friend Jeremy organises us both to meet him at the tree house. Looking at Luke he asks, 'You like Esther, don't you?'

'Aye,' Luke answers, smiling shyly.

Turning to me, Jeremy asks, 'And you like Luke, right?'

I feel my face flush as I nod.

'Well then,' Jeremy demands, 'do I have to spell it out?'

From then on, Luke and I are officially boyfriend and girlfriend. Every time I see him, he gets cuter, with his carefully styled blond hair and fit muscly body – I can hardly believe someone so gorgeous is my real-life boyfriend!

So I start spending most of my social time at Oakhill House with Luke. But unfortunately, he's into heavy metal bands like Metallica, which I don't like. Although he confides to me that he likes songs from *Dirty Dancing*, but I'm not to tell anyone that. We go for long walks in the woods together, where we sit on a log sharing a fag, while keeping an eye out for staff. He gets embarrassed by the sound of his own voice, which is low and mumbly, while I'm shy too, so we don't talk much, but it's a happy silence.

I can't believe how much my life has changed for the

better since coming to Oakhill. It's as if I'm walking on air, inside a protected bubble of blissful happiness. When the other kids complain about hating it here, saying they can't wait to leave, I don't get it. For me, it's as if I've come to a new life so wonderful, I never would have imagined it existed, let alone that I would get to live it! The others moan about the morning jobs we have to do, but compared with being pushed out into the icy Orkney winds and told not to return until I've stolen enough potatoes from next door's fields – these jobs are nothing! Or shovelling cow poo, until your arms and legs burn, that's tough, not doing a bit of tidying up or cleaning! Most of the children are here because of things that have happened to them, that have affected them emotionally. Some of the girls have been raped, sexually abused and/or beaten and it's had a big impact on their education and ability to learn. I look at some of them sometimes and I wish for their problems, which are mainly one-off incidents. Then I catch myself feeling like I've never felt my whole life – normal. I delight in wearing short socks to gym. When I go swimming now, I don't need to check my body for bruises, so I've even stopped bothering. And when I run, I hear the sound of my laughter because I'm running for fun, not trying to escape.

Sharing a room with Tracey is working out all right. Yes, she's bossy, but that's okay with me as I know exactly where I stand. Most people are nice to her face but talk about her behind her back, saying she should piss off and stop lording it over the rest of us. But I'm used to living with people and we don't disagree on much: I get mad when she uses my eyeliner without asking and it annoys her when I have the window open at night. But I need it open as otherwise I feel trapped, like there's no air getting in, while she says it lets spiders get in. Spiders are her biggest fear. I didn't realise how serious it was until one night a tiny one, not much bigger than the head of a nail, got on her bed and she went ghostly white and started screaming, while trying to climb the wall.

We get talking one night and Tracey asks me why I'm here. As I tell her the bits I don't mind people knowing, she interrupts and admits she knows she isn't supposed to still be here. 'But where can I go?' she asks plaintively.

I look back blankly, unsure what to suggest. Her social worker has given her the address of a halfway house, but that would mean she's on the way out. She wants to stay with her mum, but she won't have her – she's got a new boyfriend and he doesn't like Tracey. Suddenly Tracey doesn't seem like the biggest girl holding on to what little power she has, she seems like a desperate little girl, with nowhere to go.

Meanwhile, for me, Oakhill House feels more and more like home and I'm the newest member of a big family. When we first arrive at Oakhill House we're put into teams. These are made up of about five staff and 12 pupils, and headed by a team leader, usually a senior member of staff. Ours is Christopher Yeoman. Christopher is the science teacher here, which is my least favourite subject after maths, but he is one of my favourite members of staff. As a child, I endlessly re-read *The BFG* by Roald Dahl. I dreamed that I was Sophie and one day I would meet the Big Friendly Giant, and when I met Christopher Yeoman it seemed that I had. Christopher is tree-tall gangly in his baggy green lab coat and shabby brown cords. His huge hook nose peeks out between giant batwing ears, and his unruly strawberry-blond hair sprawls down into bushy sideburns. He talks in a low slow Liverpudlian accent and always sees the funny side of things, with his blue eyes twinkling mischievously. But what he loves talking about most is science stuff. I try my hardest to listen but thankfully he can be easily distracted by questions, and then he'll talk for ages about almost anything.

Our team meets on a Friday afternoon, just before children go home for the weekend. We discuss what's happened during the week. Have we done things we're proud of that deserve treats? Or have we done things we are sorry about, but want to make right, by doing something for the person we've upset? We are then nominated to go on what's called the Privilege List, which entitles you to do things like visiting the sweet shop in the local village and using the gypsy caravan for social time. This week Beth, the cook, nominates me for being helpful in the kitchen and, 'Just for being bright-eyed and bushy-tailed,' adding 'Esther is like a ray of morning sunshine,' and the funny thing is, when she said that, I realised that, these days, I sometimes feel like one.

After we've been at Oakhill House for a while there is an informal discussion about our progress at team meeting. Just before we go on Easter break, Christopher announces we will be looking at mine. He starts by saying he's seen me transform, butterfly-like from my chrysalis. Adding when I first arrived, I seemed to distrust everyone, but now it's as if I believe there are good people in the world. He asks me to comment on my own development. I shyly agree; I have come a long way. I put it down to lots of things but especially the art therapy I have with Meredith. She is my special member of staff. All of us pupils are assigned one when we first arrive here. We can go to our special member of staff to chat to or confide in. Meredith's large pale blue eyes underneath raised eyebrows give her a permanently surprised look, as if amazed by everything I say. But, most importantly for me, I feel like I can talk to her about anything. With her long grey plaits – flecked in multi-coloured paint specks from leaning over and checking pupils' work – she reminds me of a pretty wise owl and she always has words of wisdom, to answer any dilemma I have. It quickly feels as if I have a second mum. But I get this one all to myself, instead of having to share her between 15 siblings.

My chest swells as Christopher concludes by saying he's proud of me, as is everyone at Oakhill House. I'm applauded as I stare into my lap. He finishes by saying I must work on acknowledging how far I've come. I nod, just wanting this to be over and the attention moved on to someone else. But inside I feel as if a shooting star has exploded, and for the first time in my life, I experience a little pride.

There are a couple of surprises waiting for me when I return to Oakhill House after Easter break. I discover Tracey has finally left, and hear she went to the halfway house. But I'm devastated to discover that Meredith, my special member of staff and the art teacher has left. She didn't tell me she was leaving, as she thought it would be more painful for me. I'm not sure which grown-up I can talk to now.

There is good news on the room front, however, as I'll be sharing with Eliza. She's one of my closest friends here and she's always good fun to be around as she's got a great sense of humour. Although she's the same age as me, she seems much more grown up. Her figure is fully developed with huge boobs and wide hips, so she's allowed out of sports and swimming as she feels self-conscious. She doesn't like swimming anyway, she says it messes up her highlighted corkscrew hair and ruins her bright blue eyeliner and neon-pink lipstick, which she's forever reapplying.

I've been at Oakhill House for about five months now and I've settled into a pattern of going home every couple of weeks. While I enjoy spending time with my brothers and sisters on the farm, I'm always excited to be travelling back to Oakhill House on the Sunday afternoon. I catch myself sometimes daydreaming that, from the outside, I must look like any other ordinary 14-year-old girl. I have great friends and a boyfriend I love being with. Sometimes I even fantasise that one day I might become Mrs Luke White.

That 14-year-old girl was me for a little while. But my life was about to change, reminding me I am not normal and never will be.

CHAPTER FIVE

Overdosing

It is just after tea on a Saturday evening. I'm staying at Oakhill this weekend and I'm reading a book on one of the couches in the big sitting room. Only a few kids, maybe three or four at most, stay at the weekend. It's a different Oakhill House then, emptier but also more relaxed. If the right staff are on it's great fun, but if not, it's boring and time drags and it's then that I wish I was back home, on Crook Farm.

Adrian, a member of staff, comes in accompanied by two boys. He must be on this weekend, I mindlessly note. I find him a bit creepy as I've caught him looking at me a few times. But I don't think he's that keen on girls, as he seems to prefer spending his time with the boys, either doing woodwork or rough-and-tumbling. He's probably in his early fifties and almost as small as the boys he's with. He is super alert, darting here and there with jerky little movements – reminding me of a weasel, that's discovered itself above ground, without a tunnel to hide in. His curranty eyes dart about himself, while his large pointy nose pokes out through his grizzly black beard, nervously sniffing at the air.

They sit on the sofa opposite me, and the boys start throwing cushions on Adrian. During the week, they wouldn't be allowed to play rough on the sofas and I wonder if Adrian will tell them off. But instead, he starts throwing cushions back and soon a play fight is in full flow.

I watch for a moment, surprised at them play-fighting inside. Adrian looks up, catches my eye and winks before continuing. My stomach jolts. I've been caught out – I wish I'd never looked. I try to focus on the words in my book, but their playing and laughter reminds me of my siblings. It was in rare moments of feeling free; under Dad's rule it was only when he wasn't around that we could let ourselves go and play. Rolling around the floor, like the children we were, laughing until our stomachs ached. Pangs of homesickness wash over me – I miss my brothers and sisters; I want to go home.

I feel Adrian staring over at me and look up. 'Do you want to play?' he whispers. I shake my head. He leans over the small table dividing our sofas, grips my knee and uses it to hoist himself up. He then plonks down beside me. 'It's okay, you can, I won't bite,' he adds, in a barely audible whisper.

The boys disappear and suddenly Adrian is pushed up beside me and I feel horribly uncomfortable. I don't want to be alone with him in this room, in the whole of Oakhill.

I shift along the sofa. 'I've got to—'

Putting his finger to his lips, he says, 'Sshh, don't worry,' and with frightening ease he pulls me up and over himself so I'm on his lap, facing him. My book clunks to the floor and my stomach churns with panic and confusion about what I should be doing right now. I glimpse his eyes. From a distance they look dark brown, but now I see are a deep burnt orange. He smiles excitedly, like this awkward horribleness is normal rough and tumble. I grab the side of the couch, trying to pull myself away, but he presses my arms to my sides. Leaning into my ear he breathes, 'That's it, see, you like playing. I thought you would!' Laughing softly, he turns me towards the seat of the sofa and lays me down and suddenly he's on top of me, grinning. 'You like that?'

'No,' I hear myself meekly squeak, the words jamming in my throat.

'Come on, let's play. It can be our little secret.'

With rising terror, I realise I can't move. I'm trapped and there's nothing I can do about it. I open my mouth to scream but only gluey sounds escape. Right now I should be screaming. But Adrian is the member of staff I would be calling to – for help!

I twist my face as far away from him as possible and focus on the curvy grain of the wooden coffee table. Waves of nausea wash over me, as his hot breath burns my cheek and his hairy face burrows into my neck. Momentarily I think I might escape when he releases one of my arms. But it's only so he can pull himself further up me. Then he's sitting astride my stomach, gripping my body between his legs. 'Are you enjoying yourself?' he whispers. I continue staring at the table, because this isn't happening. It can't be. It isn't real. Not in the sitting room at Oakhill! Then with horror I realise he's reaching down behind himself, and I know why. I struggle, twisting, turning, kicking and shaking my head. 'No, no, please!' I beg in a barely audible croak. But he keeps going until I feel his hand on my private parts, pressing hard and squeezing. As I'm shaking my head, I glimpse his face, flashing a sickly sweet smile at me, as if still trying to pretend we are playing. My heart pounds so hard it feels as though it might rip from my chest, whooshing blood into my ears and everything sounds muffled. After what feels like an excruciatingly long time, the sound of someone approaching brings me back to the room. I look up at Adrian: this is my chance to escape and he knows it. Panic shoots across his face and he jumps off me. I sit up, while he hurriedly straightens himself up. Before the boys enter the room, he leans towards me and winks. 'See, that wasn't so bad was it, you should play more often Esther, you'd enjoy it!'

Adrenalin kicks in and I leap up and run from the room, past Adrian and the boys coming in, straight up to the girls' wing. Locking myself in the bathroom, I tear my clothes off and get under the shower. Tears blind me, falling with the water, as angry thoughts swirl around my mind. Why did I think I could be a normal girl? I must remember I'm not the same as other girls. How stupid to imagine I could be. I've made this happen. Adrian must have done it accidentally. He wouldn't have done it on purpose – not a care worker at Oakhill! I shouldn't have been playing rough and tumble with him anyway – what did I expect?

The following morning at breakfast, I sit on the other side of the room from Adrian. But as I'm checking round, I catch him staring over at me. I hurriedly look away. I can tell he's angry with me. It's because I made him do dirty stuff. I finish eating and am putting my breakfast dishes in the sink, when my body tenses as Adrian comes up behind me. Pressing himself into my back, he whispers, 'Morning, Esther.'

'Morning,' I murmur before sliding away.

My head is spinning as I return to my room. 'That didn't happen. It couldn't have happened,' I repeat to myself in panic. If I stay away from him, and act like nothing's going on, it can't continue, can it?

After breakfast, the staff are taking us kids out on a Sunday swimming trip. I watch where Adrian sits on the minibus and take the furthest seat from him, next to Alison. She's easy-going, so she's happy to let me sit next to the window. But as the bus pulls away, Adrian gets up and walks down the aisle, stopping to chat to people on the way, but I know it's his sneaky way to get to me. Sure enough he stops next to our seats. 'You all right, girls?' he whispers.

'Yes, fine!' I snap, not taking my eyes from the window.

He waits a moment before he speaks again. 'Alison,' he says, 'we'll have to think of something to cheer Esther up, she's not herself today.'

We pass a field of newborn baby lambs, but I still feel disgusted. I know what he's doing. I can't say it, but I know.

'We'll have a laugh at swimming, Esther,' Alison promises.

'I said I'm fine,' I reply sharply.

'Well,' Adrian continues, 'if it's something I've done, I didn't mean to upset you.'

My stomach churns. I know he's talking about what happened yesterday. He didn't mean to do it – he is truly sorry. 'It's okay,' I mumble, turning to look at him. He's just trying to care about me and be nice and I'm messing it up with my dirty thoughts. He's a member of staff, he would never do those things. Care workers don't do dirty things – they look after children.

*

79

I'm changing for bed that evening, when there's an abrupt rap at the door. Before I have time to answer, Adrian appears.

'Adrian, I'm getting dressed!' I call out in surprise.

Without taking his eyes off me, he sits on Eliza's bed. 'Esther, you've got a lovely body, you shouldn't be ashamed of it.'

I hurriedly climb into bed and pull the duvet up under my chin and wait expectantly. Without taking his eyes off me, he slowly rises and crosses the room. I instinctively push myself against the wall. Sitting on my bed, he leans towards me. 'I'm sorry about what happened yesterday, I know I was a bit rough on you,' he whispers.

My stomach clenches uneasily and I shoot a look at the door. 'Alison is coming up in a minute. She's sleeping in here, with me,' I bluff.

Adrian lets out a low laugh. 'Well, she's not here now, is she?'

'No, but she will be!' I reply defensively, my voice trembling.

He sits still for a couple of painfully uncomfortable minutes, before asking, 'We are still friends, aren't we?'

'Yes,' I lie.

He moves back a little, and I think he's about to leave, but instead he suddenly pushes his face up to mine. 'Well, let's seal it with a kiss then.' I turn my cheek, hoping he'll give it a quick peck. But he cups my face and forces me to meet his. Pressing his lips hard on mine, his tongue pushes inside my mouth. I squeeze my eyes tight shut and try to pull away. Releasing me he gets up. 'We've got a very special little secret, you and I,' he whispers, before adding, 'and I know your dad would be very proud of you!'

I tearfully scrub at my mouth with a hot flannel, trying to get rid of the feel of his lips, but my mind is stained. Later, as I'm listening to Alison gently snoring, I turn over what Adrian said. What did he mean by it? Why did he say it? What, or more importantly, who does Adrian know? And why would my dad be proud of me?

As Monday dawns, I desperately wish things will go back to the way they were only a week ago. Adrian can't do anything dirty to me as there are lots of people around, especially Luke, I reassure myself. And when Adrian is off for a couple of days, I dare to hope they were just one-off incidents and my life can return to normal.

But a week later, I'm in the laundry room one afternoon, taking my clothes out of the dryer, when I feel someone touch my bottom. I spin round. 'Well, hello, Esther, what a nice welcome!' Adrian whispers.

After that Adrian touches me whenever he gets a chance. Putting his hand between my legs or touching my boobs, always with a dirty comment or a twisted compliment: 'You have very nice boobs, Esther!' Showing him how upset, disgusted or fearful I am only seems to excite him more. When there are other people around, my stomach lurches, as he winks at me, as if we are sharing dirty secrets together.

Later that week Adrian is doing an evening shift. I go to bed before Eliza and a few minutes later, Adrian pokes his head around the door. 'Not feeling well?'

I jump, and pull the duvet up tight around myself. 'No, I'm just tired,' I mutter.

He comes in anyway and sits on the end of my bed. 'Would you like a massage?'

'No,' I reply irritably, 'I just want to sleep!'

'Well, that's not very nice, is it?' he whispers. 'I'm just being nice and looking after you. After all, that's what your dad would have wanted.'

Ice cold fear turns to relief as he stands up and goes to my bedroom door. But when he opens it, it's just to check the corridor before quietly closing it and returning to stand by my bed. 'Someone wants a kiss goodnight!' he says, pulling down his trousers to reveal his erect penis. I'm immobile with fear; I don't know what to do. 'Open your mouth, Esther, there's a good girl,' he whispers. My eyes water and his penis goes blurry.

'I just want to sleep,' I plead, turning away.

'Come on, Esther,' he whispers more aggressively, 'be a good girl, and give it a little kiss.'

Panic rises in my throat, like sick, as the acrid smell of old, warm pee hits me. He leans forward and his penis touches my lips. 'That's it; open your mouth. You're daddy's very special girl, aren't you? See, that's it, you know you want to!' He jabs and jabs, until I feel it going in, further and further, until it hits the back of my throat, and I wretch forward. He pulls the back of my head towards him and shoves faster and faster, until my mouth is flooded with hot salty liquid and my stomach starts heaving. He slumps forward, almost falling on me. Stroking my head he whispers hoarsely, 'Your dad would be very proud of you. Good girl, you did good!'

'I'm going to be sick,' I panic.

'Well, swallow it. And remember, Esther, this is our special little secret. It's best not to tell anyone else, they wouldn't understand. Besides, they're not likely to believe your word, over mine!' he smirks, pulling up his trousers. As he leaves, he clicks my light off and calls back, 'Sleep well.'

I wait to hear the door at the bottom of the stairs clang, before I bolt up and race to the toilet, to throw up what I can of the liquid and scrub my mouth out.

The next time Adrian is on night duty, I take a butter knife from the kitchen and unscrew the handle from the outside of my bedroom door. I explain to Eliza that I'm doing it because I want more privacy. I'm relieved that night when Adrian doesn't try to come into our room – not even to sit on my bed and pretend, in front of Eliza, he's just giving me a cuddle. Maybe this was the answer all along, I hope, as I drift off into a peaceful sleep.

But when Alexander Burberry asks for any other business at the end-of-morning meeting the next day, Adrian raises his hand. In his pretend caring voice, he says, 'I won't mention any names, but it came to my attention last night that someone took the handle off their bedroom door. I wouldn't be so bothered, but it's a fire hazard and not just to them, but to all the other pupils.'

'No!' Mr Burberry, agrees sternly. 'You are quite right. That certainly cannot be allowed to go on.'

All the staff nod their heads and I'm engulfed by a feeling of never-ending despair.

A few weeks later, I'm at Oakhill House for the weekend and I'm horrified to discover that Adrian will be on night duty. But worse still, I'm the only girl staying. A nervous gnawing starts in the pit of my stomach on the Friday after-noon as I watch the other girls pack. I haven't slept alone in the girls' wing since Adrian started attacking me. But I've come up with a plan. I'll go to bed much earlier than everyone else and pretend I'm asleep. And, as an added precaution, I've borrowed one of the other girls' fleecy all-in-one sleep suits that covers me, neck to toe, in a giant protective baby-gro.

But deep in the night I'm woken by a sickeningly familiar whisper. 'Esther, wake up, Esther,' Adrian says insistently, stroking my back.

I jolt upright – all plans forgotten. 'What?' I snap.

'Look!' he says, offering out his hand. 'I've got a present for you.'

In the light from the window, I see he's handing me a packet of ten Silk Cut cigarettes. 'Oh,' I say, automatically reaching for them.

'No,' he breathes, pulling them back, 'you can only have one in the staff sleep-in room.'

'I don't want one,' I mumble.

'Listen, Esther, I've got a surprise in there. Something I got especially for you!'

'No Adrian, I don't want it. I don't want to go in there.'

His orange eyes glare dangerously at me. 'I'm doing nice things for you, Esther. You don't want me telling someone you've been a bad girl, do you?' he threatens.

My mind is racing. Does he mean Dad? He can't mean anyone else. Will he tell him about me? I reluctantly sit up. I could just have a cigarette, I suppose.

He pulls me up off the bed. 'Come on,' he says encouragingly, adding, 'you'll really like what I got you.' He looks down at the fleecy baby-gro I'm wearing. 'Why are you wearing that?' he asks irritably. 'You've got a beautiful body, you shouldn't hide it.'

I reluctantly let him lead me out of my bedroom and up the corridor to the staff sleep-in room that divides the girls' and boys' wings. I walk round the large staff bed and lean out of the open window into the still moonlit night. Adrian hands me the cigarettes. 'Have one now, if you like,' he offers. My hands tremble, as I pull open the cellophane seal and tear the silver paper out, revealing two tight neat rows of dappled brown filters. I slide one out and Adrian strikes a match. His flame is steady and waiting, while I struggle to meet it.

I turn back to the night and inhale deeply. Looking out at the farm behind Oakhill House, I am torn up with jealousy at the animals, safely locked away from night predators in their little houses. Beyond the farm is the little cottage where Alexander Burberry lives with his wife and two children. I momentarily wonder what he'd say if he knew what Adrian was doing to one of his pupils in the staff sleep-in room.

Adrian comes up behind me and hands me a glass of vodka and orange. 'Drink this, it'll make you feel better,' he instructs. He's taken off most of his clothes and wears just a T-shirt and pants. He sits on the bed and pats the space beside him. I don't move, instead I sip the drink and let it slip down my throat and flood me with warmth.

The swimming feeling goes straight to my head and suddenly I'm too dizzy to stand. I need to sit, otherwise I'll fall down, so I drop to the end of the bed. Adrian is smiling and whispers, 'Come and have a cuddle.'

I stay still, in an effort to control the dizziness. His hands start pawing at me, pulling me and trying to make me lie down. The room spins faster and faster. I have to close my eyes, but I become aware of Adrian unzipping my all-in-one. 'Please, don't,' I hear myself plead.

'You want this just as much as I do, you know you do!' he whispers viciously. Then he adds, 'You've been cock-teasing me since you got here.'

I open my eyes wide with alarm, does he really believe that? 'I haven't, I swear,' I splutter defensively. But the dizziness takes over again and I must shut my eyes.

I groggily become aware that my all-in-one has been pulled off and I'm only in my pants. Adrian is climbing on top of me. 'I need to throw up,' I say, hoping it might make him stop, but instead my mouth is filled with his wet, pushing tongue. I try moving my face away, but he follows me and with one hand pulls down my pants. I struggle with renewed force when I realise in disbelief what he's going to do. His breathing is heavier and faster and he urgently asks, 'You like that, don't you?' Gripping my arms above my head he forces his body between my legs. Panic rises up my chest. WAKE UP! I scream at myself, knowing I must try to escape from the frozen cage I'm locked in. A sharp hot slicing pain shoots through my body, making me gasp for air, and suddenly it's all too real. 'Ah, that's nice. You're a dirty girl. Your daddy's dirty girl!' he whispers urgently, continuing to push himself into me, in sharp stinging stabs. He stabs at me faster and faster, before he suddenly stops and pulls back, rubbing his penis furiously and spraying hot liquid all over my stomach, before slumping over me groaning, 'That was good!' As he moves away, I pull my legs together and limply cross them. 'You make me do this,

Esther,' he says, adding, 'you love it just as much as I do!'
Later I'm vaguely aware of him carrying me back to my
room, my head still spinning.

When I wake the following morning, my head is
thumping violently. I can barely lift it from the pillow but
waves of sickness rise in my stomach, forcing me to
scramble for the bathroom. With my head over the toilet
bowl, last night flashes back to me. I burn with guilt and
shame at the memories of Adrian on top of me. His curranty
eyes smiling down at me. The disgusting things he whispered to me. The red-hot pain as he forced himself inside
me. Please God, I beg, make it not have happened. I recall
my frozen locked body – why didn't I move? I should have
tried harder to escape – but I couldn't move! My stomach
aches and the purple bruises between my thighs remind me
it wasn't a nightmare.

'How are you this morning?' Adrian asks in a mock
caring whisper, pressing his hand on my lower back, while I
sip water at breakfast.

My whole life at Oakhill seems to have become about
trying to stop Adrian sexually attacking me. Whenever there
is an opportunity he forces himself on me in some way.
When I refuse to do what he wants, he knows how to
threaten me. 'You wouldn't want your dad hearing about
what a disobedient girl you've been, would you?' I must
watch out for him everywhere, and I jump when I see him.
I try not washing my body to see if that will stop him. But
Emily, my new special member of staff, just sends me to
nurse Edith who lectures me on personal hygiene. I must tell
someone, but who? If only Meredith, the art therapist was
still at Oakhill – I'm sure I could have told her.

On a weekend home, I try refusing to go back to Oakhill. When asked why I don't want to go back, I try to talk to Mum about it, but the words choke me like gravel. I end up crying and screaming about something else. So I return to Oakhill House and to Adrian.

I can't go on like this! I've experienced the life of a normal 14-year-old girl, and I don't want to live any other way! This isn't living anyway, it's barely existing! One way or another, I decide, I'm getting out of this.

One Sunday evening on the way back to Oakhill, I buy two bottles of paracetamol, each containing 15 tablets. Then I give myself an ultimatum: either I confess to Eliza what Adrian is doing, or I take these tablets!

That evening Eliza and I are lying on our beds chatting. She's telling me about the weekend with her boyfriend, Rob. I don't say much; I'm too busy trying to work out how I'm going to tell her about Adrian. She stops mid-flow. 'Oh, by the way, why did you and Luke break up? I thought you really liked him!'

'I did!' I reply defensively. 'I mean, I do, it's just oh … I don't know,' I sigh resignedly. How can I explain that kissing Luke makes me feel sick now, or tell her how I can't bear to feel anyone touching me. 'Have you done anything with Rob?' I ask, trying to sound casual.

'Kind of,' she giggles, 'you know the usual stuff. What about you and Luke, did you …?'

'No,' I reply, 'just kissing really.'

Eliza continues, 'Oh, Rob's a great kisser—'

'Someone raped me last week!' I forcefully interject.

I stare hard at the ceiling until the silence becomes deafening and I must look at her. She's leaning towards my bed, eyes wide and mouth slack. '*What?*' Suddenly, I don't know what to say. What can I say? I knew people wouldn't believe me. I've already said too much. I desperately wish she could guess the rest for herself. 'Who, Esther, tell me who?' she asks urgently.

I can't say. I know I can't. Who would believe me? 'I don't want to talk about it!' I reply tightly.

'Esther,' she continues insistently, 'you have to tell a member of staff, you've got to talk to someone about this. This is serious!'

'No,' I reply forcefully, 'I can't!'

I jump from my bed and storm to the bathroom. Why does it feel like it's all my fault? Why can't I just tell her? Why am I making Adrian do these things? If I was a normal 14-year-old girl, he wouldn't!

When I'm sure Eliza is asleep, I return to our bedroom. I've already decided to take the tablets that lie waiting under my pillow. If I can't talk to Eliza, I don't stand a chance. Once I've taken the tablets, everything will be okay. It will be the end of it all. I won't feel anything any more. No pain. No anger. Nothing. When they find me in the morning, I'll already be dead – it's the perfect answer for everyone.

I grip one of the little white bottles tightly and carry it, as if it's a precious object, back to the bathroom. I quietly lock the door and pour myself a large glass of water and get settled down on the carpet. I gently spread the bottle's contents upon the floor. Fifteen little white discs, full of the promise of oblivion, glow up at me. I take one and swallow it. It's larger than I realised and it takes a lot of water to make the first few go down. But once I'm warmed up, I start taking two or three together – otherwise this could take for ever! No amount of water can wash away the chalky bitterness that lingers in my throat. But I keep going – I have to. When I try to take more than three at a time, they clog up, their edges jagging like giant sharp discs, against my throat lining. I experiment with different ways of taking them – filling my mouth with water and squeezing them through my pursed lips. Until finally, they are all gone. None on the floor and all in my tummy.

I return to bed and wait for the end. I wait for what seems like ages and still don't feel any different. Suddenly I have a great thirst. I go to get up – I need a drink. But giddiness washes over me and I fall back down to the bed. This is it – they must be working. I don't feel right at all. I lie where I've fallen and my eyes close over. Soon I will be finished.

I glimpse Eliza's face in mine, shaking me: 'Wake up, Esther, you're being sick, wake up!'

'Go. Away. I'm. Dying.'

Sirens. Shouting voices. Lights being forced into my eyes. Moving. Beeping, flashing bright blue lights and more shouting. Why doesn't everyone stop making so much noise and switch the lights off? Thick pipe rasping down my throat. 'What have you taken?' a man's voice angrily shouts at someone. 'What have you taken?' Drowning in words, in acid, body heaving, trying to sit up, being pushed back down, down through the bed, down through the ground, down.

I struggle to swim up through sleep. My throat is on fire. A needle is attached to my arm. I follow it to a drip. I'm in bed – not my bed. Everything is white. Last night flashes dully before my eyes. Am I dead? Hardly daring to breathe, I slowly look round the room, until I lock eyes with a nurse and attempt to sit up. 'No, don't try to get up, Miss W, everything's all right,' she reassures me, pressing me back down to the pillows. 'You're in Inverness Hospital. You've had your stomach pumped. I think we got to you in time and they got most of the pills out. But now you need to rest.' Before she's finished I'm falling back into sleep, but tears squeeze through the corners of my eyelids. I wanted to die and I've even failed at this!

The next time I wake, it's daylight and two police officers are waiting beside my bed. 'Hi, Esther, I'm Officer Burgess,' a pale-complexioned woman says in a soft Scottish voice. 'We've spoken with your friend at Oakhill House. She has told us you confided in her, about being sexually assaulted. We're here to ask you some questions about it.'

I go to open my mouth but it's as if I've swallowed broken glass. 'I don't want to talk about it!' I croak.

She smiles sympathetically. 'I'm afraid it's not that simple. Sexually assaulting a minor is a criminal offence and it has to be investigated.'

I turn away and close my eyes. In the distance, I hear her mumbling something about returning later.

But the next time I wake, it's late afternoon and a female social worker is in the room. 'Could you give me the name, or indicate, who it was that sexually assaulted you?'

I open my mouth but no words come out, so I shake my head.

'Well, I'll need to file a report and there'll be a meeting ...'

'A meeting! What for?' I whisper fearfully.

'Well, you won't be returning to Oakhill House and I'm not sure we can send you home ...'

'Why not? Why can't you send me home? I'll be okay there!' I stammer, my voice rising.

'It's not that simple, Esther. You see, you tried to kill yourself after telling a friend you'd been raped. And now you're refusing to tell anyone who it was. You must see we have limited options.'

I sit up, alarmed. 'What do you mean, limited options?'

'Well,' she continues, 'Mona Drone, your social worker, doesn't want you returning home as she suspects you might have been sexually assaulted by one of your older brothers.'

'*What?*' I gasp.

She nods, 'But, if you were to tell me something different, then we'd know, wouldn't we?'

I open my mouth to tell her about Adrian, but just as quickly remember that she's a social worker. She wouldn't believe it was one of her lot. Nobody would believe me! They'd say it was lies. And they'd say I made it up about Dad, too! And they'd let him out of jail and he would come home ... and my life would return to the hell it was before! Frustrated angry tears spring from my eyes. 'I've told you – there's nothing to say. Nothing happened!' I cry defensively.

The following morning Christopher Yeoman visits. I feel myself welling up at the sight of his friendly face. But he isn't smiling, he is pale and drawn and the rims of his eyes look unnaturally red.

'Esther,' he says gravely, and I know he's about to say something I don't want to hear, 'I've just come from a meeting about you.'

My blood runs cold. 'Have you?' I mumble.

'Yes. I'm so sorry Esther, but you're being placed in a children's centre, with higher security.'

'What?' I scream. 'No, please, Christopher, no ...'

He drops his head and now I think, maybe I could put up with Adrian. I just didn't try hard enough before, it would be better than going to a strange high-security place. With renewed hope I offer, 'I could come back to Oakhill with you, Christopher. I wouldn't do it again, I promise!'

'It's too late for that, Esther. We're so far from everything at Oakhill. We can't take that risk. What if we don't get to you in time?'

'Send me home then. I don't want to go to a strange place.'

'It's not up to me, it's up to your social worker and she doesn't think the best place for you is at home. Try not to worry though, it's only until they've done more investigations,' he adds optimistically.

We sit in silence for a few moments, before he speaks again. 'Esther, why don't you speak to someone about what's happened? You could speak to me,' he offers in his gentle Liverpudlian drawl.

Why can't he guess? Why doesn't he ask me different questions? Can't he see I can't say it? If he guesses and tells me, it means it was a bad thing and I'm not to blame. But if I have to tell him, it means it was my fault and I caused it. But he won't say it and the more I deny it, the deeper the secret buries itself within me, so far down that even I can't get to it.

'Nothing happened, Christopher, nothing. I've told everyone! Please just let me come back with you?'

His eyes well up and watery thin rivulets trickle a path

down his cheeks. 'It's not just this, Esther, you've been going downhill for a couple of months. A lot of the staff have noticed it. I don't know what it is, but something's going on with you.'

'Nothing is. I was just being stupid. Please let me come back?'

He shakes his head. 'I'm sorry.'

My eyes water. 'Okay,' I reply quietly, 'but can you come to the new place with me?'

Again he shakes his head. 'No, Esther, this is somewhere you'll have to go on your own.'

Icy fear plunges through me and I'm more frightened for myself than I've ever been before.

CHAPTER SIX

Crouchend Alley

I've lived in the country my whole life, so going to Oakhill, set in the deep wilds of the black isle, felt natural and homely. Crouchend Alley in a small grey town not far from Inverness and imprisoned within granite grey council estates. It immediately feels hostile and alien.

A male social worker drives me there from the hospital. We arrive late in the evening. Pulling up on a cement driveway, he pushes a button and reports to a woman inside that I've arrived. She buzzes us through heavy glass doors into a small porch. He presses out a security code on a metal pad that allows us access to the inner building. It is quiet and everything is in grey shadow. Plastic chairs and fire extinguishers line and dot the walls, while brown curtains provide the only soft furnishing, reminding me of the hospital I've just come from.

The man delivers me to the office where a huge woman, whose stomach rests on the desk between us, offers me a pudgy hand while raking the other through fuzzy grey hair. 'Hi, I'm Bertha, the manager here at Crouchend Alley.' She points dismissively at the black plastic bag I'm carrying. 'Just pop your things out on the table.' Her eyes beadily check through my stuff as she lists it in a 'client's belongings book'. 'So nobody leaves with anything that doesn't belong to them!' she chirrups.

'Ah, Sharon, this is Esther,' Bertha addresses a tall, slim woman who has quietly slipped behind me, 'will you show her to her room?'

On the way, Sharon stops to show me a room. 'This is the main living area and that,' she says, pointing at a large round table surrounded by chairs in the corner, 'is where you'll come down for breakfast in the morning. Before half eight, or none at all!' she adds sharply.

I don't say anything – eating is the last thing on my mind. I silently follow her through a set of heavy glass doors, up two flights of stairs and to the end of a corridor. She unlocks a white door, releasing a cold lifeless gasp.

Flicking on the light, she gestures to two plain beds. 'That's where you'll sleep, take your pick! And that's where you'll put your clothes,' she says, pointing at two narrow wardrobes. As she crosses the room, she explains, 'The windows here only open ten inches – so don't force them!' Lifting one of two chairs, she takes it over to the door, opens it, and jams it under the handle, before turning to me and warning, 'This door stays open, got it?' I nod without looking in her eyes. 'I'll be up to check on you in a little while. You better get some sleep, you're going to need it!'

I drop my black bag on one of the beds and lie on the one closest to the wall. Finally, as I exhale heavily, tears escape my eyes and fall on the pillow. I suddenly feel desperate with fear. How did I get here? Why didn't I just shut up and put up with Adrian? I look around at the rest of the room. There isn't much to see. Just four bare white walls, except for a couple of red and silver metal signs reminding me not to use Blu-Tack to attach personal items to the walls. I drift off into an exhausted sleep, the same questions going round my head: why am I the one being punished? And, why doesn't Mona Drone want me to go home?

I'm woken by chaotic banging, shouting and screaming, coming from the corridor outside my room. I look around wildly for a few moments, at this empty, unfamiliar environment. Then I recall where I am and my stomach drops. The chair has gone from under the handle and my door is shut. It was so quiet when I arrived last night, I thought I was the only child here. I wish I could hide in here for ever; I don't want to face anybody, especially people who sound like that. I jump when a woman with short spiky grey hair, wearing round sliver glasses, pokes her head around the door. 'Get yourself up and sorted and down to breakfast!' she hurriedly orders.

'Okay,' I mumble, attempting a little smile. I don't want to move but I don't want to upset anyone, especially not on my first day. I drag myself up and prepare to meet a houseful of strangers.

Twenty minutes later, I'm making my way down to the main living area where all the excited voices come from. I gently ease open the glass door, hoping not to draw attention to myself, but as I enter the voices stop. The lady with grey spiky hair comes to meet me. She takes me over to a table laden with cereal boxes, cartons of juice, bread, butter and a toaster. But I don't take any of it in, I've seen the other kids – tattooed, pierced, and angry – and I definitely don't want to be here. I force myself to pour a bowl of cornflakes and sit at the table. Focusing on my cereal, I intend to gulp it down and escape back upstairs. I'm forcing dry spoonfuls down when I become aware that the girl next to me is miming slitting her wrists to muffled guffaws of laughter from some of the other children. With horror, I realise they must all know why I'm here and I stare even more intently into my bowl. It's then that I see I'm still wearing my hospital ID bands. At Oakhill, nobody would have made a joke out of something like attempted suicide. But as I'll quickly come to realise, at Crouchend Alley, anything goes: it's all about survival.

'Daisy, quit that!' a man gruffly orders. 'If you've finished your breakfast, leave the table!' I glance up to see a dark-moustached man. 'Esther, I'm Brian,' he says in a kind Scottish voice. 'Once you've done, get yourself to the office to meet your key worker.'

A slim freckled woman with mousy brown hair and pale blue eyes barely acknowledges me as I enter the office. Motioning me to the seat opposite her, she finishes what she's writing before dropping the pen. Then she leans over the desk energetically, and her eyes crease into a smile. 'Hi, I'm Linda!' she says, in a blunt Scottish accent. 'I'll be your key worker, while you're here. Are you finding everything okay?'

I pull my hand from hers and my vision blurs. I blink furiously but my eyes still drown in tears. I shouldn't cry, not in a place like this. 'No,' I mumble, 'I don't want to be here. I want to go home!'

She comes round the desk and kneels in front of me, looking concerned. 'Esther, you're in here because it's not safe for you to go home!'

Why are they all saying the same thing? I wonder irritably. 'Why not?' I ask. 'What have I done?'

Returning to her chair, she presses her fingertips together under her chin and looks thoughtful. 'I'm not sure it's something you've done. From what your family social worker tells me, it's more something one of your brothers has done. They've been sexually abusing you. Haven't they?' she asks, sympathetically.

'NO!' I shout. Linda flinches at the aggression in my voice. 'I've already said nothing happened at home,' I add quietly.

'Then why did you attempt to kill yourself?' she replies gently, before continuing. 'It seems to me, you need time to accept what's happened.'

'But I don't want to be here. I'll go anywhere else,' I offer desperately. 'I could go back to Oakhill?'

She gives a little smile. 'It's really not so bad here, Esther, you'll see. Anyway, you're here now, so you may as well make the best of it!' Panic threatens to engulf me; it all seems so hopeless. 'I don't want to get used to it!' I cry.

'Look, I'm sure everything will get sorted out at your next panel, and what's in your best interests will be—'

'Do I have a say in any of this?' I interrupt.

'Look, Esther,' she replies firmly, 'we're all trying to do what's best for you. And, as I say, until your next panel I'm your key worker, so if you have any problems come and see me and I'll try to sort them.'

I feel numb. Nothing I say seems to matter – adults I don't know are completely in charge of me. I have no control over my life at all.

'Anyway,' Linda continues, as if everything is finalised, 'while you're with us, there are some basic rules you must follow. You do not leave Crouchend Alley unattended.

You're not to make any phone calls without permission, and bedroom lights are out by ten o'clock. Any questions?'

I don't answer, instead I continue wrestling with the ball of anger inside me. Anger at being punished for something I'm sure isn't my fault.

'Right!' Linda continues. 'I'm going to pair you up with Leanne. She's only been here a couple of weeks. She can show you around the place and you can bunk up together.'

When I meet Leanne I'm surprised that such a pretty girl is in a place like this! She is easily the best-looking girl I've ever seen, like a Barbie doll come to life. She's very slim, with delicate feminine features. Her large sparkly blue eyes beam at me as Linda introduces us, revealing two rows of perfect white teeth inside generous candy pink lips.

There isn't much for Leanne to show me, but she swishes her long, thick blond hair about as she does. The communal eating area divides two sitting rooms. The main living room is slightly larger and has a shabby brown couch in it, but apart from that, they're set out the same way. Grey plastic chairs line the walls, a couple of small paper bins are placed here and there. From the ceiling in the corner dangles a small TV from a black metal mount and both rooms look out – through reinforced glass – to a cemented exercise area.

Leanne is moving into the bedroom I slept in last night, and as I'm helping her pack her things, she asks me why I'm here. But when I hesitate to answer, she proudly reveals she's in here because, 'I tried to kill my mam with a pair of scissors!'

I recoil in horror, wondering if she's joking. Her hard-set face confirms she isn't. 'Why ... what ... why did you do that?' I enquire hesitantly.

'Because, I fucking hate the bitch, that's why!' she angrily retorts, her face colouring.

'Uh,' I numbly reply, instinctively knowing not to push it.

Leanne and I bond immediately over late-night chats and our love of all things girly, but most of all, our mutual dream, of escaping from Crouchend Alley.

I learn fast that Crouchend Alley is run by two 15 year-old boys: Derek the Drug and Calvin. They rule through fear and violence, either a slapping or stealing your stuff. Most of the staff let them get on with it – it seems to be too much hassle to stop them. In the privacy of my bed at night, where I can't be picked on for being soft, I yearn for my old life back at Oakhill. Where all the staff, apart from Adrian, were caring and supportive; at Crouchend Alley the staff have given up on us kids, they expect us to be bad. At Oakhill House the staff seemed to want to make us better, while here we're just surviving, and they get paid to watch us, until we're dumped on the streets, at 16.

I had never done drugs until I came to Crouchend but soon I'm taking anything I can get my hands on; as long as it helps me forget where I am, I'll take it. But mostly it's the kids at Crouchend Alley that are different from the ones at Oakhill. It's like they've been hurt so long, the wounds have become vicious scars, making it impossible for them to ever recover. They've become so bitter and angry they want to take revenge on the world. When I first enter Crouchend, a scared vulnerable 14-year-old girl, I don't realise that in a couple of short month I will become one of them.

All the kids in here take drugs, which they get from Derek the Drug. The harder stuff, such as crack or acid, is usually for the weekend while spliff and sniffing is a daily activity. I sniff anything that gives me a buzz. Aerosols are a favourite, because they're easy to get hold of – antiperspirants being the best. You spray them into a plastic bag, hold it over your nose and mouth and inhale deeply. The buzz gives you a pleasant zinging sensation that momentarily dissolves you into another world. Glue and nail polish are good too, because their smell quickly dissipates, so go easily undetected. You can be sitting in the main sitting room, off your face in front of the staff, and they don't even know it. But my favourite is lighter fluid as it's got a strong, long-lasting buzz. Holding the little nozzle between my teeth, I press and inhale. It makes my head swim so deep I could be anywhere. But lighter fluid is difficult to get hold of as not many shops will sell it to kids under 16 and, more importantly, it's expensive. The only problem with buzzing is the tell-tale bright red pimple rash around my nose and mouth. When it appears even the staff can't ignore what I've been up to.

But the weekends are even more relaxed with drugs as it's when the agency staff are on. Either they don't know the rules or, if they do, they don't care, they're only doing a job to get paid. So the rules are slackened and later on in the day we can be sitting around in one of the bedrooms, all getting high together. These weekends getting wasted are some of my best times at Crouchend.

Some kids are allowed home on weekend release and others, like me, never go anywhere. It's Friday and a few of us permanents are sitting in the main sitting room, trying to block out the excitement of those going home. We're being watched by Terry, Leanne's key worker. He's throwing a ball at us, which we must catch and throw back. Terry is foot-

ball mad and despite never playing it, he still squeezes his fat
frame into a sausage tight uniform of the Rangers' blue and
white strip, which he wears with jogging bottoms and
trainers. I can tell he's bored and restless and changes the
ball's direction suddenly and violently with a 'Head's up',
usually hitting one of us in the chest or on the arm. When
he catches us, he chuckles, 'Too slow by half. You'd never
make the squad!' When he's like this, he loves winding up
us kids. He'll pick on a child, find a weak spot and keep
needling at it until they crack. Thankfully, Leanne warned
me never to tell Terry anything. But Jamie is easy prey as
he's forever boasting about how much his mum loves him.
He's always saying that she'll definitely be coming to see
him this weekend – even though she never turns up. Terry
holds the ball still for a minute, before his eyes narrow. He
throws the ball. 'So Jamie,' Terry says, his voice dripping
with sarcasm, 'your mam coming to see ya again tomorrow,
is she?'

Jamie knows what's coming. He doesn't want to answer
but he'll have to, otherwise Terry will punish him. Jamie
catches the ball, his muscle vest revealing tense Indian-ink
stained arms. He drops his hedgehog-like skinhead. 'I ...' he
mumbles.

Dissatisfied, Terry returns the ball to him roughly. 'Your
mam's never coming to see ya. She's too busy we the auld
drink,' he replies, miming her throwing one back.

'She is too coming,' Jamie mutters defensively, chucking
the ball back.

'What was that, answering back are ya? Ya cheeky wee
shite!'

My stomach twists in uneasy knots, watching Jamie

unravel like soft wool. But like everyone, I'm relieved Terry isn't picking on me. His pock-marked face sneers, as he goes on, 'She canna be arsed w' ya, lad. She'll never come.'

Jamie's face has turned blotchy red and contorted as he violently chews on his inner cheek. Recognising he's about to blow, Terry goes in for the kill: 'Look, laddie, I'm only trying to help ya oot. The sooner you accept she doesn't gee a toss aboot ya, the better it'll be!'

To everyone's relief, especially Jamie's, Brian pokes his head around the door, and Terry's bullying is interrupted for the day. We all race for the door when he offers, 'Would any of you fancy a wee trip out, on the bus?'

Leanne, like me, is a permanent and desperate to go home. But she'd be happy if we just drove near her parents' house. As usual she tries to convince Brian to take a trip that way and he has to remind her she's not allowed, adding, 'It'd be more than ma job's worth, pet.' She doesn't do herself any favours though, as she tells everyone, the next chance she gets, she'll do a proper job on her mum. Me and Leanne have become very close in the three long weeks I've been here, but I've got a panel meeting next Tuesday, so only three more days and I'm off home. Although I'll be sorry to leave Leanne, I'm beyond happy to be going – as I don't know how much longer I can handle being locked up here.

On Monday morning Linda calls me to her office. She has a packet of my favourite chocolate biscuits and a carton of Ribena waiting for me. She watches me greedily tuck in for a minute, before breaking the silence: 'Well, you'll need to get ready for your panel tomorrow!'

Hoping she means my clothes, I reply animatedly, 'I am ready. I'm wearing my new purple and white striped top, you know the one I got special, with my Pepe jeans.'

'No, Esther,' she replies sharply, while eyeing me meaningfully, 'you know what I mean. You need to think about what you're going to say and not what others want you to.'

I know she's referring to Mona Drone, claiming my brothers sexually abused me, and I can't help feeling immediately defensive. 'Well, I'll just tell the truth. Nothing like that happened and I want to go home,' I say, my voice rising.

'Is it really the truth?' she asks sternly. 'I have to say I agree with your social worker. You must have attempted suicide for a very good reason, and perhaps home isn't the best option for you.'

My eyes well up in frustration at the mention of me not going home. 'I don't want to keep talking about it, Linda, we just keep going round in circles!' I cry.

'Okay, but just so you know, Esther,' and she waits until she has my attention, 'I'll be recommending you stay here in care, until you're 18.'

I stare in disbelief, my throat tightening, '*What*?' I scream. 'I hate it here. It's like a prison and I haven't done anything wrong! What have I done wrong?'

Her face is flushed as she leans determinedly over the desk. 'You won't tell anyone why you attempted suicide and you're refusing to admit what has happened to you at home.'

I slump over the desk, banging my head. 'Linda, you're not listening to me. You never listen to me!' I cry.

'Look,' she says, softening, 'if it's Crouchend Alley you

don't like, we can find an alternative. Maybe a foster placement?'

I don't have the strength to keep fighting. 'I don't want to go anywhere else. I just want to go home,' I reply weakly.

Mitch, a blond-haired, stocky social worker, is doing the afternoon shift. After staff changeover, he comes to find me, where I'm watching TV in the main sitting room. 'Esther, Linda says she wants you to write a statement for your panel tomorrow. Get it done, will you?'

I look up, annoyed at being interrupted. 'But I don't need to write a statement, I can remember what I want to say,' I reply shortly.

'Look, Linda wants you to write it down, so you'll do it!' He replies irritably.

He wheels round in the direction of the office, reappearing moments later with a pencil and a few sheets of paper. 'Come with me,' he orders. I reluctantly follow him and I soon realise where we're headed – the paddy room! All the children hate being put in there, but I've never been in before and I don't want to now. I've seen Terry needling Leanne, until she blows and starts screaming at him, to fuck off and shut up. Then he jumps her, restraining her arms and legs behind her back, shouting excitedly, 'We've a live one here! She needs a bit of calming down methinks!'

But I'm not screaming and I don't need restraining. 'Okay, okay,' I say, hoping he's only trying to scare me, 'I'll write it at the table.'

But he's already unlocked the door. 'No, you've had your chance.'

'But why do I have to go in there?' I ask desperately.

'Because you've been disobedient. Now in!' I know it's no

use, I can't fight him, so I tentatively enter the shadowy room. Handing me the pencil and paper, he orders, 'Give me a bang once you've done!' before slamming the door hard behind him.

I take in the small dark box that imprisons me. My eyes are drawn to the only light coming from a small window high up near the ceiling. Suddenly, I'm overwhelmed with a fear that I'm going to be here for ever and will never escape. Thumping at the walls I cry out, 'But I don't know what to write!'

'You know what to write, now get on with it,' Mitch calls back.

There isn't ahandle on this side of the door, so I dig my fingernails into the crack, attempting to force it open. Hopeless tears spring from my eyes before it hits me. If I write something – anything, it doesn't matter what it is – he'll let me out. I push my back into the corner of the room where the hand-sized patch of light falls upon me and grip my pencil determinedly. The question I want to ask the panel immediately comes to mind, 'Can I go home?' but just as quickly I disregard it. That definitely isn't what Linda wants.

My stomach churns nervously as the empty page stares back at me, waiting for my confession. Soon it will be too dark to write anything and I'll never get out of here, I panic. 'I would like to ...' I begin and then I stop and chew on the end of the pencil. Stars fill my eyes and I slowly smile and finish the sentence with, '... be a circus performer!' One of my childhood escape fantasies was the idea of running away to join the circus. I'd heard they took people in no matter what their backgrounds – forming a family of misfits – so I'd fit right in. Then, I do what I've always done when there's paper in front of me – I draw. I sketch Ferdinand, the little red pony my father starved to death. He wears a glittery pink saddle and bridle and a bright pink feather headdress. I balance effortlessly on his back, dressed in a matching sparkly pink leotard, performing amazing circus tricks while he proudly trots around the arena to gasps of awe and thunderous applause. I enjoy myself for a while, careful to save a couple of sheets of paper – so I can write something for Linda, later. But before I know it, I'm falling into a blissful sleep – full of circus dreams.

I'm woken by the jangle of keys. Mitch is framed in the doorway. 'Come on then, what have you got for me?' I gather the sheets and hesitantly hand them over, staring at the floor, awaiting his verdict. He examines the pictures for a moment and sighs resignedly, before pointing to the stairs. 'Just get to bed.'

The following morning I'm the first to rise. I hurriedly wash, dress and finish packing. I'm too nervous to eat anything, but I busy myself making toast for everyone else. Sue, the on-duty social worker, comes into the kitchen. We call her Lesbo Sue behind her back as she looks and acts like a man. Her closely cropped dark hair brings out the sharp pointed features of her face and enhances her intense brown eyes. 'Esther, may I have a word?'

'Yes,' I breezily reply, sitting down to butter the toast.

She sits beside me and places a cold, clammy hand on my arm. I feel her eyes boring into me, as she starts, 'There's no easy way to put this, because I know you've been looking forward to it. But it was decided, last night, that you shouldn't attend your panel meeting today!'

I stare blankly at her. 'What? What do you mean, not attend my own panel?' I become aware of anger welling up inside me. It's been there since I was first put in here. Anger at being locked up for a crime I didn't commit.

'Well,' Sue continues, 'it's believed to be in your best interests—'

Suddenly the fireball explodes and I'm possessed and lunge wildly at her. But she's pulling my arms up behind my back and grinding my face into the buttered toast. 'Now you'd better calm down, miss, or you'll find yourself in the paddy.'

I can't, my rage is red hot. I want to smash her witchy face in. I need to kick her until she breaks. I haven't even started, I think, as I kick out at her. 'YOU FUCKING LESBO BITCH! GET YOUR STINKING FUCKING HANDS OFF ME, YOU LESBO CUNT,' I screech.

I hear her shouting for help. Then there's two of them; my arms are stretched so far back they feel as though they might pop from their sockets. Then Sue and the man carry me, a twisting, spitting, snarling monster, baring my teeth and spewing threats – but they carry me all the same, and I know where we're headed. The door is unlocked and I'm thrown in. 'You can stay in here until you calm down!' Sue orders. I softly thud to the floor.

I rage against the soft walls, but I can't damage them. So I scratch at my arms, revealing long thin satisfying ditches of blood. I rip at my hair, rooting up clumps and scream until my voice runs hoarse. Sliding to the floor, I scream, 'I'm going to be here for ever!' Then, when I can't do anything else, I sob, before catching my breath and sobbing more and more until my head throbs and I've run dry of tears. Wiping my nose and eyes on my sleeves, I look down at my ruined purple and white striped top – the one I got special for today.

Hours later, Sue releases me from the paddy room. She stands aside, eyeing me cautiously, like I might attack her again. 'You're to get yourself to Linda's office,' she orders.

You fucking bitch! I want to accuse her. I bet you've told Linda everything and now I'm in loads of trouble. But when I get there I'm amazed to be greeted at the door by my older brother Jacob and Mum.

'Mum!' I cry, racing past Jacob.

She slowly lifts her head and a look of heartbreaking pain flashes across her raw tear-stained face. She awkwardly returns my cuddle before continuing to sob into a bundle of tissues.

After the initial surprise, I'm full of questions. Am I going home with them? Why is Mum crying so much? Is this nightmare finally over?

As if in answer, Linda explains, 'It was decided at your panel this morning that you'll remain at Crouchend Alley for the foreseeable future.'

'But why?' I angrily demand.

'Well,' she replies measuredly, 'it is believed to be in your best interests. As we don't know what you might do to yourself.'

'But I won't do anything to myself!' I cry, frustrated tears spilling from my eyes.

'As I say,' Linda, continues matter-of-factly, 'it's already been decided.'

A fresh wave of tears hits me, as I beg Mum, 'Please take me home with you. I just want to come home!'

'Right,' says Linda, as if everything is normal, 'you have an hour's access visit together. Would anyone like a drink?'

Nobody answers and I try to explain to Mum and Jacob why they're keeping me here. 'They say my older brothers have been sexually abusing me—'

'Esther, that's not for here. That's a matter for another time,' Linda cautions.

'But it's true,' I retort angrily, 'that's why you're keeping me here, isn't it?'

She looks at me threateningly. 'If you continue to disobey the rules of this access visit, I'll have no choice but to terminate it.'

I stifle my tears and sit quietly on the floor, putting my head in Mum's lap, where we spend the remainder of the visit in near silence. Mum eventually stops crying and gives me a present of a necklace she says she thought I'd like. 'Listen,' Mum whispers quietly, 'we're doing everything we can to get you home. Sit tight and we'll sort this mess out.'

'But why can't I just come home with you now?' I cry, 'I don't want to stay here.'

Linda interrupts. 'Access time is nearly up. Oh, and Esther, I think I'd better take that necklace for now, to make sure it's appropriate.'

I refuse to hand it over. 'Why wouldn't it be appropriate?' I argue.

'Look, you'll get it back later, but we must follow policy,' Linda insists. 'If it's okay for you to keep, I'll give it to Bertha and you can pick it up from her tomorrow morning.'

I reluctantly hand it over as I don't want to waste the time I have left with Mum and Jacob by arguing with Linda.

The rest of the visit passes in a blur. As they're leaving, Mum promises they'll try and get me legal help so I can get out of here, which makes me feel more optimistic than I have in a long time.

After Mum and Jacob have driven off, Linda steps forward, her arms outstretched, but I pull away. 'This is all your fucking fault, Linda,' I spit venomously, before escaping to my room, where I cry as the day darkens into night.

Sometime later, I'm aware of someone entering my room. I hope it isn't Linda, I think bitterly, or I'll end the day in the same way I started – in the paddy. Thankfully it's just Leanne. She sits on my bed and offers me some tissues. 'I heard you're staying now,' she says.

I don't answer. I'm not ready to admit it out loud.

'I know how you feel,' Leanne continues. 'I want to get out of here as much as you do.'

I feel a spark of annoyance. 'No, Leanne, you don't! You tried to kill your mum, I didn't. I shouldn't be in here, I've done nothing wrong!'

Leanne stays quiet, patting my shoulder. When she does speak again, she sounds excited. 'Anyway, listen, I've come up with an escape plan!'

I spring up, feeling a glimmer of hope. 'How?'

'We'll run away,' she replies brightly.

'Leanne,' I sigh, slumping back, 'don't be stupid. We're not going anywhere.'

She jumps up and clicks the light on, then checks the corridor. 'Just listen, will you? I've worked it all out. We just have to plan when we'll do it, that's all!' she replies simply.

I stare at her like she's gone mad. 'Look, first of all, there's no way out. There are locks on the doors and the office is at the front. What would we do? Disappear through the window crack?'

'No, Esther,' she replies patiently, 'we do it when we're already out – on a trip!' This stops me in my tracks. 'But,' she adds, 'it does mean waiting until the weekend.'

Now I am listening and it actually makes a crazy kind of sense. I'm surprised we've never thought of this before. For the first time, since I've been here, I think we could really do this. And at least for now, it takes my mind off the horrors of today.

Leanne and I whisper and giggle about our escape plans late into the night. We imagine how good our lives will be when Crouchend Alley is just a bad memory. Fantasising in exaggerated detail, the member of staff discovering we've disappeared and having to return without two children. We'll need to find jobs of course. Me, so I can pay my way home and Leanne, so she can move to a new city to start a different life.

The following morning, I knock at the office door. 'Come in,' Bertha's gravelly voice calls.

'Can I have my necklace back?' I ask pointedly.

Her piggy eyes don't leave my face, as she reaches over her stomach to pull out a flat tray from the side of the desk. There's a horrible scraping noise and we both look down. All the delicate pink stones in the necklace have been crushed and broken. A lump catches in my throat and I continue to look at it, unsure what to do.

'Oops,' Bertha says, slowly raising her eyes to meet mine. 'Well, we'll just have to get you another one!'

I go to pick up the pieces, and my voice is as broken as the necklace. 'But I don't want another one, I wanted this one!'

'Well,' she replies bluntly, 'there's not much can be done about it now, is there?'

I race out of the office, convinced more than ever that running away from this place and the vile people in it is my only option.

Despite Bertha breaking my necklace, the rest of the week feels like the best I've ever had in Crouchend Alley. I'm even allowed to make a supervised phone call home. Sue sits in, just in case I say anything 'inappropriate'. But I don't care, I'll soon be out of here – so fuck you, Sue, I think, returning her bore-hole stare.

Leanne has managed to sneak a peek at the staff rota, and Brian is on at the weekend. He loves getting us all out and about, so it shouldn't be too difficult to persuade him to take us on a trip. We decide on the woods just outside town as there are signposts to Inverness from there – at least then we'd know the right direction to take. Obviously, we can't take bags, so instead, we decide to wear two sets of clothes and only carry our toothbrushes. Home, here I come!

CHAPTER SEVEN

On the run

Saturday morning finally arrives. At breakfast, Leanne raises the subject of a trip out, to Brian. 'Yeah, that's a good idea,' I nonchalantly join in.

Brian says he's happy it's been suggested, as he's had the same idea himself. 'Do you have anywhere you fancy going?' he asks kindly, before adding, 'Apart from your parents' house, obviously, Leanne!'

Leanne forces a tight smile and I try not to giggle with nerves as I watch her pretending to have a think. 'Well ... mmm, what about the woods we went to before? You know the one, with the little stream in it, just outside town?'

'I can't see why not,' Brian replies breezily, 'but you'll have to persuade the others!'

So it's settled and all we have to do is get the other five kids to agree. Most of the kids love getting out, so it's not difficult convincing them and by 11 a.m., Leanne and I are nervously waiting on the minibus, doing our best to act calm.

By the time we arrive at the woods it's nearly lunchtime, so we help set out the picnic of sandwiches, crisps and drinks. We've decided the best time to go is during our after-lunch wander. Our plan is to run as far as we can, as fast as we can, and hitch lifts the rest of the way to Inverness.

I distractedly bite at a sandwich, trying to act relaxed. Leanne mentions going for a walk after we've finished lunch, causing the agency staff member to accusingly quip, 'Blimey, what's wrong with you today, you're a bit keen aren't you?'

We exchange warning glances – Leanne should be playing it cooler. Once all the picnic stuff is cleared away, Brian asks everyone to vote on which way they'd like to go and there are various calls for different paths.

The path that gets most votes is in the opposite direction to Inverness. I'm disappointedly trailing behind everyone when Leanne whispers, 'This is better, cos when we make a run for it, nobody will notice we've gone.'

We're full of excitement and desperate to get going but we must follow the others for a good 20 minutes until the staff are distracted. When we've walked behind them for what feels like ages and are surrounded by deep, dense woods, Leanne and I quietly fall back.

Once we're out of earshot, we seize our chance. Adrenalin kicks in and we bolt in the opposite direction. Cutting through brambles and batting at leaves, darting around trees and jumping over nettles, falling and scrambling and racing and tangling, until we are almost tumbling over. Running, running, running, until our legs are bandy like rubber and our bodies are sticky hot. Eventually slowing to a stumble, we listen intently, checking whether we've been followed. But apart from birdsong and crunchy leaf litter underfoot, all is silent. We must keep going. Time isn't on our side. Our only hope is to get a lift as quickly as possible.

We've been on the run for at least 15 minutes. We're being careful to stay just inside the woods, until we see a car we want to hitch in. We'd always planned to avoid hitching in lorries, as we reasoned they'd be full of old pervs. But the road is a lorry merry-go-round, similar ones continuously trundle past. We're considering a change of mind when a dark blue car races towards us. We get out on the road and stick our thumbs up enthusiastically while smiling our sweetest smiles. To our relief the car slows and stops ahead. The driver's window is wound down and a dark-haired older man asks, 'Where to, girls?'

'Inverness!' we chorus.

'Hop in,' he says, moving his case from the front seat, 'that's just where I'm headed!'

Leanne sits in front. It seems only right she would – she's more worldly wise than me and talks more easily to men. I sit in the back where a glance takes in the tidy leather upholstered space.

'Where you from?' he asks.

My stomach freezes and my mind goes blank. Thankfully Leanne pipes up, in a posh-sounding voice I've never heard her use before, 'Oh here and there, you know, we travel quite a bit.'

I stifle my giggles, knowing we'll laugh about what she's saying later. I'm hoping that's an end to the questions, when he speaks again: 'So why are you going to Inverness?'

'Well, Inverness is a wonderful place to visit,' says Leanne, sounding like a woman of the world. 'It's got the Castle and lots of historical things there.'

I cringe a little, thinking that she should shut up now. I hurriedly interrupt with something I've heard adults ask one another: 'So, what do you do then?'

He catches my eye through his mirror. 'Oh, I'm in marketing,' he replies, smiling.

Once he's explained what that means, Leanne asks, 'Do you work for anyone famous?'

'Nescafé coffee,' he replies, adding, 'is that famous enough for you?'

We both draw exaggeratedly impressed breaths, because although we don't drink it, we recognise the name.

We continue chatting to him, all the while keeping an eye out for signs and distances to Inverness, when he suddenly pulls over. Leanne looks over her shoulder at me, her face mirroring my alarm. He turns to look at Leanne, then back at me. 'Now tell me, girls,' he asks, 'what's really going on?'

Leanne opens her mouth to speak and I'm hoping she's thought of a good story, but instead she quietly replies, 'We're trying to escape from some men.'

He looks at me and I nod enthusiastically. 'Well,' he continues, 'I can see what you're getting out of this, but what's in it for me?'

We exchange confused looks. 'What I mean is, is one of you nice young girls going to make the risk worth my while?'

We watch in horror, as he starts unzipping his trousers. Leanne wordlessly goes down on him, and to the sound of wet squelching and moaning, I look out at the woods, wondering if anyone's realised we've gone yet. Eventually he lets out a moan and Leanne sits up, wiping at her mouth. He turns the radio on and we continue our journey to Inverness, with Feargal Sharkey, pleading with someone to be gentle with his heart. 'Where do you want dropping?' he asks as we enter the outskirts of Inverness.

Leanne turns to me. 'Esther, would you mind if we went round a mate of mine? We could have a shower and get something to eat?'

I nod and she instructs the man how to get there. But soon after, as we're driving through a big housing estate, Leanne suddenly demands, 'Just drop us off here.'

Leanne leaps from the car and stalks off purposefully. Struggling to keep up, I call after her, 'Where is it we're going again?' But when I glimpse her darkened face, I know. 'Oh no, Leanne, you're not going to see your mum, are you?'

'I just want to see her, that's all,' she replies in a flat faraway voice.

'But you're not supposed to. You'll get into trouble,' I warn. Her face remains rigid, as she marches on. I pull at her sleeve. 'This isn't what we ran away for!' I plead. She yanks her arm from me. 'Go away then, Esther, nobody's forcing you to come. This is something I've got to do!'

'Leanne,' I tearfully beg, 'remember what we talked about? You moving to another city and starting a new life?'

But she's far from here, in a scary place from her past and nothing I say will change her mind. 'Well, I better come with you,' I sigh resignedly, 'to make sure you don't actually kill her!' I add, pretending to laugh.

Walking through the housing estate, we turn a corner and abruptly halt at the sight of two police cars parked up on the kerb. Automatically turning around, we're faced with another one, driving up behind us. Leanne grabs my arm and pulls me into a nearby garden where we watch through the bushes at the police crawling everywhere. 'I think we should stay here a while, until it's a bit darker,' I suggest hopefully.

'No,' Leanne hisses, 'I'm going to see my mum, with or without you!'

I look at her, trying to search her light sparkly blue eyes, to see if I can talk her out of it, but they've turned a dead steel grey. 'If you hate her so much, why do you want to go and see her?' I argue.

'Because she's going to pay!' she replies aggressively, looking away.

'Pay for what, Leanne? What did she do that was so bad?' I ask urgently.

'She used me as a punchbag my whole life, that's what! Nobody stopped her, not even Dad. He turned a blind eye, pretending she loved me. "Don't say such evil things about your mum, she loves you, it's just in her own way!" So let's see how she likes it, my fucking way!' Choking back tears, she rages on, 'I'm going to make her so fucking sorry!'

I remain silent, realising that there is so much about my friend I don't know. I try to think of something helpful to say but nothing comes to mind.

'Anyway,' she says, turning to me, her face raw from crying, 'the police are always hanging about round here. They won't bother coming after us, it's like a mini east Kilbride round here!'

Looking out at the burnt car shells, boarded-up windows and the barely dressed feral-looking children, I think she could be right.

'But,' I add, 'please don't do anything stupid. We don't want to wreck everything.'

'Esther, you don't have to worry about me,' she says,

sounding more like her old self, 'I won't. I'll just give her a mouthful. You know what I'm like, I'm all talk. Once I've mouthed off, I calm down. Don't I?' she asks, her voice softening.

Feeling reassured I follow her out and we set off again, trying not to act guilty. We have the cover of early evening shadows now, and Leanne reassures me there isn't much further to go.

As we round the corner to the estate where Leanne's parents live, we're confronted by three more police cars. 'Just keep walking!' Leanne whispers. But my legs have turned to jelly and I can't help checking whether they're watching us. With a plunging sensation I realise they are. Forcing one dead leg in front of the other, I try to match Leanne's confident stride. Looking down, the pavement swims in and out of focus as I become aware of the police car doors opening and officers getting out. They are coming for us.

'Run!' shrieks Leanne. But my legs won't work. And within moments a policeman catches up to me. He yanks my floppy arms behind my back and marches me back to his car where, pushing me against the bonnet, he effortlessly clicks handcuffs around my wrists.

I watch from the back seat of a police car as Leanne puts up a much better fight. She kicks, screams and bites for all her worth. Despite being handcuffed, she continues to angrily rear up. She flings her head against the policeman's chest and kicks at his shins, all the while squealing, 'Let me go, you fucking pig!'

The policeman in the passenger seat turns to me. 'You've put everyone to a lot of trouble today, my girl. Anything could have happened to you.'

I look at him; he looks caring. 'Please don't take me back to Crouchend Alley!' I beg.

'But, there's nowhere else for you to go,' he replies. The car starts and with mounting dread I watch out for familiar signs that lead us back to Crouchend.

My stomach churns nervously, as we pull up outside. A policeman walks me in, still in handcuffs, to where Linda is waiting in the lobby. I'm staring at my shoes, as she exclaims, 'You had us all worried sick,' and grips me in a stiff embrace.

I can tell the policeman interprets my dropped head as feeling ashamed of my behaviour. 'Well, I don't think she'll be doing that again, in a hurry,' he reassures Linda.

When he's gone Linda takes me into the office and demands, 'Why did you do it, Esther?' I don't answer, but rub at my sore wrists. She continues, 'You're not doing yourself any favours, you know that don't you? Because you certainly won't be getting out of here any faster!'

I watch my tears splash the backs of my hands for a moment before answering. 'I did it, because I don't want to be here. I was trying to get home!' I cry.

'Well, unless we find you a foster family, I don't know what else we can do.'

Her words hang in the air, because the answer is obvious. Just send me home, I want to scream – but I know it's point-less. Then, as if taking pity on me, she offers, 'You can come home to my house tonight, if you want, it will give you a little break.'

I don't care where I go, as long as it's not here, so I eagerly agree. 'But Esther, you dare running away again and that's it, you've burned your bridges!'

'No,' I say with wide-eyed promise, 'I won't.'

I grab my nightie and Linda drives us the short distance to her home. She shows me to her daughter's bedroom who is away at university. I'm asleep within minutes of my head touching the pillow.

I'm startled to wake the following morning in an unfamiliar girl's bedroom. I slowly take in the posters of boy bands attached to the walls with Blu-Tack. On a pink bedside table a sparkling jewellery tree jostles for space among numerous exotic-looking perfume bottles of Poison, Charlie and Lou Lou. For a couple of minutes I pretend that this is my own bedroom, and imagine what it must feel like to be a normal teenage girl.

There's a soft knock at the door and Linda pokes her head in. 'Morning, honey pie. How did you sleep?'

'Oh, okay thanks!' I reply.

'Come through when you're ready and we'll have some breakfast,' she says in a kind voice I've never heard before. She's treating me differently. Like I'm a real girl out here, with real feelings, not a problem that has to be dealt with.

After breakfast Linda shows me through to her living room. Handing me the remote control she offers, 'You can watch some TV if you like. I just need to do a couple of things.'

But I don't turn on the TV. Instead I look at Linda's family photos. Pictures of happy, clean people. Photos of her daughter dominate – as a baby, a toddler and a toothy schoolchild. She is laughing or smiling in all of them, as if the love people felt for her has shrouded her in stardust, forming an invisible protective veil that she will always wear. But then my eye is caught by a picture of Linda hung in pride of place over the mantelpiece, beaming proudly. She wears a decorative cape around her shoulders and on her head is a flat board with a tassel. In her hands she holds an important-looking scroll.

Linda startles me when she returns and finds me examining her picture. 'Couldn't you get the remote to work? It's a bit dodgy, mind you!' she adds.

'No, it's not that,' I stammer. 'Linda, what are you doing in that photo?'

She looks at it for a minute and a soft smile spreads across her face. 'Oh, that's one of my proudest achievements. That's me with my degree.'

'What's a degree and why are you wearing that funny costume?'

She laughs, 'That's not a costume, it's a gown and mortar board. A degree is a very special thing, Esther. It's a higher education certificate that will change your life. It can take you anywhere in the world. But here's the best thing: nobody can ever take it from you!'

I silently look at her and the words 'change your life' and 'nobody can ever take it from you' repeat on a loop in my mind. In an instant I decide, that's the answer I've been looking for – I need a degree! 'How can I get a degree?' I ask.

Linda laughs again. 'Well, I don't think that's something you'll have to worry about,' she says, continuing to chuckle to herself, like I'd made a very funny joke.

When Linda's daughter visits that afternoon I felt nervous. Will she think I was trying to steal her perfect, normal life and be angry with me? But I had nothing to fear, she's friendly and welcoming and acts as if we'd known each other for ever. When Linda tells her I'm staying until Monday she just accepts it, and asks no questions about who I am and why I'm here. We all go out together to see a film, then to McDonald's and it was one of the best days I've had, in a very long time.

Monday morning comes too fast and I hate returning to Crouchend Alley, although I'm desperate to see Leanne and hear what happened to her after. I search everywhere but can't find her. Returning to our room, I find a social worker packing up her things. 'What are you doing with Leanne's stuff?' I ask, immediately concerned.

'Oh, she's been moved to a high security centre,' she replies casually.

'What?' I demand. 'Why?'

'Leanne's got problems that can't be helped here.'

'What problems? She was only going to tell her mum how she felt. She wasn't going to hurt her, not really!' I protest tearfully.

The social worker cocks her head to one side and eyes me doubtfully. Suddenly I feel sad and alone. Leanne was my best friend here and she'd been with me since day one. I lie down and bury my face in my pillow while the social worker continues her packing. 'Look, you won't be by yourself for long,' she says as if that's what I'm upset about. 'Daisy is coming in with you. There's a new girl arriving this afternoon and she needs a room by herself!'

After Leanne's things have been taken away, Daisy moves in. Her head down, she drags her feet and bag behind her. Turning her back to Leanne's old bed, she lets herself free-fall. She's back after yet another failed foster placement. She keeps running away from them, going back to the streets, where she drinks and takes drugs. As usual, she's togged from head to toe in brand-new gear. Baggy jeans, red surfer hoodie – still with creases from the packaging they came in – and the biggest, whitest trainers of anyone in Crouchend. Daisy is famous for knowing how to manipulate her key worker. If I had all those clothes, I wouldn't be that sad, I think, eyeing her enviously. She turns to me, her pale brown eyes shining bright from her dark face, and sighs dramatically. Then, as if reading my thoughts, she says, 'I don't know why I do it. I think I want a family, but when I get one, I feel caged in, like all I can think about is escaping.'

'You're mad!' I accuse. 'You're caged in here, aren't you?'

She shrugs and with a sad smile adds, 'Like they say, I'm going the same way as me mam: streets, drugs then dead!' She says it mournfully, like it can't ever change, like she's on board a train with only one destination.

Later we go down to the main sitting room where Derek, Craig and Jamie are trying to outwit each other in front of the new girl, Annabel. Derek and Craig have ganged up and are ripping the piss out of Jamie.

'You're weak as shite, Jamie, you pussy!' Derek baits.

Craig joins in, 'Aye, Jamie, you mind that time I bitch-slapped you and you fucking howled for yer mammy!'

This causes them both to fall about in gales of laughter while Jamie is scarlet. He makes a faltering attempt to give as good as he gets: 'You're twats, the both of yez, kiss my fucking arse, you homos!'

Meanwhile, Annabel sits curled up in the corner of the sofa, reading her magazine, completely unaware the boys exist, let alone that all of this is for her benefit. She's in her own world, while we look at her from our cold hard one, sizing her up and figuring her out. She looks new, but it's more than that: she's wearing the same veil of love as Linda's daughter, I can see it protectively sparkle all around her. While we have a couple of hours' schooling at Crouchend, she'll be allowed to leave here every day and go to a proper school in the uniform she's wearing now: a smart dark grey pinafore over a crisp white shirt with a gold and blue striped tie tucked down the front. Her cropped dark hair frames a slim angular face and straight nose. Of course her legs have no bruises and she wears the shortest, cleanest ankle socks and smart polished plain black shoes. Where us girls grow our hair long and cover it in lace and clips, hers is glossy, neat and understated. Our ears stretch and ache under the weight of the goldest, glitziest and biggest hoops we can bear, while Annabel wears plain gold studs. Our eyes are caked in multi-coloured sparkle but only a hint of mascara darkens her sweeping lashes. She doesn't belong here with us. I look over at the boys still vying for her attention, and I know they don't stand a chance.

The staff treat her differently too. Annabel's here, they say, because of something that's not her fault: her parents split up. She has nowhere else to stay – the place we live in permanently is her temporary last resort. She acts like she expects care, like she's someone who has people who love her, so the staff treat her with care, and we all hate her for it. We know she is loved and it highlights how we are not. She doesn't have to stay with the rest of us kids for activities, she can do her own thing. She's allowed to return to her room when she wants, where she can lock us all out.

If the boys get too lairy, Terry defends her, and if us girls get too lairy with her, he puts us in our place. Annabel must have quiet in the evenings to do her homework, so she needs one of the sitting rooms to herself. Nobody else eats the brown bread, that's for Annabel; she likes the muesli too, so leave that alone just in case Annabel fancies it. We bitch about her endlessly and boast how we'll tell her what we really think of her. But underneath it all we're all desperate for her to like us. When she smiles at me with her straight white teeth or laughs at something I've said, my tummy goes warm and I feel my face glow because I've been allowed to glimpse inside a magical other world through her, the world of normality.

I've been at Crouchend Alley for just under nine months when Linda comes and whispers in my ear at dinnertime. 'I need you to come and see me when you're done.'

I rush my food, excited at the thought of what it could be. Since staying with her that one weekend, I keep hoping she might ask me to come home with her again, but she never does. I don't ask. I don't want to hear her say no.

The air in the office is too thick and still, like the window needs opening. 'Come in, Esther, and shut the door behind you,' Linda orders in a serious voice.

My body tenses, and a surge of panic rises in my stomach. What have I done?

'I'm afraid I have some news that might upset you,' Linda continues.

I've never heard her sounding so formal and it scares me. 'What is it?' I ask urgently.

'Just a minute, I'll get to that. But first, I need you to

promise that you'll stay calm. Can you do that?' I nod, trying to imagine what would send me spiralling into an immediate rage. 'Today, all eight of your younger siblings were taken into care by the Orkney Social Work Department.'

CHAPTER EIGHT

One step forward and two steps back

An icy disbelief washes over me and the room spins. 'No!' I gasp, shaking my head. 'But why ... what ... what happened?'

'Well, I imagine, the children were taken out of their schools and the younger ones were taken from home ...' Linda replies measuredly.

'No!' I interrupt impatiently, annoyed by her calm manner, 'I mean why has this happened?'

'Well, Esther,' she says hesitantly, as if unsure how to continue, 'I thought you'd realise this was bound to happen. It's because of the suspicion surrounding you being sexually abused at home. Removing your siblings and taking them to a place of safety is the next step. It's believed to be in their best interest ...'

She is still speaking, but I've had to blank her out as the more she talks and the more I don't understand, the angrier I feel. A charge of energy shoots around my body and I lean up to her face. 'Why are you doing this, Linda?' I scream. 'Why won't you believe my brothers haven't sexually abused me? How many times have I got to tell you?' I shout hard until my voice runs out. Linda's blurry image stands up and moves towards me. 'No, don't you dare come near me!' I growl, backing towards the door. She's in on this too! I can't trust anyone! 'What will happen to them now?' I ask tearfully.

'They'll just be questioned about what has happened to them at home. Then we can give them help—'

I start laughing. 'Help?' I shout incredulously. 'Help from social workers? Nobody gets help from social workers!' I laugh until my lips are dry against my gums, recalling how I once believed in social workers.

'What is it, Esther? Speak to me. Tell me what's going through your mind.'

'No!' I angrily retort, 'I'm not telling you anything! Why the fuck would I talk to you? Just fuck off, the lot of you! Social workers have never helped me or my family!'

She quietly watches me for a while, which only makes me angrier. 'I understand you're upset about your brothers and sisters being taken into care, so I'll excuse your outburst today. Why don't you go to your room and calm down?'

I kick open my bedroom door and throw myself on my bed and cry frustrated angry tears. I'm destroying my siblings' lives! I don't understand how I'm doing it. This is all my fault. I'm making all these bad things happen. Why can't I stop the derailed train that my life has become?

A couple of hours later I've calmed down a bit and actually start to feel a little excited. If my siblings are staying in Inverness, I might be allowed to see them.

Swallowing my pride and temporarily placing my anger on hold, I go to Linda's office and gently knock. Doing my best to talk calmly, I explain, 'Linda, you know how I haven't seen my brothers and sisters in a long time? Well, could I go and see them while they're down here?'

There isn't a discussion. She's already decided. 'No, I don't think that would be a good idea. They're being questioned about possible sibling abuse at home, and you could influence the outcome, so—'

I see where this is going and my rage swells up again. 'You fucking bitch, this is so fucking unfair!' I scream, running from her office.

Three weeks pass before Linda calls me to her office again. This time it is to tell me that the Social Work Department have sent my brothers and sisters home. While I am happy for them, I can't help feeling upset over what feels like injustice: why am I still here then? At least Linda lets me phone home. Mum explains that the Social Work Department were forced to return them, as no evidence of sibling abuse was found. Predictably, our family social worker, Mona Drone, had tried to get them kept in care. But the chairwoman at the panel said that without evidence that they were being harmed at home, she could see no reason for them to be kept in care.

But my brothers and sisters being returned home has given me renewed hope. I go to Linda prepared to fight my corner. 'I've said all along I wasn't being abused at home. My brothers and sisters said they weren't and they get to go home, so why can't I? Why am I being kept here?'

I sense Linda is a little less sure of her ground, but she still churns out the familiar argument. 'It isn't that simple, there are guidelines that must be followed.'

'But,' I interrupt, 'I wasn't allowed my say at the panel

that put me in here, so why does there have to be one about me staying?'

'Look,' she says, getting visibly frustrated, 'you haven't long to wait. You'll have your say at your sixteenth birthday panel.'

She's right, my birthday is only two weeks away. But why should I believe that this panel will be any different from the last?

Time drags in here at the best of times, but it's worst when you're waiting. I feel like I'll go mad if something doesn't change, and I need it to be something big!

My panel date finally comes through – it's to be on 11 August, the day before my 16th birthday. And there's even more good news – it's to be held in Orkney! That means I'll get a chance to say what I really want and not have social workers speaking for me in what they claim to be 'my best interests!' Linda had always said she would come to my sixteenth birthday panel, and that she'd be asking for me to be held in care until I was 18. But since my brothers and sisters were returned home, she seems to have changed her mind. Instead an agency social worker I've never met before will be flying to Orkney with me. After over a year of being my key worker, Linda and I never really say goodbye. With a surreal feeling, I pull open the exit door to Crouchend Alley, when, on the way to her office, Linda calls out to me, 'See you later, Esther!'

'I hope not,' I jokingly retort.

Once the car has driven me a safe distance, I look back at the empty, grey box that is Crouchend Alley. I've experienced so much pain and misery there in the last year and I dare to wish that I'll never return.

*

The agency social worker and I sit in silence on the plane. She is reading through my file and I'm deep in thought about seeing Mum and my brothers and sisters again. It has been over a year since I last saw my mum after my first panel meeting at Crouchend, but it feels like a lifetime ago. So much has happened since then, including my brothers and sisters being taken into care. I wonder whether everyone will blame me, because I know I do!

Painful childhood memories flood through me as we drive into Kirkwall. After what happened with my dad, do I even want to live in Orkney again? I must remind myself that I'm coming back to be with my mum and family. The car winds down a small back street and pulls up outside an ordinary-looking terraced house. I look out confusedly – the driver must have got it wrong! I had been expecting a meeting room inside some office block. The agency social worker seems as unsure as me as she hesitantly knocks on the plain front door, which I'm expecting to be opened by a housewife. I'm not far wrong when a plump middle-aged woman with smiling pale blue eyes and wavy auburn hair swings it open. 'Ah, hello there,' she greets in a friendly lilting Scottish accent. 'I'm Judith Hope, the panel reporter.' I'm surprised at how normal she seems for someone in charge. Pointing out the loo and drinks machine on the way, she shows us to an empty waiting room.

The agency social worker settles down with my file, but I'm so full of energy, I pace the floor. Soon I need a wee. 'Can I go to the toilet please?'

She looks up startled. 'Of course you can. Do you remember where the reporter said it was?'

Opening the door from the waiting room, I am immediately confronted with Mum, getting herself a coffee. For a moment neither of us say a word. I stay silent, as I know the social worker won't want me talking to her. Not taking her eyes from mine, Mum lifts her polystyrene cup from the machine. I can't help comparing her to the mother I last saw over a year ago. She seems so much older. Her deep dark glossy hair has paled to a grey fuzz, and her once vibrant face has sunken into sallow skin and bone, while her dark eyes look as if they've seen too much. A golden necklace ripples upon her prominent collarbone and the layers of clothes she wears – a big jacket over a thick shirt over a couple of T-shirts – only make her seem smaller.

Gently and quietly she places her cup on the windowsill. I wait with bated breath. She opens her arms out and relief floods me. 'Come here,' she says, her voice breaking. I lean in, overwhelmed, everything is going to be all right. I luxuriate in the feeling of safety, wrapped inside my mum's arms, at last. But then I become aware of a vice-like hand, clamping my arm. It's the agency social worker. 'Come on, Esther,' she says firmly, 'we haven't had the panel's decision, yet.' Tears stream towards my chin. I've waited so long for this moment, but I must still wait for other people's permission to cuddle my own mother.

Back in the waiting room, I slump into a chair, my face wet with tears and my chest heaving with anger, while the social worker stands guard at the door. After a few minutes a woman pops her head in to say that the meeting has started and we'll be called through in due course. My stomach starts flipping so I jump up and start pacing room

– nine steps long and six steps across – while adults I've never met before this day decide my fate. Finally, after nearly an hour, the same woman pops her head in again. 'You can come through now.'

Gripping my statement, I follow the woman to the meeting room. The large oval table is surrounded by adults. I nervously glance around and catch Mum's eye; she gives me a little smile. I sit where I'm shown and tightly fold my arms and legs in an effort to control my trembling body. Looking up, I meet the eyes of the woman opposite me. 'I'm Judith Hope, the panel reporter. Remember we met before, Esther?' I nod and she goes around the table, introducing me to everyone, before getting to Mum. 'And this is your mum.' I smile, everyone else chuckles and I feel more at ease. 'Now, Esther,' she continues, 'I want you to understand what we do here. We're here to find out what's best for your future and the most important opinion on that matter is yours. Do you understand?'

Looking into her clear calm blue eyes, I nod. 'Yes,' I reply. But while I understand what she is saying, I haven't felt my opinion counted for so long. I don't know whether to believe her yet.

My stomach jolts, when Judith Hope addresses the social worker with me. 'What do you believe is in Esther's best interests?'

The woman glances down at my file. 'Well, it is generally felt that if Esther wishes to return home, we are not going to contest her decision.'

I spin round to face her. Did I hear that right? They're not going to contest my decision? I repeat it over in my mind. After over a year of them going against everything I've ever said, I don't understand what's going on. But there isn't time for that now, the meeting has moved on.

I look back at Judith Hope, who is nodding and writing something down. She turns to me. 'Now, Esther, what would you like the outcome of today's panel to be?'

I know what she is going to ask me and I interrupt. 'I want to go home!' I answer quickly and she smiles kindly. 'Okay, we've heard all we need to from you for now. Please return to the waiting room and we'll get back to you with our decision.' Giving me a friendly wink, she adds, 'Soon, I promise!'

I reluctantly return to the waiting room with the social worker, where we once again wait in silence. She is staring out into a moody August sky like she doesn't want to be here. I ask if I can go and get a drink. 'You can do what you like,' she says in a tired voice. I look at her, surprised for a moment, but then I get it. She just came here to make that statement then her job was done. I'm gripped by an impulse to shake an answer from her. Why, after all this time, didn't they contest my decision? If they really believed they had a right to keep me at Crouchend and that I was being sexually abused at home, why are they simply letting me go home now? Why have they stolen all this time from me? But she is someone I didn't know before today and I realise she hasn't got any answers. After all, she doesn't know me either, she just knows a girl from inside a thick green file.

My thoughts are interrupted by a mass rumbling and scraping of chairs. Someone is calling my name. The waiting room bursts open and I'm in Mum's arms. 'Esther, you're coming home. You're coming home!' she sobs.

I lean on Mum's shoulder and firmly grip her bony hand on the journey home to Crook Farm. As the car crunches up the familiar gravel path, I hear my brothers' and sisters' shouts and excited screams of welcome in the distance before I see them. Soon I'm surrounded by my siblings and questions are fired at me from every angle. 'What happened?' 'Are you okay?' 'Why did they take you away?' I try to answer, but I find it impossible to put my feelings into words – I'm too overcome with happiness.

I'm surprised how different life at home has become. Under Dad's rule, it was deathly quiet – as none of us wanted to draw attention to ourselves. But even without all but one of my older sisters – the others having moved down south – Crook Farm bustles with the noise and life of my younger eight brothers and sisters. There is Bella, 15, who I am beyond happy to see as she has always been my closest sister. Then there is Robin, 14, who seems to have grown into a young man since the last time I saw him. My sister Willow, 12, with her delicate bone structure and petite frame, looks like a beautiful ballet dancer, while Lawrence, ten, starts immediately joking around as he's always been the clown of the family. Then there's football-mad Sam, nine, with his great big brown eyes and the longest eyelashes I've ever seen. I have missed Holly, eight, desperately, as we've always shared a special bond. Last but not least, there are the two youngest girls, sensible Penny, five, and three-year-old Poppy.

It is instantly obvious how different their childhoods are from mine, Bella's and my older siblings. We were never allowed to bring friends home, but neighbours' children play with my brothers and sisters where once Dad's prize stinging nettles grew. Orkney's famous winds have knocked off the roof from Dad's old workshop and it now acts as a play den and obstacle course. Children race through it, kicking up the earth, as if Dad was never here at all. And, most poignantly for me, the old ruin where Ferdinand was so cruelly starved to death has brightly coloured flowers growing in it, creating a perfect sheltered garden.

Toys litter the floor, which once had to be kept clear at all costs. I learnt early in life that if I had a toy, I must hide it so Dad wouldn't break it when he got angry. One of my little brothers loves teenage ninja turtles, so he has model figures of them everywhere and posters all over his bedroom wall. My younger sisters have dolls; us older ones had real babies to look after. Their dolls look almost like the Tiny Tears I always wished for.

But the biggest difference is in Mum. She behaves like a real mum, cooking food that the children want to eat and cleaning the house. But, for me, the best thing about the change in her is being able to talk to her about the little things that bother me. The ice-cold fear that once ruled this house with a death iron grip has melted – it is now a home!

My relationship with most of my younger brothers and sisters soon becomes part of the daily routine. I'm the older sister who helps with homework and gets annoyed when they touch my stuff, but who mostly loves being back home and around them. I am relieved that my bond with Holly is still strong, but confused and hurt by Bella's attitude to me. I thought she would be over the moon I was home but she doesn't seem happy or sad – just nothing! I catch her looking at me sometimes from a distance and a darkness passes over her face, but then she will smile and in the blink of an eye everything seems like it might be okay between us again. One day I attempt to have it out with her. 'What's going on?'

She looks through me and smiles politely. 'Everything's fine,' she replies in a stilted voice, that doesn't invite conversation.

I can't help feeling upset about it and wonder if I'm expecting too much, especially after everything that's happened. Maybe I have to accept our relationship can never be the same again. But her behaviour becomes even stranger, and things start happening that I can't help but find disturbing.

After ignoring me for days she challenges me to a race from our house to the beach, about a mile down the road. I'm going to cycle and she will cut across the fields and the winner is the first person who makes it to the beach. Happy she wants to do something fun together, I agree. Once on my bike, I watch her make a start, by climbing the first fence. Determined to win, I start cycling furiously, first down the gravel path and through the gate, then on to the straight stretch that will turn right, towards the beach. I arrive nearly 15 minutes later, sweating and breathless but happy to see I've won.

Looking across the fields to check her progress, I'm surprised not to see her. I call her name a couple of times, without an answer. Then I wonder if she's already here, waiting to jump out at me. I look everywhere I think she might be, but don't find her anywhere. I skim stones until the sky over the Atlantic Ocean deepens into an inky evening blue. It's then that I become worried. What if she's had an accident on the way here? She could have fallen into a ditch and broken a leg or, worse, she might be drowning somewhere. Suddenly seized by panic, I hurriedly make my way back across the field, hoping to cover her tracks. But she isn't in the fields and all my calls go unanswered.

I am climbing the last fence, dividing our farm from next door's, when I see her. She is sitting statue-still on the grass. The evening shadows shroud her and all I can make out are the whites of her eyes that stare up at me. I should be angry but when I meet her gaze a fearful shiver ripples down my spine. 'Bella?' She continues to stare silently, and I become alarmed. 'Bella, are you all right?' I demand.

In a slow robotic voice, she asks, 'Who are you?'

Ice trickles through my veins. 'Bella you ... you know who I am,' I hesitantly reply, 'I'm your sister.'

But with a heavy heart, I realise she isn't pretending. She never has been. She doesn't know me any more and if I hadn't always known her face, I would swear we were strangers. Now I agree with Mum: Bella needs professional help. Mum has been asking for help for ages, but they haven't even done an assessment. Bella refuses to go to school and instead has been assigned a young, newly qualified social worker, Sarah Cooke. She drives a 60-mile round trip from Kirkwall to pick Bella up and take her into town a couple of times a week to talk to her. But that doesn't seem to be helping.

After living at home for a couple of months, I decide to move out. Not only is there not enough room but I need my own space. So I move to Kirkwall, Orkney's capital. While there, I work in an old people's home training to be a care assistant. I have a great time working with the old people and most of the staff are really nice too. Because of what happened with my father, and more recently with my brothers and sisters being taken into care, my family is infamous in Orkney. So the minute I say my name, most people know who I am. The majority of people are supportive, but some aren't. They are the ones who say, 'There's no smoke without fire.' Our history has cast a long shadow over my and my siblings' lives, but we are all trying to move out from under it so we can have a much better future than our past.

Since moving to town I have seen Bella a couple of times. She is usually with her social worker or on her way to the Social Work Department to see her. One day I catch sight of her in the distance and call to her. At first I don't think she hears me, so I keep calling. She turns, as if she's heard something, but runs on. I give chase. She turns again and this time I know she's seen me, but she hurries on even faster. Eventually, catching her arm, I spin her towards me and demand, 'Bella, why didn't you wait for me?'

She doesn't answer and I search her face. 'I'm in a rush,' she mumbles nervously.

'What's wrong?' I ask.

'Nothing, I'm just in a rush,' she repeats, turning away, as if growing impatient. And even though she is here right now, her voice sounds distant. 'Right,' I say awkwardly.

She looks at my hand, still gripping her arm and so do I. We both seem to know that once I let it go, it will mean the end of the bond we once shared as sisters, so I hold on for a moment longer. I'm desperate to scream at her, 'Look, it's me Esther, your sister! You've known me your whole life. What's going on with you?' But she is too far away. 'Bye, then,' I add sadly and she slips from me – like I knew she would.

I stand for a moment, watching her hurry from me to the Social Work Department, the only people she seems to talk to now, and it feels as if everything has changed for ever.

Part Three

1990–1991

CHAPTER NINE

Stolen

One of the consequences of my brothers and sisters being taken into care while I was at Crouchend Alley is that they are still under what's called a supervision order. This means that Mum has to report to a panel of people about their welfare every two weeks.

The panel is headed by the panel reporter, Judith Hope – the same woman who allowed me to come home from Crouchend. She is employed by the Secretary of State, which means she is independent of the Orkney Social Work Department. Judith is assisted by three volunteers who must be upstanding members of the community as their decisions have far-reaching consequences for the futures of the children under their supervision.

At the panel for my brothers and sisters on 31 October 1990, the reporter and panel members are so pleased with the children's progress and school reports, they want to terminate the supervision order. This would mean the end of social work contact for our family. There is only one person who disagrees: Mona Drone, our family social worker. With a sickly sweet smile she asks, 'If nobody minds, could the supervision order be extended, just a little while longer?

What harm could it do?' And, as nobody sees the harm, the supervision order is kept active.

Judith Hope then concludes the meeting by adding, 'Well, Mrs W, I just want to congratulate you on how far you and your family have come since your husband was jailed three years ago.'

Mum nods, returning her a tired smile. 'Thank you. It's been a real struggle, but I think we're finally seeing daylight.'

Mrs Hope turns to Mona Drone. 'Have you anything you would like to add, Ms Drone?'

A coldness creeps over Mum as she watches Mona's face darken. She looks around the table, her mouth pursed and eyes narrowed. 'Well,' she declares, 'I have to reiterate that as the saying goes, the abused becomes the abuser, and I still believe the best course of action for this family is to be separated and the younger ones put into care—'

'But Ms Drone,' Mrs Hope wearily interrupts, 'there is no evidence of the so-called abuse you keep referring to.'

Leaning over the table, Mona's dark eyes glitter dangerously and in a voice laden with menace, she promises, 'Well, I shall just have to find evidence then, won't I?'

Nobody knows how far Mona will go to complete her plan. But the supervision order needs to stay active, for it to work. She is going to split my family up no matter what, but to do it she will need help from the inside.

I have only lived away from home for a few weeks before I realise how much I miss it. When you've grown up in such a large family, living alone feels lonely and alien. So I move back where I give Mum some much needed help with the kids and the animals on our smallholding.

It's a few days since the children's last panel and I'm carrying two slopping buckets of water across the field to fill the trough for the sheep when I'm startled by an unfamiliar southern accent. 'Does your mum feel she'll get fair treatment from Orkney Social Work Department now Judith Hope has been suspended?'

I drop the water and spin round to see a casually dressed dark-haired man, leaning over the gate to Crook Farm. 'What? Who are you?'

His face breaks into a wide friendly smile. 'I'm sorry, the name's Pete Dockle. I'm a journalist from London.'

'Oh,' I dumbly reply. Because of my dad's imprisonment for child abuse there has been on-going media interest in my family, so I'm not completely surprised to see a journalist at the gate but they do usually phone first. 'I think you'd better come in,' I say, 'I know Mum will want to hear about this!'

'Judith Hope's been suspended?' Mum cries, ashen-faced, sinking into a chair.

Now it's Pete's turn to be surprised. 'Yes, didn't you know? It happened yesterday afternoon. My editor sent me up on the overnight train. This is turning out to be quite a case. Do you mind if I smoke?'

Mum shakes her head. 'I think I need one, but I'd prefer a stiff drink.'

'I'm sorry to be the bearer of such bad news,' Pete continues, opening his leather satchel and taking out a notepad and pen. 'I assumed you'd know.'

'No, no, I didn't,' Mum replies absent-mindedly, before asking, 'But how can they suspend her, she's independent?'

Pete gives a cynical laugh, 'It's the way little places like Orkney work, Mrs W, the council is run by its own rules.'

Mum nods. 'You're right there. But wonder why they are so desperate to get rid of her, that they'll suspend her?'

After Pete has left, Mum lets out a moan of despair and drops her head into her hands. 'Look, Mum, Pete could be right – it might all turn out okay. Anyway, what reason could they have to take the children again? Remember how well the last panel went?'

But when Mum lifts her head, her face is tear-stained and full of dread, as if she has glimpsed the future. 'Reasons don't matter. It's already too late. That awful woman Mona Drone is really going to do it,' she whispers fearfully, 'and now the council has removed the last obstacle in Judith Hope there's nothing we can do to stop her!'

Only a week after the last panel, at midday on 6 November 1990, Mona Drone leads four uniformed police officers and four social workers into Lady Mary's Primary School. They have an emergency care order, empowering them to forcibly remove all of my younger siblings and take them into care. They will forget no one; they have a list.

My brothers and sisters know what is happening. It's just over a year since they were taken into care for the first time, but that only makes it more terrifying. They know that they will ripped, crying and screaming, from everyone who loves them. And even though they know it's no use, they fight, they scream and run for their lives. Bella is taken just two days before her sixteenth birthday. Robin is at high school and is called to the headmaster's office, where two social workers wait and snatch him. Meanwhile, the younger ones are taken from their primary school. Willow and Lawrence are taken, while Holly cowers beneath her desk and is dragged out screaming and calling for Mum's help. Penny, at only five, is confused and follows them as she is told. But Sam is still haunted by a head full of horrific memories, and he makes a run for it. Locking himself in a toilet cubicle in the boys' room, he climbs upon the cistern and attempts to prise open the small window and escape. But it's no use, so instead he stays put, trembling and praying the social workers and police will leave, forgetting him. On hearing footsteps enter the bathroom, he hardly dares to breathe. But it's his teacher, who he loves and trusts. 'You can come out now Sam, it's okay.' Just the sound of her voice makes him believe that everything will be all right.

'Have the social workers gone now?' he asks tearfully.

'Yes,' she gently reassures him, 'they have gone, don't worry.'

Sam slowly climbs down, hope rising in his chest. He has escaped and they haven't got him. Tentatively sliding back the lock, he opens the door. But the faces of a policeman and a social worker loom aggressively down upon him. He tries to push the door shut, but they effortlessly bat it open. Grabbing an arm each, they drag the nine-year-old boy out and past the teacher he believed in. Looking up at her, Sam's large brown eyes are filled with fear and confusion. 'But ... but you said it was okay?'

The children are told they are being taken to a place of safety. Begging to be allowed to go home, they are driven over 30 miles to an airport. They are then put on a chartered plane and flown a further one hundred miles away. Being taken to a place of safety means nothing to them, when they felt safe at home, among their family and friends. Right now they feel more frightened and unsafe than they have ever felt in their short lives. There is no one with them who loves them, to comfort them. No one to kiss them goodbye and tell them that they will be thinking of them. No one reassures them that they will sort this mess out and bring them home to safety. They have only the school clothes they stand in, no comforters, no special teddies, nothing to remind them of home.

But Mona Drone isn't finished yet. There is one more child she is going to take. My youngest sister, Poppy. As she's just turned four years old she is not yet at school.

By late afternoon, Mona Drone arrives at Crook Farm flanked by two police officers. She bangs urgently at the front door. Mum is alone at home and nervously answers, unaware her other children have already been taken. 'Would you like to come in?' she offers.

Mona Drone returns her empty smile. 'No we won't, thank you, Mrs W. We are here following up some allegations of abuse. I have had an emergency care order issued on all your children under the age of 16. We are here to take Poppy.'

Mum clutches her chest in horror, panic flooding her body. 'NO! This isn't happening, this can't be, not again. *Please God, not again*!' she screams.

Mona stays deathly calm. 'Look, it will be best for all concerned if you hand Poppy over with the minimum of fuss.'

'NO!' Mum screams in hysterical disbelief. 'NO, please, no!' she howls, falling to the ground.

Ignoring Mum's distress, Mona Drone continues, 'Yes, Poppy is to be taken to a place of safety. We need you to tell us where she is.'

'Well, you can't take her. She isn't here. She's in town!' Mum hears herself defiantly whisper.

'You're hiding her, Mrs W, I know the signs,' Mona sneers. Turning to the police officers, she orders, 'Search the house.'

While the police search the house, Mona follows Mum into the kitchen where Mum collapses on the sofa. 'I would prefer you don't contact anyone until we've gone, Mrs W. It's easier that way. You understand,' Mona asks in a sweetly threatening voice.

Mum nods. 'But what is this about?' she asks in a barely audible whisper.

'Well, your daughter Bella has made some serious allegations of abuse to her social worker. Which have led me to believe that your children are not safe in your care. Any further details can be discussed at the panel meeting tomorrow morning,' Mona replies.

'But what kind of allegations?' Mum asks breathlessly.

Mona moves towards the door. 'Look, I'd really rather not discuss this now. As I've said, we can talk about it at the panel in the morning.'

Once the police have turned the house upside down and still not found Poppy, they prepare to leave. Mona turns back and looks down at Mum, her black eyes bulging, and in a voice dripping with sinister promise, she adds, 'Oh, and don't worry Mrs W, we'll be back later for Poppy.'

As Mona and the police drive off, it suddenly occurs to Mum that if they want Poppy, they might try to take her other children. She looks at the phone directory but the school number blurs to a distant shadow. Mum cries out, as she is struck by a needle-like stabbing sensation behind her eyes followed by a terrifying loss of vision. She phones a friend, whose number she knows by heart. 'It's Victoria!' She screams, 'Please help me, I can't see. Please get me the number for Lady Mary's Primary School!' she begs into the receiver.

'What's wrong, Victoria, what's happened?' her friend urgently replies.

'I can't explain now, there's no time,' Mum shrieks. 'I need to phone the school *now*!'

Once through, Mum asks, as calmly as she can, 'May I just check my children are okay?' The receptionist says she'll get the headmistress; Mum's guts twist. It feels like a bad sign.

'Mrs W.' Mrs Brown's usually friendly voice is professional and abrupt. 'Social workers removed your children from St Mary's Primary School at midday. I am sorry, but I'm not at liberty to discuss the matter further.'

Mum hears the handset clonk against the table leg and everything moves far away as if she is wrapped inside a thick cotton wool fog. But she can't stop now. She must act fast.

'Mrs W, are you there?' Mrs Brown squeaks as Mum replaces the handset. She dials a friend in Kirkwall. 'Marlene, please find Poppy, find her and hide her *now*!'

'Victoria, what's happened?'

'It's happening again, Marlene, they're taking the children. Please, I'm begging you, find Poppy. She's in town with her older sister, Karen. When you find her, get her away from Orkney. Do whatever it takes, Marlene, just save her!'

Marlene races round to my work, her face white and her eyes wide with fear. 'Esther, we need your help, the social workers have taken the kids again. Poppy's in town with Karen. We have to find her and get her to safety!'

Mum contacts everyone she can think of, starting with

her solicitor, Mr Moore. She is relieved when he reassures her: 'This is bloody outrageous and it's illegal. They can't just go around stealing people's children. There's no way they can get away with this! If they're not charging anyone or investigating a criminal offence, they can't do it. Try not to worry, Victoria, this'll be easily sorted out.'

Mum goes on to phone the local newspaper and journalists on the mainland, including Pete Dockle. Recalling their recent conversation, Pete gasps, 'So that's why they wanted Judith Hope out of the way! I suspected they were after taking your children, Victoria, but even I didn't think they'd work this fast.' Mum then phones the local MP and asks if he can do something. 'We need action, they need to be stopped,' she begs. She keeps wondering whether she should phone the police, surely this must be a crime? But the social workers had the police with them. The realisation hits her like an ice bullet: we are on the wrong side; we are the criminals!

Mum phones all the family friends she can think of, including Fran, the local minister's wife, and relays in horror what happened today. She explains that all of her younger children have been stolen, except her last little girl. 'I need somewhere to take her, Fran,' Mum pleads desperately. 'Maybe someone can take her away from all of this. They can't do this to her, not Poppy, she's just a baby!'

In her soft soothing voice Fran reassures Mum. 'Bring her here, Victoria, you must bring her here. Under God's roof, I promise you, she will be safe.'

When Poppy is found, she is rushed to the local church and smuggled to Mum who is waiting there for her. The press are informed of this latest development: while all of the other children from our family have been snatched and taken far from here, under an ancient Scottish law Mum is claiming sanctuary in the local church, trying to keep her youngest child.

The sky is a deep bruised purple as Mum, Poppy, Marlene, the minister and his wife hide in the shadows of the village church. They cover themselves in blankets to try and ward off the icy Orkney winter. It isn't long before the heavy metal knocker is forcefully rebounded off the church door, stirring Poppy from her slumber. 'This is the police! Open up! We want Mrs W to come out and hand over her daughter!' a man's voice demands.

'No,' Mum wails, pulling Poppy closer, 'please don't let them in.'

Fran springs to her feet. 'Don't worry, nobody is getting in here,' she promises, determinedly striding down the aisle. Opening the door a little she tells them firmly, 'What you and the Social Work Department are doing is wrong, in every way. Poppy and her mother are claiming sanctuary here, in the house of God. I forbid you from entering,' adding, 'Do I need to remind you that Poppy is a very frightened little girl? The only place she needs to be is in her mother's arms.'

A man's voice replies, relenting a little, 'Well, Poppy can stay here tonight, but her mother is expected at a panel hearing in the morning to discuss this further. If she fails to turn up, Poppy will be forcibly removed. So, do I have your word that Mrs W will be there with the little girl?'

'You have my word, officer,' Fran sighs resignedly. Rebolting the door, she returns to the little group, with the heartbreaking news.

Poppy is settled to sleep between two pews while the

adults stay up talking late into the night, trying to find a way to end this nightmare. But Mum holds on to a glimmer of hope, reminding everyone what her solicitor Mr Moore said: 'This will get quickly sorted. It isn't legal. They can't just take children.' But when he rings back, it's bad news. 'I'm so sorry, Victoria, but as the children were still under an active supervision order, the Social Work Department are allowed to take them,' Mr Moore explains, adding, 'we'll have to fight this through the courts, I'm afraid. But don't worry, it sounds worse than it is. They'll have to legally test their allegations and that's where we'll win,' he concludes triumphantly.

'Have you got children, Mr Moore?' Mum asks wearily.

'No,' he replies, 'but that hasn't got—'

'Well, I promise you,' Mum interrupts, 'that if you did you wouldn't for one second ask me to hand my last baby over to these bastards. Please, I'm begging you, Mr Moore, please find another way.'

'I'll try Mrs W, I'll do my very best,' he promises.

While I return to Crook farm, bewildered and in a state of shock at the brutal events of the past few hours, Mum sits awake through the night in the church. Watching her little girl sleep, she commits to memory the way her dark chocolate curls lie upon her forehead, framing her heart-shaped face. She notices how her long thick lashes rest on her chubby red cheeks as she gently sleeps with one arm crooked above her head, while in her other hand she clutches a soft toy. For now, in sleep, she is safe; tomorrow her sanctuary will be ripped apart. A sensation of black foreboding fills Mum, at the agonies she knows tomorrow will bring.

The morning comes fast and icy cold, with persistent drizzle that soaks to the bone. Poppy awakes startled and pulls on Mum's sleeve. 'Mum, where's Penny and Holly, where is everybody?'

Mum's throat is aching and tight. 'They've gone away for a little while, for a special holiday,' she lies.

Accepting Mum's explanation, Poppy investigates her new home. 'Look, Mum, rainbow windows!' she exclaims in delight, pointing at the stained glass that dazzles everything in multicoloured light. Mum slowly dresses her little girl for what she knows could be the last time. 'Are we going into town again today, Mummy?' Poppy asks excitedly. Mum feels the outside world closing in, and it's as if the rainbow windows have shattered and glacial winds howl through – she knows she must tell her what is about to happen.

'Poppy, listen to me,' but Poppy continues running up and down the church aisle. 'Poppy, sit down. You have to listen to Mummy. I have something very, very important to tell you,' she says firmly. Poppy sits on Mum's lap for a moment, half listening, while spying some toys from the Sunday school. 'Today you might have to go somewhere, with people you don't know.' The words choke in Mum's throat.

Poppy twists to face Mum, her face full of alarm. 'But Mummy, I don't want to go anywhere! I want to stay with you!'

Mum looks away, tears flooding her eyes. Poppy touches Mum's tear-stained cheek with her small chubby hand. 'Please don't send me away, I don't want to go!' she begs.

Mum can't continue. Handing Poppy to Fran, she runs to the bathroom. Locking the door, her body convulses with great, racking sobs. 'God have mercy, please don't let them take her. I will do anything, please protect her,' she begs the heavens.

At Crook Farm we have the heartbreaking job of packing a bag for Poppy. We try to decide what she needs for a journey to an unknown destination. Some clothes to keep her warm, of course, and her special princess dress-up clothes. In the bag go her favourite toys and some books she likes. Her potty and last but not least her night-time comfort-bear. The bag is loaded into the boot of the taxi that will take Poppy from us.

On the hour-long journey into town, Poppy sits on Mum's lap, their arms tightly woven around one another. Mum whispers urgently to her, as if trying to etch her words on to her very soul, 'Remember that I love you Poppy, I love you. Please try not to worry and don't be scared. I am always with you. Even if I'm not there in person, I am in your heart. Just remember I love you.'

With everyone crying around her, Poppy begins to whimper and grips Mum even tighter as they slowly enter Kirkwall.

The car halts on the street of terraced houses, outside the panel building. A more nondescript façade would be hard to imagine, providing the perfect disguise for the horrors within. A crowd has gathered, made up of family friends and supporters; the rest are journalists and cameras, shepherded by numerous police officers.

Holding Poppy, Mum unsteadily climbs from the car. Shielding her from the commotion of the gathered press, she carries her into the panel building. She is allowed only one other person with her in the meeting, so she takes her solicitor. Mum hesitantly enters the panel room. When Judith Hope was in charge, the place felt warm and welcoming; now it feels hard and cold.

The panel is being chaired by a temporary reporter, Gill Grubb. He looks at Mum with empty, grey eyes and informs her, 'Mrs W, your daughter Bella has made allegations of abuse. She has alleged that the local minister made wild, passionate love to her, and also a family friend, namely Marlene White, has abused her. I have read through the allegations Bella has made and I agree with the Orkney Social Work Department's decision to issue an emergency care order. Now, you must hand Poppy over. If you don't, we will be forced to remove her from you.'

Mum turns despairingly to Mr Moore, her eyes filled with fear, desperately hoping he might have a last-minute solution. Overcome with agony at what she is being asked to do, Mum screams in a pain so pure and deep, she wonders how she can still breathe.

'Just hand her over quickly,' Gill Grubb adds, his voice steel blade hard.

'No,' Mum replies, pulling Poppy closer and catching her breath, 'I have nothing to hide; there is no abuse going on. If you are going to steal my last child from me, I want the world to witness her being stolen.'

With Poppy clutched to her chest, Mum makes the dreaded journey back downstairs and outside to the pavement. Through a tear-soaked voice she tells the waiting journalists, 'I have done nothing wrong. There is no abuse going on. Yesterday they stole seven of my children and today they are taking my last.'

Poppy was always a shy child. She would want Mum to

hold her when strangers came into the house, and when they tried to speak to her she would cuddle down into Mum's chest. She is doing that now, her arms wrapped tightly around Mum's neck, burrowing her little face into Mum's jumper. All that can be seen of her is her mop of dark chocolate curls and her little legs in red woollen tights hooked around Mum's waist. She lifts her head momentarily, the whites of her huge brown eyes wide with terror, before plunging her face further into Mum's chest. There are two social workers, Sid Limey and a female social worker. The woman steps forward to take Poppy's hands from around Mum's neck. But Poppy pulls away, gripping another part of Mum's jacket, her little fists clenched, holding on for dear life. The social worker turns to a policeman. 'You,' she orders, 'take that child from this woman.'

But tears spill freely from the policeman's eyes. 'No,' he replies, choking up. 'I can't. I just can't,' he adds, turning away.

The social worker comes up behind Poppy and puts her hands around her waist, attempting to forcibly pull her off. Deep tracks of agony are etched into Mum's face as in a cracked voice she tells Poppy, 'It's okay, my darling, go with this woman. Everything is okay.'

Mum doesn't hand her over, but supports her weight as the social worker grips and pulls her, uncurling Poppy's little fingers, one by one.

Suddenly Poppy's terrified cries pierce the air. 'Mummy! Mummy, help me! Pleeeease help me! I don't want to go! Mummy!' she screams, as her heart is being broken. Her empty arms flail in the air, trying desperately to reach her mother. Poppy has lost her battle to stay with Mum, and

Mum has lost hers to keep her. Mum forces herself to look away – fighting every natural urge to grab hold of Poppy and run. For Poppy's sake, she must pretend it will all be okay, while every fibre of her being is telling her the world has changed for ever.

A vicious satisfaction spreads across the social worker's face. 'I have her, I have her,' she repeats.

Mum continues calling out to Poppy, hoping she hears her over her cries. 'I love you, I will always love you, and everything will be okay.'

No one asks for Poppy's special things, which remain in the boot of the taxi; instead a family friend hands them into the Social Work Department later, and they are handed back a copy of the rules.

The rules state that my brothers and sisters have been taken into care, under an emergency care order. This means that the Social Work Department can keep them for up to three weeks, during which time they will be questioned about the abuse they are believed to have suffered at home. All further correspondence with the children must be written and addressed to Orkney Social Work Department. The social workers will open the letters and check them. If they decide the information contained within them is 'appropriate' they will pass the letters on to the children. We are not told where the children are, or who they are with.

Mum, Marlene and I go to a friend's house, as none of us can bear the thought of returning to Crook Farm. Mum and some family friends talk of what we should do now but I'm too consumed with my own grief to add anything. I struggle for breath as the same question torments me: how can something this bad be allowed to just happen? At one point,

Mum suddenly lets out a long pain-filled sob, and soon everyone is crying again. Later, the crying turns to anger and frustration as my older brother Jacob, who drove up from down south during the night, despairingly asks nobody in particular, 'How can the Social Work Department take allegations and act as if they're real evidence?'

'Look,' Marlene points out, 'I'm one of the ones Bella has accused. I am supposedly the abusive family friend. I've tried to get them to interview me, but they won't. What else can I do?'

The following day we make the dreaded journey back to Crook Farm. It is a place deserted in panic. The gate at the end of the lane has been left open and children's clothes hang limply from the line. Inside, the November air is spiky sharp and all around is the chaotic mess left from the police's search for Poppy. Crook Farm is no longer a home; it is a dirty, violated shell.

I feel somehow detached from the physical pain that builds up in my chest and escapes through my mouth. We all gather in the kitchen, and again we cry and talk for hours. But all the words in the world change nothing. The same things are said over and over again. How could they do this? How can they get away with it? Is this legal? No background checks or social reports were done on the children, so how could they just take them? We ask one another questions but we don't have the answers.

We only get up to make coffee or use the toilet, otherwise we sit frozen into another night. But later waves of exhaustion wash over me, I need to get away from all of this. Despite myself I fall into a jumbled nightmare, full of pain, and a screaming that burns the skin from my face. I jolt awake, breathing hard and fast. There's a tick, tick, tick and it's getting louder. Suddenly fearful that something is about to explode, I frantically search for the source. I find the little white plastic alarm clock, ticking back at me. I had never realised it was so loud. There was always too much noise, people talking, shouting or laughing. Its half past five in the morning and everyone, except Mum, is asleep. She is perched, bird-like, on the edge of the couch, her head bent over yet another coffee. 'I'm going upstairs,' I mumble wearily, heaving myself from the couch.

The stairs are shrouded in the darkness of an early November morning. I step around a piece of chunky Lego that must have been left here two mornings ago. When I get to one of the children's bedrooms at the top of the stairs, the door is ajar and I glimpse the stars and moon decoration. They might still be in there fast asleep. They'd be annoyed if I woke them this early, so I gently pad past. I seem to float to the next bedroom at the end of the landing where more of them will be sleeping. I would love to see their sleep-filled faces and prove this has all been an evil nightmare. I softly open the wooden door but hollow air gasps at me. The carpet is icy beneath my feet and the small room feels echoey big. I trip forward and look down to see Lawrence's bedtime bear. My throat is tight, he would have missed that last night. Thomas the Tank engine pyjamas are strewn over the end of the other bed, and the Three Bears storybook is left open at Goldilocks trying the three chairs, never to reach a happy ending. They have nothing of home with them and that must have been how the social workers planned it. I climb into a bed so cold it's almost damp and pull up the covers. Scrunching my eyes tight shut, I wonder if I stay still and don't even breathe, will all of this still be true?

After a couple of hours of restless sleep, I go to the bathroom to face yet more reminders of them. The children's unused toothbrushes are lined up alongside an open tube of toothpaste. And their dirty washing is thrown in the direction of the washing basket. I hurriedly gather their clothes up and take them upstairs so there is one less thing for Mum to face.

We can't go to the police about this crime. The newspapers aren't allowed legally to identify us. But sitting around doing nothing, hoping that the Social Work Department will start behaving decently, is unbearable. We must do something. A family friend hits upon an idea: 'You can identify yourselves, can't you?' An A4 leaflet is scrambled together. Underneath a photo of Mum and my younger siblings, it explains: 'My children have been stolen by the Orkney Social Work Department, from their school, crying and protesting. They were dragged out in front of staff and fellow pupils. My four-year-old daughter was ripped from my arms. Please protest: no crime on earth justifies treating children this way. They were flown to God knows where in a chartered plane. Why aren't my children in Orkney? Where is my baby girl? Please help me get justice, fetch my children home to Orkney.' We spread the leaflets all over Kirkwall, in shop windows, on car windscreens, on lampposts and walls, and hand them out to everyone we come across. Mum also takes one around to her solicitor's office. 'Could you put this in your window, please Mr Moore?'

On seeing the poster, he looks horrified. 'NO, Mrs W, NO!' he thunders. 'This isn't the right way! You can't identify yourself, or your children and you definitely shouldn't be going about telling everybody what's happened. There are proper legal channels for these things.'

'Mr Moore,' Mum replies defiantly, 'it's too late for that. They've already identified my children, by stealing them. And if you can see what's legal about that, then please tell me, because I can't. Furthermore, I refuse to hide and act guilty. My children have been stolen from me and I intend to do everything I can to get them back.'

Family friends rally round and help in every way they can, both practically and emotionally. They contact the press, who from then on identify us as the 'W' family. Journalists travel from as far afield as Australia to report on this shocking case. They write of my brothers and sisters being ripped from their family, by Orkney Social Work Department on unproven allegations. They want to know, what we've been asking all along, how can the legal system let the Orkney Social Work Department get away with this?

We write letters to the children but we are not allowed to express any negative feelings towards Orkney Social Work Department, about their behaviour, or the fact that we want the children home. If we do, the letters simply won't be passed on. We can't write about how desperately heart-breaking all of this is. And, without being able to state the obvious, it's difficult to know what to write. So you make things up, you write about things that don't matter. You remind them we're still here; we haven't forgotten them. We tell them we love them and everybody is doing their best to get this mess sorted out.

I mainly write to Holly, who I've had an almost motherly bond with since the day she was born. I write about the weather. I tell her how Merrylegs, our little pony, is doing, how he's getting fat and missing her and her brothers and sisters. I make up a list of what I'm hoping to get for Christmas – without mentioning what I wish for most. I create a little cartoon called the Love Heart family and I illustrate the everyday antics of Mr and Mrs Love Heart and their baby Love Heart. Mum makes up poems, while others send photos and cards, mentioning things they remember about them. We struggle daily over what to write and how to put it, in case it offends the Social Work Department.

But it would be some months and hundreds of pounds spent on presents before we discover that we had been wasting our time. Not one letter, card or present will be passed on to the children. Instead they were being kept by Orkney Social Work Department, where they were being interpreted as containing evidence of satanic sex abuse. Later those letters, including my imaginary Love Heart family, would be used as evidence against us.

CHAPTER TEN

Finding our family

Nightmare days drag on, and soon the children have been gone for two painfully long weeks. Then Mum receives a letter from Orkney Social Work Department. A date has been set for the children's panel. It is to be on the last possible day of the three weeks they can hold on to the children without seeking court permission.

Despite everything that's happened, we feel optimistic about the panel's outcome. Nobody has been charged with abuse or even questioned, so we can't see on what grounds they can keep the children. We feel confident the result will be an apology from Orkney Social Work Department and the children will be immediately returned home.

On the day of the panel, a few family friends accompany Mum, my older brother and me into town. But only three people are allowed into the panel room, so Mum, her solicitor and Marlene go in. The rest of us wait anxiously at a nearby cafe for what we believe will be wonderful news.

Mum's heart lurches as she enters the ordinary-looking terrace house that was witness to extreme tragedy only three short weeks ago. They wait a torturous 15 minutes before a woman Mum doesn't recognise curtly orders them through. 'Mr Grubb will see you now.'

Mum begins to involuntarily shake, partly because so much depends on this panel's outcome but also because she finds Gill Grubb intimidating. Collapsing into a seat at the oval table, her bangles knock against the wood. Clenching her wrist tightly, she forces herself to face Gill Grubb who sits between two new panel members Mum has never laid eyes on. Fear skitters through Mum at a horrifying realisation: during the last three weeks all of the people in charge of whether or not she is allowed to see her children again have changed!

Mr Grubb doesn't greet Mum, instead he continues to focus on the thick sheaf of papers in front of him. All is uncomfortably quiet and Mum catches herself staring at the long white strands of hair carefully arranged over Mr Grubb's impossibly shiny scalp. He coughs, she jumps and he finally lifts his head. Readjusting his oversized glasses, he slowly takes in the people around the table. He doesn't greet anyone, but instead reads, in a cold detached voice, from a prepared statement. 'Mrs W, your children have been removed from you because they are believed to be at risk in your home. At present they are undergoing disclosure therapy with the RSPCC. It is believed to be in their best interests that we continue the supervision order and hold them in care—'

'NO, you can't do this! It isn't right!' Marlene screams.

But Mum is pressed hard into her chair, as if the force of his words have knocked her backwards, a look of shock across her face. She opens her mouth, but releases only choking sounds.

'Look!' her solicitor starts to say. 'You can't legally—'

'I think you'll find, Mr Moore, we can,' Mr Grubb interrupts forcefully. 'The W children were still under a super-vision order, so yes, we can!'

'And do I have any say in this?' Mum whispers.

'Mrs W, you are always free to appeal. Put it in writing and we will contact you with an appeal date in due course.'

Gill Grubb fades to a blur with the rest of the room, as Mum unsteadily climbs to her feet. 'Mr Grubb,' she shakily addresses him, 'I do not believe for a minute you are independent of Orkney Social Work Department. So I can't see the point in me sitting here, listening to your rubber-stamped decision.' The room spins and Mum strug-gles to breathe, as she searches for the exit. Her stomach lifts and heaves, she needs to get out of here, *now*. Finding the door at last, she falls through it and stumbles blindly downstairs. Her screams bounce off the walls. She is vaguely aware of someone calling her name but she doesn't stop. She needs to get as far away from here, as quickly as possible. Once out on the street, she keeps running and screaming. People turn to stare, but Mum doesn't care. Over an hour later, she finds herself at a friend's house on the other end of town. She's hysterical. Mum is taken to hospital, where she receives treatment for shock and is sedated with tranquillisers.

But even on a dusty, inhospitable, war-torn desert like this, a tiny beautiful white flower of hope grows, as before racing from the panel room after Mum, Marlene seized a copy of the social worker's report, and when reading through it later, we discover the addresses of all the homes and foster placements the children are in.

*

Meanwhile over a hundred miles away in Inverness, the children's lives have become a terrifying replay of the last time they were taken. Holly, at only eight years of age, is confused and frightened. She keeps asking the social workers, 'Why have you taken us away?'

The answer is always the same, and just as confusing: 'You have been taken to a place of safety, so we can talk to you.'

The children were only allowed to stay together for a little while. Traumatised at being taken so violently, they clung to each other for support. But at Inverness airport they were forced apart and separated into different cars with different destinations. Holly is put into a car with Penny and Poppy. When the car stops, her two sisters are taken out. Holly goes to clamber out after them, but a social worker blocks her. 'No, you're to stay in the car.'

Holly looks up at her, bewildered. 'Please can I go with them?' she asks tearfully.

'No, I'm sorry,' the social worker replies. 'That family only wants two girls.'

Holly watches despairingly from the back window as her sisters disappear, trying to remember where they live. Now totally alone, with only a strange social worker and none of her siblings around her, Holly feels more sick and frightened than she can ever remember. 'Where are you taking me?' she asks fearfully.

'You're going to a nice children's home!' the social worker replies brightly.

Holly tries not to cry, she tries to be brave, but the tears won't stop falling.

They drive for what feels like hours, before finally

arriving at Mine Park Children's Home. There are a few other children here, but none as young as Holly. She has no belongings with her, no clothes, nothing special and nobody to turn to. No matter how hard she tries not to, because she knows it annoys them, she asks again, 'Please, can I go home now? I want my Mum!' She remembers a story about a very bad child who was so naughty she got taken away from her family, so she tries to recall the thing she has done, the thing so bad it's got her sent away.

Holly discovers a little window at Mine Park Children's Home. It looks out across a granite city, over windy roads and play parks dotted here and there. But far off into the distance, if she looks closely, she can make out a little grey, pebble-dashed house with a red door. 'That's where they left my little sisters!' Holly recalls tearfully. She finds comfort in going to the window and finding the little house and watching it intently, hoping somehow to see Penny and Poppy, wishing that one day she can get there, back to her family. The days here are not only painful and full of tears, but also long and boring. She doesn't know anyone here and there's nothing to fill her days. She isn't allowed to go outside and play in the park by herself, and there's rarely anyone who wants to take her there. Soon she will be taken out, she will be taken out on trips to a play centre – but it won't be to play!

The children have been stolen from us for five agonising weeks. We've had the addresses of where they are staying for a couple of those. But so far, we haven't decided what to do with this information. The Social Work Department haven't mentioned that they know we know. This could mean one of two things: either they really don't know we know, or they do but feel confident we've been threatened so much we won't dare use the information. But Mum argues, 'Even from a distance, we can tell them we love them and we're all thinking of them!'

So an undercover trip is planned. Mum, Marlene and Fran will travel to Inverness on the morning ferry, using assumed names and the cover of darkness, while I'll stay home at Crook Farm to look after the animals. None of us believe they'll really get to see the children, but everyone agrees that anything is better than this endless sitting and waiting.

The three women reach Inverness by late afternoon. They use the remaining daylight to locate the first two children's homes on the list. Lawrence and Sam are staying in a home called Bridgeport End Children's Home. With just the address to go on, Fran nervously skirts around Inverness in her little turquoise Fiesta, while Mum and Marlene pore over unfamiliar maps, looking for signs to places they've never been before. They daren't ask anyone for directions, in case the police catch on to them. It's gone 9 p.m. by the time they've found the first two homes. Fran parks up in a lay-by a couple of streets from the first home, where they drink coffee and take turns to try and get some sleep inside Fran's tiny car.

After enduring a cramped and freezing December night, they creep out, one by one, to stretch their legs. Marlene suggests they park near the first home early, so they don't stand out and look suspicious. So around 7 a.m. they drive the short distance and park directly across the road. Beyond catching sight of Lawrence and Sam there is no plan, so they eagerly watch the doors and windows of the big square grey building.

The street buzzes with early morning traffic and inside the confined car, the tension is almost unbearable. They try to distract themselves with talk of other things, but the conversation keeps returning to what they'll do if they get caught. Should they brave it out, now they've come this far, deny it's them at all or follow their natural instincts and make a run for it? Nearly two hours drag by and most of the early morning traffic has tailed off.

Excited hope has turned to fed-up dismay, when suddenly children's voices are calling their names. They look up and see Lawrence and Sam leaning out from one of the upstairs windows, waving and shouting, 'Mum! Marlene! Fran!'

They hurriedly wave back, while winding down the windows: 'Are you okay?' calls Fran.

Without answering, Sam urgently calls, 'We want to come home! Can we come with you?'

A sob catches in Mum's throat. 'I'm sorry, love, not just now. You must be brave and remember we're doing everything we can to get you back. We love you!'

They've waited so long to speak to them and Sam and Lawrence could disappear at any moment, their messages come out fast, gabbled and repeated. Marlene calls up, 'Have you been getting the letters we've sent you?'

The boys look confused. 'No,' they reply in unison.

The women exchange puzzled looks, before Marlene adds, 'What, not even the presents?'

'We haven't heard anything from you. We thought you'd forgotten us!' Lawrence calls, his voice full of hurt.

'Of course we haven't, we'd never forget you,' Fran reassures determinedly, before adding, 'Don't worry, boys, we're fighting to get you home where you belong!'

A couple of figures appear behind Sam and Lawrence and the boys are pulled back inside, before the windows are yanked shut and the curtains tightly drawn.

Suddenly Mum, Marlene and Fran are alone again. Joy at seeing Sam and Lawrence overwhelms them and they smile and cry excitedly at each other, before rehashing, in detail, what just happened. 'They must have recognised my car!' Fran exclaims, delightedly. It was so much more than they could have hoped for. But their happiness is soon replaced by a disturbing realisation: not only are they being kept inside the home, against their will, but they haven't received anything – not one message of love and hope, not one present. Fran jolts Mum and Marlene back to reality: if they want to get to any of the other homes, they'll have to get moving as the police will most likely have been alerted.

Stopping at a telephone box, Marlene calls home to share the good news, and for a moment we all celebrate. Having seen and spoken to Lawrence and Sam is wonderful in itself, but it's also a little victory over the Orkney Social Work Department, who forbade us from seeing them. Today a little battle has been won – but a war still rages on. Marlene explains that, even though they suspect the police might have been called, they are going to keep going. They are on their way to the second home to see Robin.

It isn't much longer than a year since I was living at Crouchend Alley. The building stands isolated at the top of a cul-de-sac, so can only be approached from the front. Fran attempts to squeeze her bright blue car inconspicuously among the others parked close by, and again they sit, wait and pray. They feel sure they've had all the luck they could have today, but all agree to wait a while: even if they eventually have to give up, at least they will have tried.

The three women are watching the building's entrance lost inside their own thoughts when an urgent banging on the passenger window causes them to jump. Robin's brown eyes are wide with amazement as he peers down into the car. A member of staff is attached to his arm and is trying to pull him away. Coming back from a supervised walk, he had instantly recognised Fran's car. Instead of winding the window down this time, Mum throws open her door, ignoring Marlene's cautions: 'Victoria, stay in the car, it's too dangerous!'

Mum wraps her arms around Robin, while the member of staff warns, 'Robin, I've already asked you to come inside. You're getting yourself in trouble, young man!'

They silently hug for a while, before Mum pulls away, her face red and tear-stained. She grips his shoulders. 'Listen to me!' she urges, looking into his dark haunted eyes. 'Have you had any of the letters or presents we've sent you?'

Robin stops crying for a moment and frowns – it's obvious he hasn't.

Mum adds, 'There isn't time to explain, but you need to know we've been sending you letters and presents ever since you were taken. For some reason the Social Work Department haven't been passing them on to you. We love you and everyone at home is doing everything they can to get you out of here!'

Police sirens pierce the distant air and Mum pulls him close one last time. Then cupping his face, which seems so much older and sadder than just a few weeks ago, she whispers, 'I love you, Robin, please remember, I love you.'

Two more staff members are crossing the road towards them. Robin bends down, attempting to climb into Fran's car but Marlene stops him. 'Robin, I'm so sorry, but we have to do this the right way. If we step out of line, it gives them reasons not to let us see you again!'

Robin's eyes burst with tears, as he is pulled away. The sirens are getting louder. 'Victoria, get in the car!' Fran screams. Reluctantly, Mum gets in and they speed off in the opposite direction. From the back window, Mum watches Robin's lonely little figure being dragged back into the home, struggling against three social workers for all his worth.

After getting coffees from a drive-thru, they nurse them in silence. A heavy sadness has descended over all three women. It's Marlene who breaks it. 'Shall we just go home? Surely we've seen and heard enough, haven't we?' she asks wearily.

Mum turns to her, her eyes wet. 'I wish I could, Marlene, but I've got to keep going. We have to try and see the girls!'

They eventually find the small semi-detached house where Penny and Poppy are being fostered and Fran drives past it a couple of times. Despite there being a car parked outside, there aren't any obvious signs of life. Parking in view of the house they hope, pray and wait. All the curtains are tightly drawn, which seems odd during the day. After nearly an hour of waiting, they reluctantly accept that Penny and Poppy can't be in. Fran starts the engine. 'Well look, Victoria, at least we—' she says, but she's distracted by a curtain at one of the front windows, twitching.

'That was a hand, that was definitely a hand,' Marlene whispers frantically to Mum, who also stares, goggle-eyed. The movement at the window brings new hope and the engine is turned off. But a few minutes later they freeze as they watch a police car crawling up the street towards them. It passes the house and draws nearer. They hardly dare breathe as it drives closer still. Then, with alarm, they realise it's headed straight for them. '*Drive, Fran, Drive*! Someone in that house is on to us!' Mum screams.

Fran, who was always known for her exasperatingly careful driving, pulls out sharply and reverses towards the oncoming police car, does a tight U-turn and speeds off – breaking suburban limits all the way.

Once they've recovered from the excitement and disappointment of trying to visit the two youngest girls, they're feeling braver, as if they could tackle anything. They decide to try one more visit, to Holly. It's only half past four in the afternoon, but dark clouds are already gathering, promising a wet and icy night. After the next visit, they decide they'll have to call it a day. They chat about whether they could bear to spend another night in the car or could they risk getting a room at a B&B and leave early tomorrow morning?

On the way to Holly's, they pull into a petrol station. After filling the tank, Fran goes inside to pay. Meanwhile Mum and Marlene discuss the plan of action for getting to Holly's when there's a knock on the passenger side window. They turn round and stare up in horror. Mum screams, 'It's a policeman!'

He glowers at Mum, then pushes his head further into the car, until he's squarely eyeing Marlene. 'You've been very busy girls today, haven't you?' he asks sternly. Mum and Marlene are dumbstruck, as he continues, 'You've been visiting people you shouldn't be visiting and going to places you shouldn't be going, haven't you?'

Mum dumbly nods, while Marlene, having recovered herself, hotly denies his charge. 'I'm not sure what you mean, officer. We've only been visiting Inverness and that wasn't a crime last time I looked!'

Ignoring Marlene's protests, he growls, 'I want you to stop it, or we'll be forced to stop you. Do I make myself clear?'

Now even Marlene nods submissively and before they have a chance to speak, he slides into the passenger seat of a waiting police car and roars off. As she returns, Fran glances nervously at the departing police car, unaware what's just happened. Mum relays everything while Marlene has grown annoyed. 'This is intimidation, plain and simple. The police are just trying to scare us off!'

A white and trembling Fran shakily replies, 'Well, Marlene, I must say it's worked!'

With mixed emotions, Mum, Marlene and Fran are forced to abandon another visit and make their way home. If only they had managed to visit Holly. At only eight years of age, she was the youngest to be without any siblings, and desperately in need of comfort. It was only a short while before they started driving her the sickeningly long journey to a play centre she came to know as the 'Question Place'.

Holly is being taken to dark brown brick building with long thin windows. Inside the Question Place is a room full of colourful toys and books. It is fun to play in there until two women come to talk to her. The main one is Renee Stubbs, a 55-year-old woman who has been contracted by Orkney Social Work Department to head the team that are undertaking disclosure therapy with my younger brothers and sisters. Renee's large asthmatic frame makes it difficult for her to bend down to question children. But once she is on their level, she wheezes her way through questions on dickies, fannies, devils and demons as if chatting about favourite biscuits and ice-cream flavours.

At first Holly didn't mind her as Renee would talk about what Holly wanted to talk about and play at what she wanted to play at, but soon Renee Stubbs just wants to play what she calls 'The Question Game', which is always about dirty stuff. When Renee Stubbs is asking questions one day, Holly asks her one back, a question she'd been trying to get the answer to for a long time. 'Why am I here?'

Without missing a beat, Renee Stubbs assures her, 'Horrible things have happened to you at home!'

Looking up from the toy she's playing with, Holly frowns in confusion. 'But, what horrible things have happened to me?'

Renee Stubbs looks as if she's also trying to remember. 'Well, what kinds of things happened to you at home that you didn't like?'

Holly tries to think, as nothing instantly comes to mind.

Renee Stubbs continues. 'What would someone, say one of your brothers, do to you that you didn't like?'

For a moment Holly tries to remember for Renee, who seems convinced there is something Holly should know. But this game is boring and Holly doesn't want to play it any more. She gets a book and asks, 'Can you read me a story, please?' But Renee Stubbs doesn't want to waste her time reading children stories, she wants information, so the questions continue. 'Where on your body did your brothers touch you that felt horrible?'

Holly tries to tell her: 'Nothing happened, nobody touched my body.'

The interrogation sessions go on for over an hour and take place lots of times a week. Holly quickly realises that 'no' is never the right answer. Renee Stubbs doesn't like it when she says nothing has happened to her, it makes her unhappy. Holly doesn't want to make Renee Stubbs unhappy, and if Holly doesn't try and think of something, she won't be allowed to play.

By the time Mum, Marlene and Fran return to Crook Farm, any feelings of victory have long been overshadowed by the discovery that none of the children are being given any of the things we're sending. Since they were taken into care, countless cards, letters and hundreds of pounds' worth of birthday and Christmas presents have been sent, but none have ever left Orkney Social Work Department. The one and only comfort we'd had was writing about the things we thought they'd like to hear and finding things we thought they'd like playing with before wrapping them with love and sending them. If not receiving anything from home had made Sam and Lawrence think they'd been forgotten, it must be having an even more devastating effect on the younger ones. It seems almost inconceivable that the Social Work Department said they would pass on our letters and they never have. They just let us continue writing them and sending presents. And as painful as it has been, we have done our best to follow their rules.

We talk late into the night. We feel we have been duped by the Orkney Social Work Department. Are we being lied to? Are we being set up? If they aren't following the rules, then why should we?

So we open the gates and let the press in. We give interviews to get as much publicity for our plight as possible. And, through doing this, we get help from unexpected sources. Dr John Butler, a criminologist from a leading London university, is an expert in questioning methods and techniques and he wants to help. From a contact of his, he has managed to get copies of the interview tapes. Having listened to them, he believes the social workers' interview techniques are fundamentally flawed. 'They are manipulating and directing the children to get them to say things that fit in with the allegations they want to make,' he points out.

Meanwhile, *Panorama* has been asking to make a documentary about the children being taken into care. Fearful it would have a detrimental effect on getting the children returned, Mum had refused up until now. But, desperately feeling that we have nothing more to lose, Mum agrees to talk to them. The journalists from the programme explain they've been investigating the Social Work Department. They claim to have damning footage of the interview techniques used by the social workers.

A couple of months later, the TV at Crook Farm is turned to BBC1 and we all nervously gather round. We watch in disbelief, mostly from behind our hands and through floods of tears. It is still truly horrifying to realise how often they are interviewing the children – sometimes up to four times a week – and the manipulative techniques they use are as shocking as they are painful to watch. They show a videotape of an interview between one of my younger sisters, Penny, five, and her interviewer, Renee Stubbs.

Renee is shown drawing a stick figure on a large sheet of paper and asks Penny, 'Where are the dickies and the fannies?'

Penny: 'I don't know.'

Renee Stubbs: 'Can you write the word?'

Penny: 'No.'

Renee Stubbs: 'A word for when the dickie goes into a fanny?'

Penny: 'Don't know.'

Renee Stubbs: 'Would you like to whisper?'

Penny: 'No.'

Renee Stubbs: 'Is it yucky inside and outside … is there any other word?'

Penny: 'Gooey?'

Renee Stubbs: (laughs) 'Oh, that's a good word, what does gooey feel like?'

Penny: 'Here, this.' (Penny puts her finger in her mouth and makes a pop sound.)

Renee Stubbs: 'What happened to gooey?'

Penny: 'Don't know.'

Renee Stubbs: 'Has it got a colour?'

Penny: '1 … 2 … 3 … 4 …'

Renee Stubbs: (continuing) 'I wonder what gooey is. Can you tell me?'

Penny: 'No.'

Renee Stubbs: 'When you put the dickie into the fanny…'

Penny: (tearfully) 'No. Now can I play please? I'm going to get my red car. This is boring!' (Penny gets a car and begins to play) 'Can you get me some toys please?'

Renee Stubbs: (ignoring her, continues) 'When you put the dickie into the fanny, it's yucky and gooey and disgusting. Who hurts the most?'

Penny: 'No one did it to me ...'

Renee Stubbs: 'We won't write it down.'

Penny: 'No one has been doing it to me.' (breaks into a scream) 'NOBODY HAS BEEN DOING IT TO ME!'

Renee Stubbs: 'You can play with the red car. We won't write it down if you want to whisper it ...'

Penny: (shouting even louder) 'I AM NOT GOING TO WRITE IT DOWN.'

Renee Stubbs: 'If it's a name and you see it written down, you can point to it.' (She shows Penny a list of people's names.) 'Is it a name you see written down?'

Penny: (still shouting) 'No, I don't have to tell, no one has been doing those things to me.'

The room falls silent. Penny can be seen rocking in a chair, staring at her inquisitors. The tape ends.

The programme looks into my family history. It explains how a social worker from Orkney Social Work Department interpreted what my sister Bella, a very disturbed girl with a history of abuse, had said and how it was twisted it into allegations of abuse. It spoke about other flawed social work cases, similar to ours, where the same methods were used. It finishes by poignantly asking, 'Why aren't these children at home, where they belong?'

The programme gets a very positive reaction and we get a lot of public support, which is comforting, especially when you live in a place like Orkney that often feels cut off from the rest of the world.

Not long after the programme is shown, we receive

another little boost in the form of a letter. It is addressed to Mum, in a child's handwriting, and has an Inverness post-mark on it. Marlene and I watch intently as Mum, with trembling hands, carefully opens the envelope. Inside is a letter from Robin, written from Crouchend Alley Care Home. It's obviously a hurriedly scrawled note. 'Dear Mum,' Robin writes, 'I hope you had a lovely Christmas, because I spent Christmas in a room, simply because I will not enjoy myself without you being near. This letter is not supposed to see you, so I smuggled it out. Lots of love to you and all the ones at Crook Farm xxxxxxxxxxxxxxxxxxxxxxxxxxxxxxx'

There's excited disbelief as we read and reread the short note. It's wonderful to hear from him, but painful to hear how sad he is. Mum passes the letter on to the solicitor, just in case it can help with the appeal case. How much more obvious can Robin make it – he is desperate to come home.

Meanwhile, for Holly, in a sickening repeat of what we saw her younger sister being put through on the *Panorama* programme, Renee Stubbs brings in large sheets of paper for her and asks Holly in her most syrupy voice, 'What about you draw some nice pictures for me?'

Holly loves drawing and she likes making Renee Stubbs happy. Renee Stubbs asks Holly to draw things that remind her of home. Holly draws herself sitting on the family pony, Merrylegs. This isn't what Renee Stubbs meant. 'No, how about you draw something else?' So Holly draws her and her brother Sam playing football together. 'No!' This still isn't right either. Holly looks up at her, confused, 'What should I draw?'

Renee has a folder with her, and opening it, she shows Holly a large piece of paper with a pencil drawing of circles and people around them. Returning the picture to her folder, she looks at Holly expectantly. 'Does that help?'

'Shall I draw a circle?' Holly asks.

'If you think it would help,' Renee Stubbs prompts in a sickly sweet voice.

Holly draws a circle, and Renee Stubbs, at last, smiles, adding, 'Do you want to draw people round it?'

Holly begins drawing people. 'Why don't you draw them as stick people, it'll be faster,' Renee Stubbs urges.

After Holly has completed the picture, the way Renee Stubbs wants it, she is rewarded with the promised chocolate bar.

The next time they interview Holly, the picture is brought out and she is asked to give names to the stick people. She says she doesn't know who they are, but when told she drew them, she tries to think up names. 'Maybe people from back home,' her interviewer helpfully prompts. When she starts giving them names, her interviewer likes that – she likes it a lot. These innocent drawings are kept, and will be used later, as crucial evidence, to prove the existence of a widespread satanic sex abuse ring operating on the island of South Ronaldsay.

Meanwhile, in Orkney, our campaign to get the children home continues. A letter to the Social Work Services Group and the Local Government Ombudsman has been put together. It sets out serious breaches of the Social Work Act and demonstrates how Scottish Office guidelines haven't been observed. It lists five first-hand witnesses who are prepared to testify in a court of law. This letter is waiting to be checked by Mum's solicitor and will be sent on Monday

27 February 1991. But the letter is never sent. As of that Monday morning, everything will have changed, because that is the day the other four families' children are taken.

The moment the other families' children were taken, my family's case was moved to the back burner. For them, there was no murky past with a convicted child abuser. But crucially, if it wasn't for their involvement with my family, their children would never have been taken in the first place.

CHAPTER ELEVEN

Balloons, cameras and a bagpipe player

As we did when the children from our family were stolen, the other four families actively seek as much publicity for their case as possible. Most of the articles written about them are accompanied by a picture of the parents with their backs to camera as the press aren't allowed to identify them. Holding hands, they form a human chain, standing at the edge of the infamous quarry, where the satanic rituals are alleged to have taken place. But one link is missing – my family!

Similar to our case again, their children have been taken into care under an emergency place of safety order. This means that the Social Work Department can keep them for seven days while they gather evidence from the children. The Social Work Department is meant to set up a panel meeting within those seven days to discuss their findings. The Social Work (Scotland) Act states that the hearing should be held, wherever possible, on the first working day after the child has been removed from home. In their case that would be Tuesday 28 February 1991. This procedure is designed to minimise the time spent apart for both parent and child, thereby decreasing stress as far as possible. Under acting panel reporter Gill Grubb the panel will be held on the last possible date of those seven days: 5 March 1991.

All of the parents, like Mum does when she goes to panels, have the legal right to be accompanied by a representative for support. On the morning of 5 March, a representative for one of the families is on his way from Edinburgh. South Ronaldsay is buzzing with press, and more and more pour in every day, booking every available seat on the planes, so the representative has trouble getting a flight – and won't be able to arrive for the 10 a.m. start. Gill Grubb is asked to postpone the meeting by just one hour. He refuses: the meeting will begin at 10 a.m. and that is that! The family in question is desperate, and like most parents who go to a panel, feel it crucial to their case that they have the right representation. They contact their solicitor, who in turn contacts Jim Wallace, Orkney's MP at the House of Commons. They ask Mr Wallace if surely on this occasion, when a child's future is at stake, could they please just have a one-hour extension. Mr Wallace immediately faxes a letter back, which is hand-delivered to Gill Grubb. Finally, but not without taking it up to the very last minute, Grubb reluctantly agrees to the one-hour postponement.

None of the families' nine children are allowed back to Orkney to attend their own panel, which by law they should have been.

As the other families' panel begins, a large orderly crowd of family members, neighbours, friends and well-wishers have gathered outside. Some carry placards or hold up posters demanding justice for the stolen children. Journalists and cameras go in among them to gauge the public's mood. Along with the feeling of disbelief that the Orkney Social Work Department can get away with doing this, there is mainly anger and outrage about this unthinkable crime committed against innocent children, and they demand their immediate return.

At their meeting, the parents discover, in each case just as in ours, that no background reports had been carried out on any of their children before they were taken into care. Their GPs were not consulted, nor were the teachers at their schools spoken to. Their children have just been snatched, purely on allegations.

Unsurprisingly, the outcome of the panel is a 21-day extension of the place of safety order so that the Social Work Department can further investigate satanic ritual sexual abuse allegations. This leaves the parents, understandably, devastated.

Everyone in the Orkney Islands knows the satanic sex ring allegations are ridiculous, and most journalists realise it the minute they set foot in Orkney. The flat barren landscape doesn't lend itself to hidden ways of life – especially since the favourite local pastime is watching your neighbours. The only possible way there could be a satanic sex circle is if everyone – all 400 residents on the island – knew about it and were somehow involved in keeping it secret.

Initially when newspapers reported on the satanic sex ring case they mentioned the other families and our family in the same breath. But the division between them and us is getting wider. No one says it directly but they don't have to. We are not invited to meetings or told of developments. The information we'd been receiving about how their case was proceeding slows to a trickle, before stopping completely. It seems they believe that any contact with us will be detrimental to their case.

But then we have all become suspicious of each other's motives, which isn't helped by being continually watched. Police cars are stationed at the end of most roads, including ours. Our phone makes strange hollow clicking noises, convincing us we are bugged. Sometimes when I go out to the barn, I smell cigarette smoke and I have even found recently stubbed-out butts. It makes day-to-day life frightening and stressful.

The whole situation is upside down and back to front. The Social Work Department removed our children, then the other families' children, before investigating so-called allegations, and now they are trying to collect the 'evidence' needed to keep them. They are searching for a satanic sex circle, but of course they are wasting their time. It seems that all they are really trying to do is prove they haven't made a major cock-up – which of course they have.

Like ours, the other family's lives revolve around children's panel meetings. Their second panel is on 26 March, and again, illegally, their children don't come to that one either. True to form, Gill Grubb threatens to throw a couple of the parents' representatives out, accusing them of deliberately disrupting the meeting, by referring to the law. As expected, he again extends the place of safety order for a further 21 days, to keep the children in care for further satanic abuse questioning.

As the parents have not accepted the grounds for referral – that their children are at risk of being ritually abused in satanic sex circles – their case is going to what is called a proof hearing. This means their case will be heard by a sheriff (similar to a judge in England) who will decide whether the grounds for referral are right or wrong.

Meanwhile, Cathy Buxton, who had been on the children's panel for 12 years, making her one of the longest-serving members, speaks out. She states that Gill Grubb needs to be stopped. While he is supposed to be independent of the Social Work Department, Cathy believes he openly toes their line. She stated that the panel system in Orkney has deteriorated since the suspension of Judith Hope. She wrote to the Secretary of State the previous November when our children had been taken into care, expressing her concerns, but no action was taken.

The other families' proof hearing is to be held on 3 April 1991 and will be heard by a Sheriff Kellie. It's an all-or-nothing situation. If Sheriff Kellie decides the grounds for referral were justified, it means the families will once again have to face the unscrupulous Gill Grubb. But if Sheriff Kellie decides the grounds for referral were unjustified, it could mean the collapse of the whole satanic sex ring case and their children could be returned home. We desperately hope the sheriff decides the grounds for referral were unjustified, not only for the families and their children, but it could impact positively upon our case.

The local and national eyes are out in force, to hear Sheriff Kellie's decision. We stay away, as we don't want to detract attention from them. Besides, it's hard not to believe we bring bad luck to whoever has the misfortune to be friends with our family!

The first part of the proof hearing is held in private, but after two days, Sheriff Kellie instructs that the remainder of it be opened to the public and the press. There, he openly criticises Orkney's children's panel system. He announces he will have to consider the handling of the case overnight, to decide whether he believed it had been handled competently. He will be passing his judgement the following morning at 10 a.m.

On the morning of 5 April, Sheriff Kellie looks tired and drawn – as he points out, he has deliberated over this case until the early hours. He has listened to the taped interviews of the nine children in care and read the transcripts. He says he has also been made aware that the children haven't had any contact with friends or family since being taken into care, under this supposed place of safety order.

He states that far from being in a place of safety, the children have, in fact, been taken to a place where they were cross-examined in a way designed to make them break down and admit to being abused. In short, the children from the other families had been subjected to the same interview techniques as my siblings, which had produced the original allegations. In the few weeks since the other families' children had been taken, a couple of them had even admitted to the existence of a satanic sex-abuse ring.

Poignantly, Sheriff Kellie believes that the three original statements from the W children, which led to the uplift of the other nine children, could not be said to have been made spontaneously, pointing out that the transcripts from the interviews of my brothers and sisters, although containing similarities, also contain marked variations. Referring to a comment Holly had made to her interviewer after they had collected the so-called evidence of a satanic sex ring, she had asked in a clear voice, 'Did you know that all of this was a lie?' But this comment was just brushed aside as it didn't fit in with the evidence they were after.

He cites an interview with a child that the Social Work Department had used to demonstrate satanic sexual abuse, between Renee Stubbs and one of the children from the four families.

Renee Stubbs: 'And what would he prod them with?'

Child: 'The stick!'

Renee Stubbs: 'Just the stick?'

Child: 'Yeah and his hand and fingers.'

Renee Stubbs: 'His fingers – I'm not surprised it's sore. What's the worst feeling when it's happening?'

Child: 'I don't really know, cos it's never happened to me.'

Renee Stubbs: 'Who have you seen it happen to?'

Child: 'Haven't seen anyone.'

Sheriff Kellie says the statements of evidence from the children amounted to repeated coaching. He pointed out obvious discrepancies, such as the 'ritualistic music' that was referred to, which changed depending on the child who was interviewed.

In summing up, he goes for the jugular: 'The proceedings by Orkney child care authorities were fundamentally flawed.'

To everyone's disbelief and amazement Sheriff Kellie concludes by saying he hopes the Orkney Social Work Department and the panel reporter will now make the right decision: to return the nine children home immediately. He has effectively thrown Orkney Social Work Department's case out of court as bearing no legal integrity.

Having become accustomed to dealing with Orkney Social Work Department's random and often illegal ways of doing things, the other families had geared themselves up to fighting a long and impossible war. Now suddenly to be dealing with someone who not only speaks common sense but also the truth, the relief is palpable.

But momentary elation soon turns to anger and they want to hear what Orkney Social Work Department are going to do about it. About 60 family, friends and supporters storm on foot to the social work offices and burst through the main doors. The receptionist momentarily queries them and some social workers are blocking the path, but it looks like the others have run and locked themselves safely inside their offices. 'Where is the director Keith Pratt's office?' they demand of those in their way. With sheet-white faces they are meekly pointed in the right direction.

The mob for justice forces its way into Keith Pratt's office. He stares up in wide-eyed terror, gibbering incoherently about rules and regulations. Five weeks of angry frustration, pain and heartache, hopes being built up, only to be shattered, are spewed down upon him.

'You have stolen our children and we demand you return them to us, at once!' an angry mother's voice bellows through the din.

'I can't, there's got to be—' Keith Pratt flusters.

But another parent shouts him down, her voice laden with bitter contempt. 'What you have done, Mr Pratt, is illegal. You have stolen our children from us. You have tortured them and questioned them like criminals. You have even given them medical examinations without consent! You will charter a plane, the way you did to steal them from us, and bring them back today!'

A visibly trembling Mr Pratt nervously assures them that their children will be back in Orkney by nightfall.

Families, friends, journalists and hordes of well-wishers cram Kirkwall's tiny airport to capacity. They all want to be there when the children finally touch home soil. Cameras film the tiny chartered plane, bravely fighting a wet dark Orkney evening. It dramatically appears through thick grey mist, its engines plupping gallantly as it comes to land. Wild shrieks of joy drown the droning of a kilted bagpipe player. The wheels on the little plane have barely stopped spinning when the door bursts open under the pressure from the eager children inside. Breaking out of the plane, they race across the tarmac and fling themselves into the outstretched arms of their waiting parents. Sobs of joyous relief and celebratory cheers ring out as emotional reunion scenes are beamed on local and national news channels around the world. A fitting end to the five-week nightmare that four families and their nine children have endured.

While my family and I are ecstatic for the other families, it is difficult not to ask why aren't our children returning home? What have they done that is so wrong that they should be punished this way? Aren't they too just innocent children?

Now my family and I must fight alone. The nightmare has become a way of life.

CHAPTER TWELVE

A nightmare way of life

While the other four families continue their cele-brations, there is mounting pressure from them and the community for a public inquiry. Their worlds have been shaken to the core and they are demanding answers. Rumours circulate that Orkney Social Work Department could strike again at any moment. There are whispers that they have a list, with over a hundred chil-dren's names on – nobody is safe. They nervously ask each other, how could this be allowed to happen? Where did these satanic sex ring allegations come from? And most importantly of all, how can children be taken from innocent parents without any legal process?

My family knows the answers to those questions and more. When my father was jailed, it seemed our whole family had been found guilty by association. From then on our social worker Mona Drone seemed determined to rip us apart. So we, probably more than anyone, would welcome a public inquiry as everyone would have to listen to the truth. Then we would get justice – wouldn't we?

But in the meantime, Orkney Social Work Department still refuses to legally test the older sibling abuse allegations concerning my seven younger siblings. And without the police questioning or arresting anyone, we remain in a netherworld of suspicion, smoke and lies, and every day it becomes more difficult to live here.

After five long months in care, without any contact and any progress, we have a tiny breakthrough. Our family, understandably, have no faith or trust in the Orkney Social Work Department. Mum has been repeatedly asking them, since the children were taken into care, for psychological reports to be done on the children. The children could tell a third party what their lives at home were really like and whether anyone had abused them.

A child psychiatrist, Dr Dimitri Petrovski, has finally been employed for the task. He is to carry out an overall assessment of the whole case. As well as speaking to my siblings, he will interview the social workers involved. He will also interview Gill Grubb and, most importantly, the people giving my brothers and sisters so-called disclosure therapy.

First, Dr Petrovski wants to find out why the children are not allowed to see Mum. He interviews Sarah Cooke, Bella's old social worker. She emphatically states it is because Mum is an abuser – despite the fact that Mum has never been accused or convicted of any child abuse.

Dr Petrovski discovers that apart from the children that live together, Sam and Lawrence and Poppy and Penny, none of the children are allowed to see one another. This is not an official decision: this segregation is simply done on the whim of social workers. He states that he believes the children's rights are being infringed through lack of contact with one another and further infringed by the severe restriction of letters, photographs and gifts. Gill Grubb, the acting panel reporter, argues that this is because the children are abusing one another. The fact that there is no evidence of this doesn't stop it being treated as if it were true.

He interviews my brother Robin, 14. His key worker describes him as confused, disorientated, tearful and constantly questioning them about his mother and his siblings. In the five months he's been in care, he has been allowed only two postcards from family friends – but nothing from his mother or siblings.

He went on to interview Willow and she emphatically tells him she wants to return home and see her mother. Again, she has received no correspondence or gifts from home, including Christmas gifts and cards. Before being taken into care she had been described in her school report as 'happy in school' and 'getting on fine with her class-mates'. She was said to have 'no behavioural problems and no educational problems'. After five months in care, she is described in reports as tired, listless, underweight and always worrying about schoolwork. She is also reported to cry out at night, suffering from recurring nightmares. Shortly after they had all been snatched, Mum had been told Willow had a subversive attitude as she had called a social worker a 'liar' and had said that not being allowed to see her brothers and sisters was 'sick!'

He then interviewed Lawrence, 11, and Sam, 10, together at Bridgeport End Children's Home. Neither of them mentioned sibling or satanic abuse to him. As well as having no access to their mother or siblings, they hadn't received any correspondence or gifts since being taken into care. Lawrence said he felt under pressure to answer questions, which Dr Petrovski describes as 'Significantly affecting any interpretation of information gained in the disclosure process.' As if to make sure Dr Petrovski knows exactly how he feels about what had happened to him, Lawrence calls after him, 'The social workers have ruined my life!'

Despite only being eight years of age, when he interviews Holly, she is able to make her wishes clear: she wants 'To go home to Orkney!' Although, she adds, she doesn't want to see her sister Bella who she believes has caused her and her siblings to be taken away by saying people had been doing things to them. She asks Dr Petrovski why she isn't even allowed to see her siblings, but he can't answer her.

He goes on to assess my two youngest sisters Penny and Poppy, who are now aged five and seven. Both are reported as suffering from sleeping difficulties and constant nightmares. Poppy, who has just started school, is, unsurprisingly, due to the violent way she was ripped from Mum's arms at only four years of age, reported to spend much of her time alone, utterly inconsolable. Interviewed together, neither girl expresses any particular disquiet about their siblings. Their foster parents confirm they have never mentioned abuse. Penny wants to go back to Orkney and asks Dr Petrovski if he is going to take her with him now? Both children confirm they have received no letters, gifts or cards from home. When asked what she thinks of her mother, Poppy replies, 'My mummy? Do you mean my real mummy? Oh, she's dead!'

When Dr Petrovski sees Bella he quickly diagnoses her as having a constitutional vulnerability that predisposes her towards mental illness. He finds her agitated, indecisive, confused and unable to commit herself to a decision. Dr Petrovski further diagnoses her as having a borderline personality state, probably resulting in transient states. If required to do so, he adds, she would not make a reliable witness in a legal setting.

Dr Petrovski concludes that the allegations should be tried in a legal setting through a court case. He believes the five months the Social Work Department have kept the children separated from one another and their family, to do disclosure therapy, is unacceptable. And, not allowing children to see their mother is poor childcare practice. The children, he believes, are under pressure and duress and their best interests are not being served by their treatment. He suggests letters, gifts and photographs should be exchanged and recommends unrestricted, unsupervised access.

Despite Dr Petrovski's recommendations, nothing changes. Our case is so complex and not able to be neatly tied up with a bow, that the press no longer report progress on a daily basis. Besides, all the innocent families have got their children back, haven't they? Mum continues appealing, but with Gill Grub in charge our case has stalled.

We do, however, have a glimmer of hope. On 19 May, Ian Lang, the Secretary of State for Scotland, announces there will be a full judicial inquiry into why the four families' children were removed. Then, on 23 May, Ian Lang rules that the council's case for Judith Hope's suspension is illegal. She is fully and unconditionally reinstated. Mum promptly drops the appeal she has in the pipeline with Gill Grubb, and officially requests that Judith Hope be in charge of our family's panel hearings, from now on.

But again things aren't straightforward. Judith Hope asks Councillor Richard Thomas for the keys to enter her panel offices. But he refuses to hand them over, arguing she has no need for them yet. After successive attempts to get them she is forced to ask a member of her staff to let her into the premises that she is supposedly in charge of.

The following week, in the dead of night, the panel office's front door is forced open. Some of my family's files are stolen. The police are pointed in the direction of Judith Hope, someone who it appears has been desperate to gain entry to the offices. Judith is accused of trying to improperly gain access to our family's files. As usual, the allegations stop short of criminal charges but the cloud of suspicion hangs heavy.

Judith Hope feels concerned enough to contact the Under-Secretary of State, Neil Campbell, and share her fears that there is a dirty tricks campaign being mounted against her. Neil Campbell, in turn, informs Judith that he has been told by the Orkney Island Council that she should not start work until a suitable contract has been drawn up. Judith admits she now feels the situation is worse than ever and believes the campaign against her will continue until she is forced back out of office.

She doesn't have long to wait for developments. The next day she receives the minutes of her reinstatement meeting of the 25 May. She is shocked to discover the dates appear to have been changed. Her start date has been taken out and instead an entry has been put in to exclude a specific start date. Also several other conditions have been added, which had never before been discussed.

My family aren't aware of all these bewildering developments as they happen, but on 6 May, my younger siblings are finally allowed to see one another for the first time since being separated in November 1990. The venue is a children's home, over a hundred miles from Crook Farm, and they are heavily supervised by four social workers.

Then on 5 June, after seven months of enforced separation from her two youngest daughters, and despite Dr Petrovski's recommendation to access months earlier, Mum travels to Inverness to supervise five-year-old Poppy having some teeth extracted. In the hospital car park, Mum sees Poppy for the first time since she was forcibly ripped from her arms by social workers. Poppy's uncertainty and confusion is heartbreakingly obvious. We found out later that on the car journey to meet Mum, Poppy had turned to the supervising social worker and asked her, 'Are you my mum? My real mum?'

During the dentist appointment, Mum tries to reassure Poppy and Penny that she is and always will be their real mum. She tells them over and over that she loves them and everyone at home loves them too and we are always thinking of them. After the dentistry has finished, a dazed Poppy comes round from the anaesthetic and, still bleeding profusely, begs Mum, 'Please come back soon, Mum, will you? Do you promise?'

Her eyes watery and with a heavy heart, Mum does her best to reassure her little girl she will be back very soon, all the while knowing the decision is not in her hands. She tries to instil in them as much love as she can before she is forced to leave, knowing it could be a very long time before Orkney Social Work Department lets her see them again. She is right: it will be seven long weeks before they find it possible to arrange another access visit between Mum and her two youngest daughters.

Meanwhile, Willow has a panel coming up and Judith Hope campaigns for her to be allowed to attend. It will be the first time she has been at one of her own panels since being taken into care. Orkney Social Work Department are not going to make it easy, however, as they point blank refuse to finance it.

In July, things at Orkney Council take an even more sinister turn. Judith Hope returns from holiday mid-month to discover that someone has been in her office and hundreds of confidential files – the contents of four filing cabinets – have been stolen, including all of my family's files. And just as before, the Social Work Department and the council deny all knowledge of the theft. Judith Hope reports it to the police. But it is not until it is written up in the local newspaper that it gets investigated: a member of the public had told the reporter they had seen a suspicious-looking man carrying boxes out of the panel building during the night. The police are once again pointed in Judith's direction. It is now her husband's turn to be hauled into the police station and questioned for eight hours over his whereabouts on that date. No evidence is ever looked for elsewhere, so none is ever found. Once again, it is hushed up. Judith Hope now has to go about the painstaking process of trying to replace my family's files by asking a very hostile Social Work Department for copies.

We are in despair: we don't know what to think or who to turn to. The fact that our files have been stolen seems outrageous on the one hand, but on the other it is typical of how our case is being handled. It feels like just another chapter in a catalogue of corruption.

One document Judith manages to retrieve a copy of is an

Orkney Social Work Department report done on my family in January 1991. Interestingly, it has been recently marked for the attention of Renee Stubbs – the woman in charge of getting information out of my siblings in Inverness. The top sheet is missing and new notes have been added. Notes claiming there was abuse, where not only had none ever happened, but none had ever been legally tested. A lie about an older brother assaulting a younger sibling. Another lie that I had been raped by one of my brothers. An untrue claim that my alleged rape had been corroborated by my little sister, Holly. A further lie that Jacob, one of my older brothers, had been charged with sexually abusing a young child. And finally a note from one of the social workers that claimed all of this had been explained to Judith Hope – Orkney's Panel Reporter – which predictably was not true. The authorities in Inverness were being fed highly misleading information. Suspicions were positioned as facts and had coloured the way they had attempted to extract information from my siblings in their so-called disclosure therapy sessions.

In trying to gain copies of their medical records, Judith contacts the Orkney Social Work Department and asks for help. She doesn't get a response. She writes again, explaining she is in the process of drafting new grounds for the W children for referral to a children's hearing. She will need the reports so they can be sent to the sheriff's court and hopefully, at last, the allegations can be presented in a legal setting. Again she doesn't receive a reply, and all of her subsequent requests for help are ignored and unanswered. What were they nervous about – that there was no evidence of abuse in those medical records?

Getting no help from the Orkney Social Work Department, in August Judith Hope contacts the social workers looking after my siblings in Inverness but once more her requests for information and help fall on deaf ears.

A line has been drawn in the sand: it is them and us, and they intend to make it impossible for our family to ever be reunited. Without paperwork, our case is extremely difficult to progress as there is nothing to go on. We have effectively been pushed back to square one.

It is then that we have a much-needed stroke of good fortune. A family friend very generously pays for a prominent child psychiatrist from London to carry out assessments on all of my siblings, as well as interview all of the social workers involved with the case. The aim is to use these assessments in court, in lieu of the evidence that has been stolen.

On 27 August 1991, Dr John Rumney is formally invited by the children's panel hearing to prepare reports on all of my younger brothers and sisters. Of course, being totally independent, he will find his path littered with obstacles. Despite asking the local psychological services for help, Dr Rumney is in no way assisted. It is later revealed they are acting on official instructions.

Along with the continual fight to get justice, day-to-day life for me and my family is becoming increasingly difficult. We have become outcasts in the only place I have ever known as home. The other families, that were previously our friends, have turned away. I can't find a job, as when I go for interviews, the minute I mention my name, the job is no longer available. I can't imagine a promising future for myself. I visit the doctor and he prescribes antidepressants, which he says will help. But what will they change?

One night I'm talking to Mum – explaining that I think my only option is to move away – when I come up with what seems like a great plan. 'What if I go and find Bella?'

Mum looks stunned. 'What do you mean?'

Excited by the idea, I add, 'I know Inverness, don't I? I could go there and find out where she's living. Then I'll ask her what she said to the social workers. What do you think?'

'Well, if I'm honest, I think it sounds mad. Not to mention the amount of trouble you could get into.'

'Seriously, Mum,' I say despairingly, 'look at me. I can't get a job here and we're not getting anywhere with our case. What do I have to lose?'

Mum looks dubious. But, the more I think about it, the more sense it makes. If I can just speak to Bella face to face, I'll get her to tell everyone the truth. Then they'll have to listen – won't they? But I can't help anxiously wondering: will Bella even listen to me?

Part Four

1991–1992

CHAPTER THIRTEEN

Finding love

Inverness looks unchanged since I visited it while in care. The wide-open streets are loomed over by decorative historic buildings. American tourists still bustle about, excitedly photographing the clean shiny surface. But my eyes see Inverness's ugly underbelly. I see the invisible people – just like the girls and boys I was in care with – taking shelter in the walls of the Castle and the historic buildings that are so eagerly snapped.

I'm crossing a bridge into town when I hear a friendly voice. 'Esther, how's it going?' Her once large liquid brown eyes are streaky red and her short dark hair, which she once would spend hours teasing and sculpting into waxed tendrils, is a thick, fuzzy, unkempt mess. But I still recognise her. 'Daisy!' I call back. I'm careful to readjust my shocked expression, as I approach her. She smiles, revealing a mouthful of rotting teeth. Suddenly she seems aware of herself, how different the dirty rags that barely cover her must seem, compared with the head-to-toe designer gear she used to blag from her key worker. She covers her mouth, but the smell of decay still lingers between us. 'How are you?' I tentatively ask.

'Och, I'm doing fine, just fine!' she replies cheerfully. But when she registers my uncertainly, she adds, 'Getting better, that's for sure. I don't touch the hard gear any more. No, I never touch the crack! Just the buzz!' she says, lifting her arm to reveal the top of an antiperspirant can peeking from her sleeve. 'D'ya fancy a huff?' she offers sociably.

'No, you're all right, Daisy, I won't just now. I ... I need to be somewhere. You know how it is?' I leave her there, eking out her survival on the edge of society, most likely by menacing American tourists out of their spare change. I recall her as she used to be, desperately trying to survive in Crouchend Alley, and now she's on the streets after being dumped out into the real world.

Suddenly I see what I have to lose. It isn't much, but it's so much more than Daisy. I promise myself not to let that happen to me. Feeling motivated, I trawl shops, restaurants, hotels and old people's homes searching for work. But as afternoon drifts into evening, I'm exhausted and unsuccessful. I've given up for the day, when on the way back to my B&B, I pass a bar called Mr G's and go in on the off-chance. They're setting up for the night and my work inquiry is at last met with enthusiasm. The manger says I need to be over 18 and offers me cash in hand for bar work – if I can start tonight. I eagerly agree, even though I've no bar experience and I'm only 17! But, none of that matters yet, I'm in Inverness to do a much more important job. But that evening, I fall in love. I don't mean to – it just happens.

Adam is my first customer. I visibly tremble as I pull the pump handle towards me, pouring him the first of over ten pints he will drink that evening. I'm nice to him, as instructed, and it works: he buys me a drink every time he gets one for himself. His mates get fed up waiting and leave. The other girls behind the bar advise me, 'Ignore him, he's just a drunk!' but Adam says he likes me and tells me I'm pretty.

When I finish work, Adam and I have a couple of drinks together and he tells me about himself. At 24 he seems much older and wiser than me. He's good-looking and tells me people say he looks like Bruce Willis. I can see the similarity, only to me he's better-looking. He makes me laugh with his drunk Elvis Presley impressions. After we finish our drinks, he walks me the long way back to my B&B. The landlady has warned I'll be out on my ear if I ever bring a man back, but Adam has nowhere to go so we plan he'll leave at first light. We stay up for hours, whispering and laughing about everything and anything, him propped up on a pillow on the floor and me on my bed. I'm careful what I say and of course I don't tell him who I really am. To Adam, I am just what I want to be: a normal girl, dreaming of bigger things than can be found on a tiny island in Orkney.

I don't know when it happens, but we fall asleep and it's past eight when I'm sneaking him out through the fire exit. We are holding hands and making plans for our date later tonight when he pulls me up to his warm muscly chest and I hear his heart beating. He wraps me inside his strong arms where I dissolve. Bending his head down, I tilt mine up and we kiss, releasing a buzz of warmth all through my body and suddenly I'm wide awake. With a huge silly smile across my face, I watch him until he disappears.

But I wait a moment too long to pull the fire exit door closed and lock eyes with the landlady's daughter, who is leaving for work through the front door. She glowers at me. 'You're playing with fire, young lady!' But any fears of what might happen are replaced with a happiness I've never experienced before. I can't be scared, not today, not on the day I've fallen in love!

All day little bubbles of happiness rise in my tummy and burst like liquid bubble wrap, pop, pop, pop! My hands shake as I carefully apply my make-up. My stomach-churning excitement means I must stop to steady my hand. And when I forget for a moment, because I'm doing something else, butterflies flutter up and catch me unaware. Then a face-splitting smile lights me up from inside as I replay the memories from last night. I'm useless for anything else, so I spend the day getting ready for our date. I change my outfit more than five times and reapply my make-up until it's just so. But I worry most over the shoes I should wear as Adam is only a couple of inches taller than me and I don't want to tower above him.

When he arrives – on time – he's better-looking than I remember. He grins at me and I beam back, heat rushing from my toes to my cheeks. I smell beer and sweet currant buns as I walk through the door that he holds open for me. Brushing past him, I linger, yearning to feel his touch again.

He takes me to the pictures; we watch Macaulay Culkin in *My Girl*. The theme tune becomes our song. But during the film, no matter how hard I nudge him, Adam keeps falling asleep, until eventually he slips from his seat altogether and rolls into the aisle. I laugh so hard my stomach aches. It's our first date and I will never forget it. I didn't know it then, but Adam was already blind drunk when he picked me up. I have been given a warning of things to come, but it is already too late – I am in love with him.

We quickly decide to move in together. I have to move out fast from the B&B and Adam is sick of his boring life in the country with his dad. We want to be with each other all the time so it's the perfect answer for both of us. We find a flat and I get a proper job – working in an old people's home – and Adam gets a job cutting grass for the council. We don't have much money, but we don't care. It's not about what we have in our pockets, it's about being together.

The only thing I want to change is Adam's love of drink, which quickly becomes a third person in our intimate little relationship. He must drink at least ten pints every day. But he doesn't see a problem in it, and maybe he's right. We're both young, he argues, what else would we do? Soon drinking becomes a big part of our lives. As long as we have enough money to have a good time, nothing else matters. Adam drinks lager and any spirits he can get his hands on, and I'll drink anything white and sparkly.

I wear Adam's T-shirt to bed to be wrapped up in him as I sleep. We love waking up together, where we call each other by pet names. He's accepted me inside a normal world where I've always longed to belong and I've never known such happiness. We live together, we sleep together, and we spend almost 24 hours a day together. But Adam doesn't really know me at all. He knows nothing about me, who I am or was, or what made the raging messed-up little girl who loses it over the simplest of things. And I can't tell him ever – because I need us to be my new beginning.

I'm sick of waking up confused and struggling to remember what happened the night before. How did I get to bed, let alone home? And it's getting worse. This morning I woke up desperate for a wee. As usual I had the violent spinning that's become a normal part of my life these days, so I stayed still for a moment, gripping my head in my hands, waiting for everything to slow down. But on folding back the duvet, my brain registers disgust and surprise at a thick dark-green slime. It's everywhere: stuck to my legs, on the duvet and even leaking on to the floor. Gingerly climbing from my bed, I become more bewildered, at splatters of it on the carpet and streaks on the walls that lead all the way to the bathroom. Placing myself delicately upon the toilet, I let burning wee burst from me. When I have gathered up enough strength, I reach out to the little sink, to hoist myself up. Slowly uncurling, I look in the mirror, to assess last night's damage. I immediately recoil – the slime is coming from me! It is smeared from my mouth and wears itself over my chest like a deep-green crochet blanket.

Once I recover enough, I go to the doctor. I burn with embarrassment as I confide something so filthy as the slime to this flowery, shiny lady. She tries a little smile at me but she doesn't mean it; I disgust her, I can tell. Her pretty nose wrinkles from my cigarette- and dirty-living smell, which stinks even stronger in here, like a rubbish bag split open on a clean kitchen floor. She asks about my lifestyle and I admit I have a few drinks every now and then. She doesn't believe me and says, 'It's got to be more than a few drinks, if that's what's coming from your insides!'

Tears spill from my eyes. 'Yes,' I confess, 'it's more!'

'How much more?' She demands.

'Every day,' I say quietly, dropping my head.

'Can you imagine what damage you're doing to yourself? Don't you care about yourself at all?'

I cry tears of self-disgust and promise to change.

'You're very young, Esther. If you stop now – and I mean now – you won't have done too much damage.'

I nod agreeably. What am I doing, have I no self-respect? She gives me some tablets to help stop the drinking and refers me to the AA.

My sense of shame and self-loathing burns bright within me all the way home from the doctor's office. It is still with me as I down a couple of vodkas that afternoon. But it has dissolved completely by the time I remember: I don't give a flying fuck about myself, let me rot from inside out, let me pickle, what the fuck do I matter?

Adam and I have become the last people to leave the pub, and even then we must be thrown out. Our stumble home usually takes in a drunken brawl outside the chippie. Adam will say something offensive to someone, or someone will say something offensive to him; either way, he will get hit and I will step in to try to defend him and be swatted aside like an annoying fly, and flail drunkenly to the pavement. From where, moments later, I'll hear the wet bony crunch of Adam's face, being slapped down to join me.

It's funny how everything seems better after a few drinks and nothing seems to matter as much as you thought it once did. Each day is harsh, cold and unforgiving before the warm drink of the afternoon gets inside you and changes everything like magic.

A few weeks after my doctor's appointment, it's as if I have a permanent hangover and the sickness never stops. I try to ignore it, assuming it's the drink from the night before. But I can't keep anything down and I'm always exhausted. I go back to the doctor. At first she thinks it's the drink too. She asks me if I've stopped drinking. I can't lie to her, and she says she'll run some tests.

A few days later, she calls Adam and me in to see her. 'Esther,' she says gravely. 'I have some news for you. You're pregnant.'

Adam and I look at each other, momentarily shocked, before I feel a protective urge to look after whatever is growing inside me.

The doctor asks, 'So, what do you want to do?'

'About what?' I reply confused.

'About the baby!'

'Well, I'm not sure, I'll see when it comes.'

'Oh,' says the doctor.

Adam has a great big grin on his face. Everything is going to be all right, we can do this – it's meant to be.

This baby will make everything all right, I'm sure of it. On the walk home I'm already making plans in my head. How we'll look after the baby and how long I can continue working before I get so big I'll have to stop. 'Maybe tomorrow, we can go and look at some baby clothes,' I squeal excitedly.

Adam smiles back. 'Esther, there's plenty of time for all that.'

'I know, but I just want to look!'

We're walking past one of our usual pub haunts and Adam gestures to it. 'I'll just nip in for a couple!'

'But the doctor said we've got to stop drinking!'

'No, Esther,' he laughs, 'she meant *you've* got to stop drinking. You're the pregnant one, not me!'

I sit in the pub with him and try and make him come home after just a couple, but it doesn't work – he needs his usual ten pints. But it will get better soon. It must. It has to.

Sometimes I like to imagine I didn't exist until I met Adam. But my old life has ways of creeping up and pulling me back when I least expect it. One misty autumn evening Adam and I are taking a walk up near Inverness Castle. The bright orange lights surrounding the castle flare up dramatically, like hot flames into the cold dark blue sky. Not that we notice; we only have eyes for each other, our arms entwined, shutting the world out. But a girl's voice breaks our spell. 'Esther!' the high-pitched voice calls. 'I thought it was you!'

'Oh, hi Daisy,' I stutter, feeling embarrassed by her dirty holey jeans and raggedy T-shirt appearance.

Daisy seems agitated and impatient, looking around, as if watching out for someone. Her voice is high and wrong, and when she looks at me I realise I am staring into the huge glassy eyes of crack. 'Well, what are you doing with yourself? Have you settled in Inverness now?' she asks excitedly, shooting random glances about herself.

'Yes,' I hesitantly reply, turning to Adam, who looks bewildered at Daisy's tone and appearance.

Seeing my new life unravelling before my eyes, I panic. 'Daisy, look, we've really got to go, we're on our way—'

'Well, nice that, isn't it!' she interrupts aggressively. 'You haven't got time for an old mate?'

Suddenly remembering our history, I feel sorry for her, and my voice softens. 'Well, it's just we're in a bit of a—'

'Fine,' she interrupts abruptly before trotting out her line: 'You wouldn't happen to have some spare change, would you?'

'Yes,' I reply, digging into my pockets, 'I think I've a couple of pounds you can have.'

Adam shifts about restlessly, trying to pull me in the opposite direction. I place all the change I have in her dirty outstretched palm and she drops the coins into her pocket. 'Thanks for that, girlfriend,' she says cheerily, adding, 'See you again!' before disappearing back into the shadows.

As we continue on I can feel Adam's disgusted gaze upon me. 'Where the hell do you know her from?'

'She's a nobody,' I hastily lie. 'When I first came to Inverness, I bumped into her on the street one day and she asked my name and like an idiot, I told her. Now whenever she sees me, she asks me for money.'

'Oh,' he replies, seeming convinced.

So when I try to find my sister – I know I must do it by myself.

I haven't seen Bella in nearly two years. It's the longest we've ever gone without seeing each other. It's only been the last couple of years I've been just Esther, not EstherandBella like we used to be when we were kids. We spent almost our whole lives together. There is only 11 months between us, so we were almost twins, although we couldn't look more different. Where I was pale-skinned with fine mousy brown hair and hazel eyes, Bella had thick chestnut hair, olive-coloured skin and large chocolate button eyes. She smiled often, revealing a distinctive gap between her front teeth. From my earliest memories it's the two of us trying to escape from Dad, or the two of us playing and laughing together. We helped to look after the animals on our farm, but most of them scared me – especially the cows – but they didn't bother Bella. She was much braver than me and would walk in front as we passed, shooing them away while reassuring me, 'It's okay, Esther, they won't hurt you.'

I hated getting cold or wet, but Bella didn't care, so if there was a jacket, I'd get to wear it. When people said horrible things to us, Bella would tell me not to listen, they were just stupid. And as we got older Bella was the only one telling me I was pretty – when all I'd ever felt was ugly.

But Bella's and my relationship changed when I was 12 and she was 11. For the first time in our lives we were separated when I went to secondary school. That's when I started noticing the strange things Bella would say and do. One day, she pointed at a poster of a pop star and fearfully whispered, 'Esther, he called me stupid!'

I didn't even consider she truly believed it, instead I felt annoyed she was saying silly things for attention and shot back, 'Well, stop being stupid then, and posters won't talk to you!'

Looking for Bella one day, I followed a strange sad moaning and cracking sound coming from the cow barn. I discovered Bella inside, on her knees, trying to smash an already broken radio against the concrete floor. Looking up at my confused face, she explained desperately, 'It's playing bad music inside my head and I can't make it stop.'

I turned away because I didn't know what to say. It was getting more difficult to convince myself that Bella was just seeking attention. But worse was to come: going to sleep one night she leapt from her bed screaming in terror and pointed up at the skylight. 'Look, there's an evil witch flying in the sky.'

Alarmed, I jumped up beside her and squinted into the darkness. I followed her shaking finger but could only see dense blackness. 'You're such an idiot, Bella, go back to sleep and don't you dare wake me up again!' I growled. But then I felt her trembling and heard her fast breathing and I too was scared – scared that she, my strong sister, was frightened of things that only she could see.

After a while Bella stopped telling me things – I think she knew I didn't believe in her any more. After she was taken, I wished I'd listened and tried to help her more, for all those years she helped me.

But now I need Bella's help again, more than I ever have. This is my family's last hope. I must find her and discover what really happened. I need to hear what Bella said to make the social workers take her and all of my siblings away.

Even though we got the addresses of the other children, we've never been able to find out where Bella lives. So I have only one option – to contact Inverness Social Work Department and pretend to be a social worker from Orkney. Once I'm through to Bella's social worker, I've prepared a list of questions I want to ask, starting with asking how Bella is. Then I want to find out if she wants to see her brothers and sisters and, the most important one, where she lives. I nervously calm my breathing and try to still my trembling hands. The trouble I could get into flits through my mind. But, I reason, the worst they can do is put the phone down on me!

I unsteadily dial the number and it's answered immediately. I launch into who I am and what I want, before I hear the switchboard woman repeating herself, 'Inverness City Council, how may I help you?'

'Sorry!' I reply. 'Could you put me through to the Social Work Department please?'

She transfers me to a woman, who in turn passes me to the social worker handling our family's case.

'Hi,' I start, attempting to sound relaxed. 'It's Mona Drone here, from the Orkney Social Work Department. I'm just ringing for an update on Bella W.'

The short wait for her reply stretches out torturously. 'Oh, hi Mona. Actually, I was out seeing Bella just the other week. I could fax you over my new care plan, if you'd like?'

I'm thrown. Of all the answers I expected, it wasn't that one. I don't want anything being sent to anyone! 'No,' I say, a little too forcefully, 'no need for that. I don't want to put you to any trouble. I just thought it'd be nice to talk to someone and hear how she is, that's all!'

'Oh well,' she continues lightly, 'you'd be better off speaking to her foster mother, Anne.'

'Yes,' I say, beginning to lose my nerve and becoming aware my pretend Scottish accent is slipping, 'you could be right there. I know I've got her number here somewhere,' I add vaguely.

'Well,' she says, 'I have it in front of me, if that's of any help?'

The receiver slips and falls from my ear down my shoulder while my trembling hands scrabble about for a pen and paper, which seem to have disappeared! I hear myself replying, in a robotically calm voice, 'Yes, that would be very helpful, thank you.'

Repeating the number back to her, I thank her, before very firmly replacing the handset. 'AAAAAHHHHH!' I scream, allowing my tensed body to slacken and slide down the wall.

From the edge of the sofa, I stare at Bella's phone number, repeating it to myself. Quietly at first, then out loud. After all this time of knowing nothing about my sister, not where she is or even if she's okay, I suddenly know two big things: the name of her foster mum and her phone number! A tight pain squeezes my chest from inside and I fall forward into shoulder-heaving sobs. After a few minutes it dawns on me that this might not be her real number at all. Of course it isn't. It can't be that easy. I must dial it, just to check, and once I hear it ringing, I'll be happy. I focus hard and carefully dial the number. It rings instantly and then reality hits me. What am I doing? This isn't pretend – not like my Scottish accent. I only have one chance at this! Panic rises in my stomach; what will I say if she answers? I'm not prepared. I've come closer to Bella than I ever could have dreamed. If I blow this chance of hearing about her, I'll never forgive myself!

Three rings in and a cheery woman's voice takes me by surprise. My throat's gone dry and I momentarily forget, why I'm even ringing. 'Hello, there!' she repeats insistently.

Then it kicks in, I have no safety net – I must finish what I've started. 'Oh hello, sorry Anne, it's Mona Drone here. The W family social worker. I'm just ringing to check how Bella is?'

'Oh, hello, Mona. Bella is doing just fine.'

My mind is racing as I try to figure out how I'm going to work my questions into the conversation. 'That's great, Anne. I just wanted to ask, has she mentioned her family at all? You know, wanting to have contact with them perhaps?' Barely holding back the tears that threaten at my eyes, I add, 'Does she ever talk about them?'

Anne considers this for a minute. 'Well ... I would have to say no, not really. I think she's just settled in her own wee routine you know, and God forbid it should change!'

Disappointment covers me like a heavy grey blanket, and I just want to stop. I need to get off the phone – my chest feels as though it's being crushed. I thought I'd love hearing about Bella, but I can't do this – it hurts too much.

I go to finish the conversation. 'Well, as long as she's—' but Anne continues, 'She has her horse riding on Mondays, which she loves, oh, and she's also started doing a bit of helping out at the Red Cross on Wednesdays. Then on Thursdays she's all day at the psychiatric respite unit. That gives me a wee break and means I can get a few jobs done around the house.'

I feel as if I've been punched right in my belly, causing me to gasp. My sister in a psychiatric unit? I couldn't have heard her properly! 'What? Sorry Anne, what was that? Psychiatric unit – what for?'

Anne stops mid-flow and I sense she might be taken aback by my abrupt response. I hastily remind myself I'm supposed to be Mona Drone, who would already know this information, so I change my tone, adding 'And does she enjoy it there?'

But Anne seems unaware of my shock and goes on conversationally. 'Ah well, yes, they're ever so good with her there. They do all different crafts with them and take them for days out. It's the new one, you know the Joseph Belling Unit. She's really taken to a couple of staff there.'

At this point I've stopped listening; I'm thinking about my sister. My strong, independent Bella in a psychiatric unit. I absent-mindedly note down the name and the day she goes while Anne keeps up her cheerful chatter. I've kept this up for as long as I can; I need to get off the phone, or she'll be on to me. Speaking as I've heard many social workers before, I say, 'You have been very helpful, Anne. I'll put all this down in her notes,' and I gently replace the handset.

The following Thursday morning, I'm on the bus to the unit. After giving the driver the address I need to get to, he promises to let me know when we're close. How will Bella feel about seeing me again – happy, angry or, as I've dared to dream, has she been waiting all this time for me to come and rescue her? I am the older sister, after all. I clutch my stomach and inhale deeply, trying to swallow my fears.

Petrol fumes invade my nostrils and waves of sickness rise up in my stomach as the bus winds through gut-twistingly familiar scenery. Crouchend Alley Children's Home is nearby, so I know the built-up city will soon open to sprawling suburbia, which will give way to fields of sheep and cows. The town will then appear as a slate grey spread of identical council houses, ripped into an ugly ribbon of charity shops, bargain booze outlets and boarded-up buildings. After vowing never to return, it's less than two short years later and here I am again.

I remind myself I'm here to find my sister but as the memories flood back so too do the fears and soon my heart is racing and my hands are shaking. My life has moved on so much in the last two years. Maybe I'll tell Bella I'm going to be a mum and she's going to be an auntie. Then we can share squeals of excitement that we're going to be a family again. A different one than before – but still a family! I bet she'll understand why I want to keep this baby. Nobody else does. They say at 17, I'm not ready, I'm too young. But they don't know that I've looked after babies my whole life. Anyway, Adam and I are in love. If I could stop him drinking, perhaps one day Bella could live with us? I dare to hope that one day soon we might again be EstherandBella.

CHAPTER FOURTEEN

Kidnapping Bella

The bus driver's voice brings me back to earth with a jolt. 'Here's the place you'll be wanting!'

I climb down from the bus and immediately see a Council sign, for the Joseph Belling Psychiatric Unit. There's an institutional feel about the place, with lots of signs, cement slopes, fire doors and windows. Beige curtains are pulled open at the front window, revealing a wall of motionless people in high-backed chairs. My stomach churns and my mouth is dry. I better do this before I lose my nerve! I set off towards the front door, covered in official-looking notices. But then I see an open fire door and stop. Would it hurt if I just took a peek? I'd regret it if they say no when I ask to see Bella. With my heart lurching in my chest, I carefully tread through the fire door and find myself in a central foyer. Now I can see inside the room and sitting there, between a snoring middle-aged man and an elderly woman, is Bella!

Although the fire door is open, the air in here is thick and still. Children's nursery rhymes tinkle out optimistically from a cassette player. 'Twinkle twinkle little star' has never sounded so hopeless. Seeing Bella like this, I go from nervous excitement to heavy black sadness. With only a room between us, she has never seemed further away. Her chocolate brown eyes stare vacantly at something in the far distance, while she slowly sways her thick dark head of hair out of time to the music, her hands collapsed upon her lap.

It takes everything in me not to cry out, 'What is my sister doing here?' It feels like an end-of-the-road place – everything and everyone has stopped. Apart from a couple of people mumbling to themselves, it is eerily quiet. While most of the patients look like the older people I've worked with in nursing homes, my sister looks young and wrong in here. High-pitched laughter pierces the air and I jump. I check about myself then I realise it's two nurses, laughing in a little kitchen off to the side. I'm reminded how dangerous what I'm doing is and that I could get caught any moment – and maybe even done for breaking and entry. I must move fast. Without daring to breathe, I glide across the room to Bella. Kneeling down beside her, a couple of the other people glance at me before returning to their own worlds. Bella doesn't register me at first and I have to tell her, 'Bella, it's me, Esther!'

She looks at me sharply, like a startled wild deer. I feel panicky; it must be true what they said – she doesn't even remember she has a family? But then, it's like she's searching her memory for my name before she declares, 'Esther it's you!' in a high sing-song voice.

Tears well up in my eyes. 'Yes, it's me!' I reply gently, stroking her hand. Apart from some weight she's gained and very long nails when once she bit them incessantly, she looks the same.

'Esther!' she repeats, her voice getting louder.

'Ssshhh,' I whisper, putting my finger to my lips. 'Are you okay?'

She smiles dreamily. 'Yes, I'm here, and you're here!'

Now a couple of the other people are openly staring at us. I decide that it'll be safer to talk to her outside. 'Bella,' I quietly ask, 'do you want to go for a little walk?'

'Okay, I will!' she answers, again in a high voice.

I stand up, but she remains seated. I'm confused. Doesn't she understand? I bend down and take her arm. 'Bella?' She looks up at me, as if she's seeing me anew. 'Come on then, come with me,' I instruct.

'Okay,' she says, and she lets me lead her the short walk across the room where I'm certain someone will shout out at any moment. But they don't and before I know it we are at the door. We are walking through the door! Then we are standing on the pavement, I look her up and down and it's then I realise she's wearing slippers – fluffy old lady slippers. But now we're out of there, I don't want her to go back in. So, firmly holding her arm, I get us walking. I don't know where we're going – I just know where we're going from. As we walk, I ask her why they put her in there, but she doesn't seem to know. I ask what she's doing with her life now, but again she seems unsure.

From sitting so still while she was inside the unit, she now lurches about randomly. She suddenly races towards things without a thought for the road between them. When she sees a phone box, she exclaims delightedly, 'Look, a red phone box!' before releasing my hand and belting towards it to examine it close up. I end up taking a firm hold of her hand and holding on for dear life.

I wish she would go back to being her old self when we were little girls, knowing all the answers and being the one in charge. I realise with panic that I haven't got a clue what

I'm doing. Then I get an idea: maybe if I move her into the flat with me and Adam, I can look after her, then she'll be okay! Suddenly feeling excited, I ask, 'Bella, would you like to come home with me?'

'Okay,' she says simply.

So I take her to the bus stop, where, much to my relief, we only have to wait a few minutes before a bus back to Inverness turns up. Once on it, I get her to sit beside the window and try to distract her by pointing at things outside. But, as I feared, she wants to stand up and wander about. I struggle to hem her in – but she effortlessly clambers over me and starts skipping up and down the bus aisle.

'Bella!' I warn in a stern parent-like voice. 'You must sit in your seat or the bus driver will tell you off!'

I try pulling her back to where I'm sitting. 'No,' she squeaks, 'I want to have a seat all by myself.'

I sit behind her, resignedly watching her draw pictures in the misted-up windows. I realise with a sudden jolt that I can't cope with her. What am I doing? People are looking at her and then at me. Although she is 16, she is behaving more like a five-year-old, her attention flitting from one thing to another, and speaking in a high, loud voice. 'Talk quieter!' I sharply reprimand, but she just keeps doing it.

She turns around from her seat. 'I love your scarf, can I wear it?'

'If you stay still and be quiet, you can!' I bargain.

'Okay,' she says, wrapping my scarf around her neck, squealing excitedly, 'this is soft, very soft!'

I'm tired and relieved by the time the bus pulls into Inverness Station. But Bella seems scared. She looks around herself, bewildered, as if suddenly realising where she is.

'It's all right!' I reassure her. 'You're coming back to my flat, remember? I'm Esther, your sister.' A flicker of recognition passes over her eyes. 'Come on then, come with me,' I urge, trying to sound calmer than I feel.

The flat where Adam and I live is only a few minutes' walk from the bus station but it takes much longer to coax Bella to it. Crossing the road is a job in itself as Bella seems to find the cars too loud and fast. She stares at them fearfully, holding her hands flat over her ears. And getting her up the three flights of stairs to our flat is another exhausting task. Halfway up she suddenly becomes annoyed and starts demanding, 'I want water, I'm thirsty! I'm hungry!' With promises of lots of food and water at the top, we finally fall through my door. I go straight to my kitchen and get out bread, butter and jam, but she grabs the loaf from me. 'No, just bread, I eat bread!' she says, pulling at it and eating clumps. She downs a couple of cups of water, and hands me the cup, 'More water!'

I sit down at the table. 'Bella, do you mind if I ask you something?'

She looks at me blankly, before running through to the sitting room. I follow her, but she won't settle, she's becoming more agitated. I realise this is probably not the time to bring up what she said, or didn't say, to the Orkney Social Work Department as I can't even make her focus on sitting down, let alone talking about the past.

She continues wandering about restlessly, looking into cupboards and pulling things out. 'What's this?' she'll ask, or, 'What does that do?' It's as if she's searching for something she can't find.

I change the subject and start talking about myself. I tell her about Adam and me and even about the baby we're expecting, but she doesn't take any of it in. I'm not even sure she knows that I'm her sister and not just someone she asks to help her today. What am I going to do with her? I wonder. I can't look after her, she needs people who know what they're doing. Maybe even the people I took her away from!

We've been home a while and I'm exhausted. 'I'm tired Bella, do you want a little sleep?'

'Okay,' she replies and for once she actually sits on the sofa, while I get us a couple of blankets. She closes her eyes and I look over at her – it's like I have a much younger sister now. Soon she falls asleep and the second I close my eyes, so do I.

'Hiya, is anyone home?'

I wake up to Harry, our landlord, calling from our open front door. Something feels not right and it isn't just because it's darker, and I'm shivering. It's something else. Then my stomach falls. Bella – where's Bella? She's not there on the couch and the blanket she had on her lies rumpled on the floor. I jump up and run through, explaining to Harry as I go, 'My young sister is staying and she's not very well. She's gone. She's out on the streets somewhere!' I scream hysterically.

'Don't worry, Esther, calm down, I'll help you find her,' he offers reassuringly.

We check our bedroom, bathroom and kitchen, search under the bed, and inside the wardrobe, but she's long gone and the truth thumps me – she's been trying to escape from me since the moment I took her. We race downstairs and into the indoor market. On the way I tell Harry that Adam must never know about this. He seems confused at first, so I explain, 'He's never got on with my family because they don't like his drinking. Why do you think I had to have my sister around while he's at work?' I ask.

Harry nods knowingly before confiding some of his own domestic issues as we poke our heads into cafes, run-down lanes, search around shops, all the while me knowing that we won't find her – she doesn't want me to. After searching everywhere we can think of for over an hour, we finally admit defeat and return to the flat.

Sometime later there's an urgent banging at the front door. I run to it, suddenly hopeful that Bella might have remembered me and where I live and come back. But two police officers are waiting on the other side. As I open the door, they stride past me. 'We have reason to believe you have kidnapped your sister!' one says.

'What? Kidnapped who?' I splutter, turning to Harry, who in turn looks dumbfounded.

'Look, wait a minute, officer—' Harry starts to say.

'Sir, stand aside, please. We have a warrant to search this property.'

They search every room and when they can't find her, they demand to know what I've done with her. I explain everything from start to finish, Harry standing by, his mouth gaping. I finish by angrily blurting, 'And how can I be accused of kidnapping my own sister? She's less than a year younger than me!'

'That's as may be, madam,' one of the police officers coldly replies, 'but your sister is a vulnerable adult. You should never have taken her from that unit. She was obviously in there for a very good reason!'

Tears spill from my eyes. 'I'm sorry, I didn't mean to hurt her. I just needed to know what she'd said,' I reply, truly full of remorse, because now I know, as much as I hated seeing her in there, it was the right place for her.

'Well then,' one of them adds, 'you better pray we find her and that she's all right!'

To my relief, a couple of hours later the police phone to say they've found Bella safe and well and she's been returned to her foster mother. 'But,' the policeman warns, 'if you want to see your sister again, you must go down the correct channels. Because if this happens again, I promise you, you will be charged with kidnap!'

Harry stays with me for the evening. His shock at what I revealed about my past confirms what I suspected: it's best not to tell anyone about myself, and for once I'm grateful Adam stays out at the pub for the evening.

Where Adam's drinking has gone pretty much unchanged since my pregnancy, I feel like I'm finally getting a handle on mine and I've managed to stop. I had to go cold turkey; I can't take the tablets as they might harm the baby. On Monday Adam promises he'll stop, but come Thursday, he's back on the weekend bender. He drinks at home, he drinks at the pub, he even drinks when he's supposed to be at work. But when he starts stealing the rent money for drink – I know something has got to give.

I've got a 12-week doctor's appointment and Adam is coming with me. I insist he stays in the waiting room, as the doctor might smell the drink on his breath. The second I enter the doctor's surgery I know this isn't a routine appointment. It's her face, it's shadowy, serious and a little bit scared – it's the face of a person who has found out who I am. 'Come on in, Esther. Take a seat,' she says in an official-sounding voice, then turns back to her desk and looks at my file.

Without taking my eyes off her, I sit down. My mind is turning over and over, trying to figure out what's going on.

'I'll get straight to the point. I had concerns of care issues, so I've been in touch with social services about your pregnancy.'

My jaw drops and the blood drains from my face. I feel cold, but red-hot anger surges through me at the same time. 'What? What does "concerns of care issues" mean?' I ask, climbing to my feet. 'And why would you be in touch with social services about my pregnancy?'

'Look, Esther, sit back down and I'll explain. You must see I had no choice,' she says, before brightly adding 'and anyway, they might even be able to help. It's just with your history and your present circumstances—'

'But what does my history have to do with anything?' I interrupt.

She smiles awkwardly. 'Everything, I'm afraid. Look: I have to consider the welfare of the baby. They'll make an assessment of you and see whether you're capable of looking after the child. Or if further options have to be explored.'

I look at her, confused. I'm not in care any more, why would they have to assess me? Why would they have to look at my history? 'This is because of my past isn't it?' I demand. 'You're never going to let me move on, are you? You won't ever let me have a family of my own. You'll take this baby as well, won't you?'

She looks startled. 'I'm not saying that, I'm just saying an assessment will—'

'NO,' I scream, 'I don't want any more assessments. I don't ever want any of your lot near me *again*!'

'Miss W, sit back down!' she barks. 'We'll work together and figure out—'

I perch on the edge of the seat. 'But why isn't me keeping the baby the best option?' I stammer.

She waits a moment. 'You're very young, Esther, and you've had a lot to deal with in your life. Not to mention your partner's problems with alcohol—'

I spring back up. 'So what you're saying is, you think I should give my baby up?' Her silence answers my question. 'I'll never let you bastards steal this baby off me, *never*!' I shout, yanking the surgery door open.

'The social worker will be in touch and we'll go from there,' she calls after me.

Tears blind me as I stumble from the surgery. I'm aware of Adam running after me. 'Esther, stop, what's wrong?'

I keep running, but I can't ever run fast enough to get away from her and the social workers – somehow they always catch me.

I feel Adam's hand grab my arm and spin me towards him. 'What happened in there?'

How can I tell him, my past is ruining our future? My past that he doesn't even know existed?

CHAPTER FIFTEEN

Falling to pieces

T he doctor makes the arrangements and says, 'It's probably for the best.'

And she's right, we would have been the worst parents in the world. Me, a fucked-up abused girl, just out of care, and him an alcoholic – what could we offer a child? How could he be a father, when his first love is drink, and I don't feel a thing – let alone love. I haven't got the right to sadness, there's nothing to be sad about. So why can't I stop crying? And why does my heart feel like it won't ever stop breaking?

Adam was supposed to come to the hospital with me; he promised he would. But either he'd left the flat before I woke up, or he didn't come home last night. I was hungry and thirsty – but I did as the letter said. I haven't eaten or drunk anything since nine o'clock last night.

I got a bus to the hospital, and made my way to the ward. A scary-looking nurse with shiny dark hair scraped back into a tight ponytail shows me to a bed. Sweeping a pastel-coloured curtain around us, she orders, 'Just pop your nightie on and the doctor will be with you in a bit.'

Without looking down at my body, my swollen breasts and what, until a few days ago, I had admired as the hint of a baby belly, I pull on my nightie. I don't want to spend a second alone with myself, so I tear back the curtain to reveal rows of beds facing each other. I squint confusedly for a moment at a strange high-pitched kittenish cry that fills the air. Then I realise, with horror, that we who are getting rid of our babies are separated only by a corridor from those who are keeping theirs!

I steal glances at the other waiting girls and, except for one sobbing, we're all silent. Most of them have boyfriends, friends or mothers with them – sharply stabbing home my solitary state. Energy darts through my body – I need a change of scenery – I can't stay here with my thoughts. I get out of bed without knowing where I'm going. But spying a couple of girls in their nighties leaving the ward armed with fags, I search my pockets before sighing despairingly: that's another thing I've forgotten. I follow them to the smoking room anyway; anything is better than sitting here listening to a sobbing girl and newborn babies crying. In the tiny yellow smoking room, one of the girls offers me a cigarette. I take it, mumbling my thanks. We sit in silence, shooting each other little smiles of comfort. They're both older than me – in their early twenties, I think – and seem sophisticated, with their shiny make-up and nail polish, while at 17 I feel too small and young to be doing something this big and scary by myself. I'm glad we don't speak; instead I stare down, focusing on my unpainted bitten nails.

When we return to the ward, the sobbing girl has been joined by a man, and she's not sobbing any more. She is whispering something to him and he's listening. Then he whispers back and she listens. Suddenly they are smiling and cuddling and now they are almost laughing. Leaping from her bed, she heaves her trousers on and shrugs her jacket over her nightie before slipping into her trainers. The nurse returns and on seeing her dressed demands, 'And, where do you think you're going?'

'We've decided to keep the baby!' the now happy girl replies, beaming around at the rest of us.

There are lots of forced cheery aahs for them, and me and one of my cigarette friends exchange tight smiles and shoulder shrugs, as if we weren't in this place at all. The happy couple, with baby on the way, skip out of the ward, hand in hand to their future, while the rest of us are trying to turn back time and pretend this never happened.

I'm bursting for a wee when I wake from the operation. I manage to make it to the loo just in time, and a torrent of blood gushes from me. There's a stock of large thick sanitary pads by the loo. I wedge one in my knickers and put the rest in my bag for later. Once I'm back in bed, I ask a passing male nurse whether Adam came to see me while I was having the operation. 'No, nobody's been for you.' he tells me gently. My vision is blurred, but I can still see he's looking at me caringly. 'You mustn't upset yourself,' he says. 'Just try and get some sleep and you'll feel better.'

But when I wake so early the next morning the blinds are still down, I don't feel any better. I search around in the shadows for signs Adam has visited – grapes or maybe even a card. Why didn't he run in at the last minute, like the sobbing girl's partner? We could have been a family. Our love could have kept the nosy doctor and social services away, couldn't it? But he probably went out drinking yesterday and forgot the time. Drink comes first in our relationship. My body feels hurt from deep inside as I struggle back into the clothes I wore here yesterday, clothes from another lifetime. There are no nurses around, and nobody to say goodbye to, so I leave by the signs that brought me here, all the while knowing I've left something behind I won't ever forget.

At home from the hospital, I'm trying to get through to Mum on the phone. But it won't work – there's a stop-start sound, like it's engaged. We're three flights up and I'm too tired to go back out and use a public phone. I sit just inside the front door, with my back against the wall. I haven't moved since I got in. The pungent smell of wee and disinfectant from the men peeing in the stairwell just outside the bookies downstairs wafts up under the door in little cold gasps. I think maybe I should get up, but I'm too tired. It was a long walk home, over two miles. I tried to work out the bus timetable, but the words and numbers got mashed up together.

I was hot when I got back, but now I'm too cold – I really should try to get up. But I can't, my jeans feel too hard to stand up in. Blood has soaked through the fabric and made them stiff and when fresh blood comes out, I feel it searching for a place to go. I can see the toilet from here, only a few steps away, but it's still too far. Anyway, I need to talk to Mum before I get up, I want her to say something. I'm not sure what – maybe something about how it's all going to be okay. I examine the itchy dark green carpet and it seems my world has become tightly woven in among all the other knots. In slow motion I fling my head back against the wall. Thudding heavily, the sensation reverberates through me, but I'm surprised I can't really feel it. I must do it again. Bang. Bang, I can't stop myself – I need to wake up. Finally a burning pain seeps through to me and I reach round to feel a warm wet stickiness. I show myself my red fingers, to prove it – see, I am real – there is blood in there. Unsteadily rolling onto my hands and knees, I crawl through to the bedroom; climbing on the bed, I'm instantly asleep.

The familiar sound of keys jangling against wood and male laughter wakes me from a deep sleep. Before he stumbles through the door, I'm up and racing at him. We collide. Grunting like a wild animal, I jump on him. Gripping his ears, I bite into his skull, but my teeth struggle to get a hold, so I scratch and scrape at anything my fingers touch and kick anywhere my feet land. I need to hurt him. He folds to the floor, retracting into a ball, leaving me with just his back. I punch into it, hard at first, until my fists become too heavy and, from a faraway place, I hear a little girl scream, 'Why weren't you there for me? You were supposed to be there!'

Eventually he keels over, his bloodshot eyes glazing up at me. His jaw hangs slack, releasing the putrid stench of stale beer, as if he's about to say something and for a moment I hope he's got the answer. But, as I have so many times before, I watch with dismay, as his eyes roll back into his head and close over, and soon he escapes into sleep. I collapse over the drunken lump of a man in front of me, and cry. I cry because now I know that if the drink can win today then we don't stand a chance.

I wake, drowning in thick water. I struggle frantically for a while before realising it's easier if I don't move and let myself return to the nothingness of sleep. When I wake again my stomach aches and I feel wet. I idly examine myself in the darkened light and see map-like patches on my

T-shirt. Panicking, I snap the side light on and whip my T-shirt up, revealing thick creamy beads of liquid falling from my nipples, like pearls from a snapped string necklace. I watch with detached curiosity for a few moments, because it feels as if it's happening to someone else, before I fall back down to the mattress.

I catch glimpses of Adam, asking me if I'm all right and if I want something. But it's not like real living at all, it's more like watching myself on television. Every now and then, strands of reality float about me, like dust particles in sunlight. I attempt to grasp them, but their reason for mattering disappears before I reach them. There's a soft nothingness, not nice, not horrible, and over time I come to wonder if something has stolen my feelings and left an empty shell.

One day I get out of bed and sit on the sofa in the living room. I push myself back into the silky suede material and lean forward over my lap – to minimise the amount of spiky air getting to my skin. I can see out of the window from here. There is a hill in the distance and when the morning light comes, a lot of people walk up it. Every morning I watch until I see a girl walking up the hill. I recognise her from her long red coat and wavy shoulder-length brown hair. That girl is me and she's going to work, but she's left her shell here, sitting still on this brown sofa. It momentarily flits through me that I should call after her to come back.

A nice doctor comes to the house. She gives me tablets to take, lots of tablets. Small black tablets, pink round tablets, white tiny tablets and long thick yellow squishy capsules called temazepams and, after a while, I realise they are the best.

With the help of strong doses of temazepam over the next few weeks, the cloud of blackness that got trapped inside me is released. And with Adam's help I can even leave the flat without feeling as though my skin has been ripped off. And eventually I know that no matter how fast my heart races and short my breath gets, I won't have a heart attack.

A few months later, I even start thinking about what I want from my life. From the moment I saw Linda's degree photograph while in care, I have wanted one. I see it as my ticket to where I want to get in life. I have no qualifications, so a careers adviser tells me the first step would be getting my GCSEs. I enrol to do English and maths at the local college. I enjoy the courses and when I get a part-time job cleaning at the hospital through a student friend called Big Andy, it seems like everything might finally be clicking into place.

Adam has always been jealous of other boys, so the first couple of weeks I'm working up at the hospital he comes and collects me. But he doesn't mind me talking to Big Andy. Big Andy is a larger-than-life character and the centre of the evening cleaning world at the hospital. He's almost as wide as he is tall, with a crown of gel-spiky dark hair, making him taller still. He's openly gay, and laughingly threatens the other male cleaners with 'a good bumming' if they don't behave themselves. For the most part, all of us cleaners have a great laugh. But for me, it's more than that, it's the feeling of carefree laughter, one I haven't experienced in a long time.

There's good news from home as well. Dr John Rumney's assessments have come back and they support my brothers and sisters being returned home.

One of the first people Dr John Rumney interviewed was Ms Enid Blood, who, along with Renee Stubbs, was responsible for getting the satanic sex ring allegations from my brothers and sisters. He found her bubbling over with allegations of abuse. She immediately made it clear she was totally opposed to Mum being given any access to my brothers and sisters. She was emphatic that the four youngest children should not go home and should immediately be freed up for adoption. She thought Lawrence, a boy who had always been bright and articulate, should be placed in a home for the mentally handicapped. She also confided that the elder brothers in our family, family friends, and neighbours, had all abused the children, and Mum knew about it. She added that Bella had not only been abused by a neighbour, but that she had also been abused by Mum – who, according to her, had also abused the other children.

Dr Rumney asked to see the statements verifying her allegations, but Ms Blood was unable to produce any. And when pressed, she had to admit that she herself had never seen such statements.

Dr Rumney then assessed my siblings individually, and found that two themes ran through the assessments of them all. Firstly, despite the disclosure therapy, none of them appeared to have any idea why they were in care. Secondly, they had all been told a similar lie – by social workers – that our father, on leaving jail, would be returning home. This was a lie of evil proportions. The emotionally damaging and wicked threat was that if they were to return home, he would be there to abuse them, all over again. Momentarily putting aside the moral reasons of saying such a lie to children, Dad wouldn't legally be allowed to return home, as part of his sentencing was the condition that he stay a certain distance away from all of us children, should he ever leave prison.

When Dr Rumney visited Sam, he took the opportunity to also speak with his teacher. She said she had witnessed his dramatic deterioration since first entering care in November 1990. Initially he had been a bright, healthy, outgoing boy, but he now seemed 'in a dream'. When left to work on his own, he just switched off. Sam's support teacher, like his class teacher, thought he needed a psychological assessment, but gained the impression the psychologist had been told to 'lay off'. The carer at Bridgeport End Children's Home, where Lawrence and Sam were staying, described him as 'bright', but wondered why he and Lawrence were the only children there not to have any contact with their parents. Sam confided in Dr Rumney that he loved his mother and the rest of his family. Describing the days of physical abuse when Dad was at home, he spoke of his mother crying and how an older brother of his had 'thumped Dad in the face'.

Lawrence immediately told Dr Rumney he also wanted to go home to see his brothers and sisters, and spoke warmly of family friends. He said he thought of home a lot and the good times he'd had there. The bad times, he pointed out, 'were with Dad, and they are over'. Of his elder brother, he told Dr Rumney, unasked, 'Nothing happened to me, the social workers lied.' Up to this point, Lawrence had not been allowed phone calls home, and now when he was, they were always supervised, with a social worker standing with a finger poised over the button. Even this little bit of family access was heavily supervised, a situation Dr Rumney considered absurdly artificial.

On visiting Holly at her foster home, Dr Rumney learnt of her anxieties over Dad being allowed to get out of jail and come home. Holly's two teachers told Dr Rumney that she was very aggressive when she had first arrived at school, particularly after disclosure therapy sessions. Another teacher drew Dr Rumney's attention to Holly's role-playing and her sexualised drawings. Holly was clear with Dr Rumney that it was her father who had done bad things and 'the sexual things'. According to the teacher, Holly had never mentioned sibling sexual abuse. Holly stressed to Dr Rumney that she missed all her siblings, particularly me who, as she pointed out, had once voluntarily taken a beating from Dad, intended for her. Holly told Dr Rumney, 'I'd like to live with my mum and I miss my mum.' She was worried, as Mona Drone had told her she was to be adopted and she pointed out, 'My mother has to sign a paper if I'm going to be adopted. Being adopted is for ever. I don't want to be adopted, I want to stay with my own mum.' When asked about her father, Holly stated that he was coming out of jail and 'He'll come home.' Asked how she knew this, she confirmed, 'The social worker told me – my dad is coming home.'

The head teacher, at the school where my two youngest sisters Penny and Poppy attended until June 1991, also informed Dr Rumney the pair were about to adopted by new foster parents and their names had been changed. The teacher had also been informed that when the father of the children was released from jail, he was going home to Orkney. Asked about the children, the teacher said she saw signs of deterioration in Penny when she returned from disclosure sessions. Poppy, the teacher said, was exceptionally quiet and withdrawn and avoided all eye contact.

Dr Rumney met the two children at their new school. Despite having had her name changed, Penny firmly insisted she wished to return home 'I want to go back to Orkney,' adding, 'My mum is kind and nice, she's got black hair, and wears trousers and red socks.' Asked about her brothers and sisters, Penny told Dr Rumney, 'Social workers say they hurt me, but they didn't, if they did I would tell.'

Poppy was described by Dr Rumney as a very quiet, almost withdrawn child, who was losing identification with her family. She knew only that she had one sister – no one else.

Finally, when Dr Rumney visited Bella, he found her to be suffering from a psychotic mental state. Strangely, no mention of this psychosis appeared in any social work reports.

Dr Rumney concluded that social workers didn't want to acknowledge the obvious affection between our mother and her children. He noted that when the children discussed their mother, they did so with warmth and affection. He pointed out that the social workers were unqualified to do psychological assessments, which is what they had been doing. He believed the children had not been treated with dignity and respect. Changing children's names, without discussion or request, he considered a tactic that was used to lessen the child's identification with their family. Handing them over to strangers was not, he believed, the right way forward for these children. Access between the children should be positively encouraged and removing the children from their mother had never been the answer. Fostering and adopting the children could not and would not solve any problems, adding that the opportunity should now be given to the mother and the children to recover from the pain they had thus far suffered. In short – he was recommending my siblings be returned home!

Meanwhile, up at the hospital, my past is causing me problems once again. Big Andy has his own tight-knit gossip circle, which makes me feel warm and protected when I'm inside it. But our supervisor Carol has changed our wards around and she put me on maternity. I am only just coping working at the hospital, let alone being on the ward where 'it' happened so recently. I momentarily wonder if I should just not turn up for work the next day. But I love working at the hospital, the banter and camaraderie has become a big part of my life. I go to Carol and quickly blurt out why I can't work in that ward. In a kind voice, she replies, 'Don't worry, I'll sort it.'

The following evening I come to work to find Andy won't speak to me. The others say that he says that I've stolen his front reception job from him. They say Carol told him I specifically requested my ward be changed to front reception – meaning Andy is now on maternity and he isn't happy. I try to explain to them, so they can explain to him, that I don't care which ward I work on, so long as it isn't maternity. But it's too late, I've pissed off Big Andy and that's something you don't do if you value enjoying your job up at the hospital. The damage has been done and, as I've seen him do countless times before, I know he'll make me pay.

He freezes me out and I am no longer one of the bitchy gaggle in the smoking room. I don't like it, but, I reason, I can survive without Andy speaking to me. What I don't know is that he hasn't finished with me – he's just waiting until he's got something good on me.

Just a couple of weeks later I'm cleaning the floor of one of the cubicles in reception when I hear the scrape and slop of a metal mop bucket. I spin round to see Big Andy smiling strangely at me, his dark, deep-set eyes glinting brightly. Supporting his bulk on his mop handle, he leans down to me and whispers in a voice full of venom, 'I know who you are! You're from the W family. That weird satanic sex lot up in Orkney!'

I wait too long to deny it and his smile widens. My blood runs cold. How did he find out? As if in answer, he continues, 'One of the boys that started work here the other day is from Orkney, and he recognises you. I'm going to tell everyone who you really are, Miss. I choose where I want to fucking work!'

Turning on his heel, the nylon curtain billows in his wake. 'No, Andy, wait!' I call. But I know it is already too late, this gossip is too good for him.

Emptying my locker at the end of my shift, I know I won't be coming back. On the bus journey home I already hear Andy's whispers spiking the air and feel the accusing eyes burning holes into me. But before Andy can blab to everyone, there is one person who deserves to hear it from me.

'I am one of the W children, from the Orkney satanic sex ring.'

Adam looks as if I've slapped him. He knows immediately what I'm talking about. 'But when we met, I asked you if you knew anything about it, and you said you didn't! Why did you lie to me?'

Tears course down my cheeks as I insist, 'I didn't lie. I just didn't tell you!'

But no matter what I say, it sounds as if I'm trying desperately to convince him and myself that there's a difference between outright lying and leaving out the truth about me and my family. 'I just wanted to be someone else, a normal girl. I've always been that little abused girl. I didn't want you to see me that way!'

His face changes. He sees who I really am for the first time. His eyes narrow with suspicion and a little fear. And even though I try explaining about Andy threatening me and how I had to tell him, although I wished I never had to, it doesn't change a thing. Even as I offer him a solution to our problems, I know we're over.

'Maybe we could run away together?' I plead. 'I can't go back to the job at the hospital now and soon everyone at college will know. We could start a new life somewhere else, somewhere people don't know who I am.'

He looks at me, and his eyes are brimming with tears. 'But I don't know you, Esther, you're not who I thought you were,' and he pulls himself from me as if in pain and storms to the door.

When he looks back, like I know he will, his words are angry. 'Maybe you should just go,' he shouts, banging the door on his way out.

Deep down, I know he's right. We can barely get through an hour without fighting and maybe it is all because of who I am. My past has ruined everything, like it always does and my normal life is over.

CHAPTER SIXTEEN

Running away to London

Whitney Houston's 'I Will Always Love You' muffles out the wild seas on the boat home to Orkney and the bitter Antarctic wind whips my cheeks. I'm returning to Crook Farm a failure. I failed in love, and I failed in what I set out to do: find Bella and make everything right. The sharp salty air stings my eyes and I wish, by some miracle, that my family's situation will have changed for the better.

But once home I find that the storm is raging as strong as ever. Last week Orkney Social Work Department called an emergency hearing for my two youngest sisters. It was their first hearing in over ten months. Despite nearly a year's separation, the girls were reported to be thrilled to see Mum. Mrs Hope described them as 'clinging to their mother like limpets on a rock' and 'wrapping their arms tightly around her, refusing to relax their grip, kissing her over and over again'. But all the affection in the world couldn't cushion the crushing blow for Mum of hearing Penny and Poppy call their foster carers 'Mummy' and 'Daddy'.

Both Dr Rumney and Dr Seth Newton – an eminent consultant paediatrician – attended the meeting and voiced their astonishment at the prejudicial treatment being dealt to my family and younger siblings. Dr Rumney was championing access and a need for our family to be reunited as soon as possible, while Dr Newton pointed out to the hearing that he had examined the children and could see no evidence of anything sexually abnormal.

But none of this would affect the outcome. Mum was informed that all access to her two youngest children would be terminated. Renee Stubbs claimed the decision was based on the children being upset following access with their mother. When it was suggested that this might simply be because they missed their mother and hated being apart from her, she appeared unable to reply, as if the idea of a normal family relationship was an alien concept to her.

Mona Drone again impressed upon everyone at the hearing that the younger ones had suffered 'abuse at the hands of their older siblings'. However, when she was asked to produce evidence, she was forced to admit she had none to hand. After learning the result of the hearing, Mum asked Mona Drone whether the Social Work Department had any plans to adopt Penny and Poppy. She assured Mum and the hearing that adoption definitely wasn't on the agenda.

Meanwhile, our family is dealt another major setback. The inquiry into the satanic sex ring allegations has begun and we have been informed that none of us, not even Mum, will be called to give evidence. From the moment an inquiry was announced, we had pinned our hopes upon its outcome. Naively, we believed it would search for and at long last expose the truth. We thought that it would have to start at the beginning where the satanic sex allegations came from – which would, of course, lead back to our family. Once the inquiry had examined the manner in which the allegations had been gathered, we felt certain, like the *Panorama* programme had before, it would expose the Orkney Social Work Department's shameful system, and their case against us would be seen as the fiction it is. We imagined the inquiry would demand, 'But why haven't such serious allegations been tried in a legal setting and somebody been charged already?' The whole inquiry would then conclude, with the fairy-tale ending of the W children being freed from captivity.

Instead, the judge in charge wants to start the inquiry from the point at which the other families' children were taken. In short, he only wants to examine the effect and not the cause. He points that there's a convicted child abuser, our father, in our history, and explains our story is just too complicated to go into – which begs the question: what is the purpose of an inquiry?

The list of people being called includes all of the parents from the four other families, as well as the local minister and his wife. But most painful of all, it also includes all of the social workers involved, including Mona Drone. While they will all get to have their say, nobody from my family will get to testify about what really happened and why. So in effect, we are being edited from our own life story.

Feeling defiant one day, me, Mum and a family friend travel to Kirkwall to sit in on the inquiry. With her olive skin, long black hair and golden earrings studding the curve of her ear, Mum stands out in a small conservative place like Kirkwall. And as we make our way through the city centre, I hear the little hissing fires we set off from strangers whispering about us. Although we can't legally be stopped from going in, by the time we push open the heavy squeaking door to the inquiry room, my paper-thin bravery has evaporated and I meekly take a seat next to Mum in the public gallery area, feeling vulnerable and guilty. It is some time before I dare look up around the cavernous inquiry room. The long rectangular table at its heart is surrounded by important-looking people in long black cloaks and white curly wigs, and it is headed by an even more superior-looking judge. A social worker from Inverness is being questioned and seems nervous and hesitant in her replies. But it quickly becomes apparent there are no answers to be found here for my family, as no questions are being asked about us. We have made our little protest, and I'm relieved when it is suggested we leave. As if it wasn't already obvious, me and my family will be blamed for everything that has happened, but we are not allowed a platform to defend ourselves on.

Worse is still to come: on 25 September Judith Hope resigns as panel reporter. She says she would rather resign than become party to this flawed and damaging system. She prefers to keep her hands clean and she suspects that if she doesn't agree then she'd be forced to leave. She succinctly expresses her worst fears when interviewed by the *Orcadian*, the local newspaper, 'I was harassed and menaced out of my job.'

When I accompany Mum to Inverness on what is to be her last access visit to Penny and Poppy, only Poppy turns up. It is the first time I've seen her in over a year, and she has since started school. But she still seems so small, or maybe her navy blue school uniform is too big. She doesn't speak like she used to, but instead points at the things she wants. The carer with her explains she hasn't spoken properly since she was put into care – over 12 months ago.

*

On the journey home from the access visit my stomach churns with a hollow sadness as Orkney's landscape appears over the watery horizon; flat, isolated and without protection from the vicious elements. I look over at Mum and gently tap her arm; she turns to me, as if woken from a deep sleep.

'Mum, I'm really sorry, but I don't want to come back to Orkney. I never want to go back there!' I cry.

Her large brown eyes shine with tears, like she already knew what I was about to say. 'But where will you go?'

'I don't know yet. I'm not sure it matters, as long as it's as far away from here as possible.'

'But why all of a sudden—'

'No!' I interrupt. 'It's not just seeing Poppy like that today that's upset me, it's everything! There's no chance of the children ever coming back, it's only you that refuses to see it. And now Judith Hope's been forced out, we're back to the beginning,' I reply, desperately trying to ignore the feeling that I'm deserting Mum when she needs me most.

Seeing Mum's sad face, I continue trying to justify my decision. 'It's the drudgery of nothing ever getting better for our family. I need to go somewhere with a possibility of happiness. I want to be around normal people. People who don't know anything about me and not be seen as just one of those screwed-up W children. I just want to be somebody new!' I rant.

Mum nods. 'I understand. It's just I'm going to miss you.'

We grip each other in a long silent hug.

'I'll miss you too, but I wish you didn't have to keep fighting, it's just so bloody pointless,' I add bitterly.

'I don't have a choice, Esther, I'm their mother. But you do, so you're right, you must go. Anyway that criminologist, Dr Butler, is coming up again from London tomorrow and he'll help. This could be the turning point we've been waiting for!'

I wearily nod. 'Yes, Mum, hopefully it will be,' I say, not believing it for a minute.

Later, Mum is on the phone with Pete Dockle. She relays that I'm desperate to get away from Orkney and he suggests I move down to London. He adds helpfully that he knows somebody who runs a nursing agency and they are always on the lookout for care assistants. He promises to have a word and line me up an interview. I'm excited at the thought of going to London, since I was eight years old I've harboured a fantasy about running away there. It started when I watched Princess Diana getting married in St Paul's Cathedral. It childishly flits through my mind that I might even meet her. Putting silly thoughts aside, I've heard people say you can go to London and completely disappear and that's what I need to do; I have to start life again – as a nobody. But this time, I intend to keep it that way, and that means being on my guard and not letting people get close.

A week later I'm waving goodbye to Mum and family friends. As upset as I am at leaving Mum, a bigger part of me is happier to be putting space between me and the cesspit that is Orkney. I watch her faded brown slopes and drizzly grey skies disappear and welcome the sign for John O'Groats. From there I take a train to Inverness and make my way to the pub, where I've arranged to meet up with Adam.

The familiar stench of stale beer, sweat and his bloodshot eyes remind me how desperate our life together used to be and for the first time I am happy we broke up.

We share a few lagers and recall how we met and fell in love. After a few too many, Adam gets emotional and breaks down. 'Look, Esther, I've thought about this a lot and, well, I forgive you!'

I struggle to see him straight, I think I know what he's talking about – but I need to hear him say it. 'You forgive me! What for?'

He grins stupidly. 'I forgive you for, you know … being you! And the family you come from. I thought we could get back together and move somewhere, like you wanted. But we wouldn't tell people who you are, obviously!'

I wait and wait until the silence becomes deafening. I don't know how to answer him. My mind is working out how I feel about what he's saying. Should I change my plans? Does him now forgiving me and being okay with who I am make everything all right?

'But Adam, I didn't do anything wrong,' I finally say.

'I know you didn't,' he replies, cocking his head, in a let's pretend kind of way, 'but you didn't tell me who you were. You weren't honest with me!'

With barely suppressed irritation, I snap, 'But you know why I didn't. I was scared. I didn't think you would still love me. And I was right, wasn't I?'

He grins again, like this is old news. 'Not exactly, it was just a lot to take in. But I think I could be okay with it all now.'

I should be relieved. I wished so hard and waited so long to hear those words – but now I'm not sure they mean a thing. Suddenly all the time I've wasted hits me. All those months trying to get this man's love but, more than that, his acceptance. His message is loud and clear: he will love me, as long as I pretend I'm not me. And I realise with a mixture of joy and sadness that I don't think that's enough for me any more.

'Say something,' he cajoles, 'it isn't too late, is it?'

I look at him, all drunk and desperate, and my anger dissolves to pity. I am moving on from his hold over me and he is scared. 'No, Adam,' I reply gently but firmly. 'I don't want you to leave your home and family for me.'

'But it wouldn't just be for you, it would be for me too! I need to go somewhere else and make a fresh start. I could stop the drinking in a new place. I know I could!' he promises desperately.

'I'm sorry,' I begin, and he drops his head, like I've already ended my sentence.

At the station, Adam grasps my hands in his and promises to write every day. The sounds of trains and tannoy announcements fill the gap, while he nervously awaits my response. 'Me too,' I reply half-heartedly. 'Is that my train?' I leap up as a train sweeps alongside us.

His hands fall from mine. 'No, it isn't! You can't wait to get going, can you? I bet you won't even miss me?' he accuses.

'Of course I will,' I reply. 'It's just I thought we should ... you know, both get on with our new lives.'

'Fine,' he says, slumping back on the bench. 'So this is it then?' he asks, folding his arms across his chest and pursing his lips. His voice is rising and I feel people beginning to stare. Adam never let being in public stop a good argument.

'I do everything I can for you. I even try to give up drink! But what does it get me? Fuck all!'

'I didn't ask you to give up drinking for me,' I mumble, unable to resist the same old bait. 'Look,' I try to reason, 'it never works out with us, we're just too different!'

'You're too bloody different, you mean.'

'Fine, Adam,' I reply hotly, 'it's me. The problem is always me.'

'Yes, it is you. You're the reason we broke up! Just face it, Esther, you're not capable of a proper relationship. What I need is a nice normal girl!'

My stomach falls and my eyes water; he knows how much that will hurt.

'Well, I need to find myself someone whose not a loser drunk!' I retort.

'I'm better than your lot at any rate.'

I look at him, feeling swollen with anger and spite. 'What do you mean my lot? It's you that's the alky!'

He's hurt, but he hasn't given up yet. 'Well, it's better than being a druggie,' he shoots.

'I'm not a druggie, you dickhead!'

'No,' he replies, 'but your bezzie mate up at the castle was. The dark beggar girl who ODed the other week! She couldn't even be a proper druggie,' he snorts contemptuously.

He knows he has won from my expression. An icy sadness crawls all over me – I know he means Daisy. I recall her squashy sad face and prediction, 'Same way as me mam, street, drugs, then dead!'

Tears burst from my eyes. 'Fuck off, Adam, you fucking bastard. Just fuck off!' I shout, turning away.

As the sleeper train to my new life pulls into the station, it suddenly hits me: I'm 18 and travelling to a huge strange city where I don't know anyone and I'm scared to death. Sensing my panic, Adam offers to come with me. And for a moment I wish all the badness that's cleaved a gulf between us had never happened. Can't we simply be two young lovers at the beginning, with all our memories still to make? But just as quickly I remember and tear my eyes away. 'No, it's best we both have a new start.' I regret my quick response, as now we must wait together for the train to pull off. 'Look, Adam, you're tired, why don't you go home?' I ask hopefully.

'No, I want to wave you off,' he insists.

I wonder how he can't see that I'm already miles away.

After a rickety overnight journey, the train pulls into London Euston at 8 a.m. Coming from the tiny island of Orkney, with a resident count of less than 20,000, to the middle of London's morning rush hour, with a population of over seven million, is mind-blowing. I'm a spinning top as colours, lights and sounds blend into one. People march through me, eyes focused forwards, on their destination. Cars beep their horns and bright neon signs wink at me from every direction. As instructed, I distractedly make my way to the underground, which is a dusty reflection of the world above. Finally, over an hour late, after following directions from people too busy to stop, I report to the London Cares Agency just off Oxford Street.

'Hello, darling!' Dale Jones, the manager of the nursing agency, extends a soft hand and greets me in a dramatic whisper. I hand my application over and he gestures to the chair in front of his desk, 'Take a seat.' Catching the dangling half-moon spectacles from the fine golden chain around his neck, he delicately places them upon his nose and examines my application. I watch his eyes move across the page and my stomach lurches nervously as I wait to be told whether I'm good enough. I'm desperate for a cigarette, but I make do with the second-hand smoke from the long slim one Dale absentmindedly taps on the edge of a crystal ashtray. Finally he looks up and takes a sip from an over-large china cup, before beaming me a smile: 'Well, you've certainly done this sort of work before, haven't you?'

'Yes,' I nod.

'But tell me, what kind of work are you after? The elderly or those with mental health problems, or more general nursing in hospitals?'

'I'll do anything,' I stammer, surprised at being asked my preference.

Dale Jones accepts me into his agency and it's straight to work. The phone call could come at any time, so I need to be ready to respond. As I'm leaving for the nurses' residence, where I'll live, Dale calls after me, 'Oh, Esther, there isn't anything you need to tell me, is there? No nasty secrets lurking about, from your past? You know, reasons you might not be allowed to work with vulnerable people?'

I think of Orkney Social Work Department and their allegations that accuse me and my whole family of being child abusers and satanic sex fiends. The police keeping surveillance on us, and the fact that I was very nearly charged with kidnapping my sister, Bella. I momentarily wonder whether I should try to explain myself. Should I say something like, 'Yes ... well, I might have been accused of something by someone, but I'm not really sure what it is. Or who it is I'm supposed to have done something to. The Orkney Social Work Department are vague about these things. But then they're allowed to be. Allegations can be made up casually and used as evidence, don't you know? So perhaps the answer is, more a maybe!' Realising how ridiculous I would sound, when I can't decipher it myself, I firmly reply, 'No, nothing I can think of.'

'Okay,' Dale replies, before adding with a laugh, 'You'll go far in this game, if you really are willing to do anything.'

And I am. I take all the jobs the agency gives me and do anything they ask. I'm just grateful they don't care who I am or where I'm from. All they want from me is to turn up at the right address on time, work hard and cause no hassle. And I make sure to do different jobs all over London – so people don't get to know me.

When I meet people, I stick to the same cover story. I'm an 18-year-old girl who lived in Scotland before I moved here. Thankfully I'm average in every way, looks, height and build, with medium-length wavy brown hair and hazel-coloured eyes. I have a couple of safe subjects I can talk freely about. One is clothes, although to see me you wouldn't know it, as I mainly rotate two mint green care assistant uniforms on top of jeans. I can also talk about make-up – I'm not supposed to wear any to work, but I smear on a little sparkly eye shadow and a dab of lip gloss. If I'm questioned about my family, I can say I'm one of four children, two brothers and one sister. If they pry further, I'll tell them my mum is a single parent and she lives far, far away in a tiny cottage, on a distant island – the furthest north you can go. Saved for last, which usually stops further probing, I'll tell them my dad is dead. He died when I was very little, and no, I don't remember anything about him.

I phone Mum from London often, but rarely hear good news. The inquiry into Orkney's alleged ritualistic satanic sex abuse ring is over and they have reported their findings. The report recommends 194 changes to the social work law. These recommendations are designed to form the basis for a comprehensive and radical review of the child care system in Scotland. Hopefully, the report will help those who come after us, but for my family it's too little, too late.

Lord Clyde, who presided over the inquiry, stated that there should still be an emergency place of safety order. It will allow social workers to remove children from their parents and take them to a place of safety. But, he stressed, the only occasion it should ever be used is when there is a real, urgent and immediate risk that the child is going to suffer significant harm. Then the parent or guardian should have an opportunity within the next seven days to have the order varied or cancelled.

He pointed out that social workers should not have interfered with the correspondence of letters, cards and presents, and children should be encouraged to write home. He also said there were inevitable dangers to have the same interviewers investigating both our children and the other families' children.

But what Lord Clyde was especially damning of was the way the information had been taken from the children to prove the existence of a satanic sex ring. The leading questions used demonstrated that the social workers already believed the allegations and were only seeking corroboration, without a strategy to deal with denials. He concluded by saying the Social Work Department were wrong to snatch the other families' children. The inquiry has taken over 11 months and cost over 6 million pounds, but it discovered nothing about my family – the family who began it! Adding insult to injury, Renee Stubbs takes voluntary redundancy – no price paid or penance for the irreparable damage she caused. She can just disappear off to a new life, free to terrorise children about dickies and fannies whenever the fancy takes her.

Hearing the bad news from home makes me even more determined to make a success of my new life in London. It feels like it's going well. I get loads of work and a couple of the old people's homes have started asking for me personally. I quickly get a reputation for doing the horrible jobs – the ones other care assistants won't do.

I've only been in London a couple of months when I'm booked to do a bed bath for a Dr Brown in Paddington. Nobody likes doing Dr Brown's bed baths as he's got a fierce reputation as a grumpy and particular old man who works his care assistants like dogs. I get nervous going on new jobs, but it's even worse when you hear negative things about a placement before you even arrive. I phone the agency, panicking. 'I've never done a bed bath,' I fluster.

'Look, darling,' Dale replies, 'just wing it. I'm sure Dr Brown will put you right – he knows exactly what he likes!'

Torrential summer rain had continued from the night before, so when I arrive at Dr Brown's house, I'm late and soaked through. The Asian girl who answers the door looks about the same age as me, so I'm surprised when she introduces herself as Dr Brown's assistant. She explains she used to do his bed baths, but now she's been promoted, she doesn't have to. But she helps me undress him and we hoist him up to a sitting position. I look away as they share a kiss before she disappears from the room. I steal a panicked glance at his thin, hairless body, wondering where the hell I should start. But he fixes me with watery grey eyes and instructs me exactly on how I'll perform his bed bath. I'm to use colour-coded flannels on different parts of his body. The water has to be almost unbearably hot and soapy and I'm not to wear gloves. I'm to scrub him in a circular motion, starting at the top of his head and work my way down to his feet. At first I rub gently as I'm nervous I might tear his papery skin, but he irritably orders, 'Harder!' His eyes follow my every move and when I accidentally stray past a body part with the wrong-coloured flannel, there's a gruff, 'Uh uh, wrong flannel, try again!'

After nearly two hours of this back-breaking work, I'm finally down to his feet. He allows me to sit at the end of his bed for what turns out to be the most disgusting part. Scrubbing the dead skin from his heels before sliding a hot soapy cotton bud behind each cracked yellowing toenail, I'm relieved to be finally drying him and am about to dress him when he unsteadily reaches into his bedside drawer and pulls out a large bottle of moisturising lotion.

CHAPTER SEVENTEEN

Princess Diana would have saved us

This morning's bed bath had been one of the worst mornings I've had since I've been in London, but this afternoon was going to be the best!

It's 11.30 by the time I'm riding the tube back to the nurses' residence. I'm mindlessly scanning a discarded newspaper when I read that Princess Diana is going to be at the Café Royal in Piccadilly this afternoon at 2 p.m.! Princess Diana in real life, just written in a newspaper, like that's normal! Since the first time I saw Princess Diana, she was my heroine. When she stepped down from the golden horse-drawn carriage in her gigantic frilly white wedding dress, with the longest train I'd ever seen, Princess Diana became, for me, a true fairy-tale princess.

After a journey that feels like it takes an eternity, I arrive at Piccadilly. I find the Café Royal. It's a proper royal-looking building, castle-like, built from huge sand-coloured stone with a glittering golden double-door entrance set inside dark wooden frames. A few people are already waiting and, over the road, police officers unload crash barriers from the back of a van. So it is true, she really is coming! It's 12.30 now, so there's only one and a half hours to go, and she'll be here! My nervous energy makes waiting around impossible, so I wander around Piccadilly without seeing a thing.

When I return, there's over 20 people gathered and almost as many press and police. I get myself positioned as near to the Café's entrance as I can and grip onto the crash barrier. More and more people turn up. Some know she's going to be here and they bring flowers, while others ask who's coming and, when told, join the crowd. But I'm expecting someone to come out of those golden doors at any minute to announce that there's been a mistake. They'll say, 'Go home and don't be so silly.' It can't be true, can it – Princess Diana in real life?

I was eight years old and living in Orkney, on an island called Rousay, while the Royal Wedding was happening in a beautiful big church in a magical faraway land called London. It was then that I realised there was another world, separate from mine, and it was a wonderful one. It was where dreams came true, and I wished that some day I would run away there. Diana looked and acted exactly how a princess should. She wore a sparkly jewelled tiara upon her head and smiled and waved to her cheering crowds – I was captivated. I read everything I could about her, discovering that, as well as being breathtakingly beautiful, she was also caring, just like a true princess. Looking at her sometimes, I could almost believe magic was real and maybe, one day, I could grow up into a princess, like Diana. But then Dad would call me his princess while he was doing dirty stuff on me, and I knew I could never really be a princess, because dirty stuff isn't in fairy tales. But if Princess Diana had found out about my life, she would have saved me, and my brothers and sisters.

Loud whispers say Princess Diana is inside the dark black car being driven towards us. The car shimmers as the cameras flash and police officers on walkie-talkies surround it. There's a tight pressing on my back as collective excitement from the crowd propels us into the barriers. The car crawls past and it's in that moment I get my first real live glimpse of her. From the back seat of the car, her hair is a golden halo, and her big, blue eyes look up at me, while a little smile plays on her glossy pink lips.

The car stops and a dark-suited man gets out, leans back and opens her door. The bubble of quiet waiting bursts into frantic noise. Multicoloured action is released from every direction, 'Diana, Diana, ma'am, ma'am!' She's much thinner and taller than in pictures, and faster: she's up and out from the car in one move. As always, she's elegantly dressed – today in a slim-fitting light beige jacket and skirt suit, matched with tan shoes and handbag. The wall of photographers jostle and surge towards her. 'Ma'am, ma'am, ma'am, this way. Diana, this way, ma'am, ma'am.' She gives them a little smile and wave, before turning to us, her eager crowd. And suddenly there's only a little sea of stretched-out wriggling hands between us. I don't put mine forward. I need to hold on to the crash barrier as my legs have turned to jelly and threaten to buckle, but I'm happy just to study her this close, in real life. I stare up at the familiar face. It's deeply tanned and much pointier close up, while those massive blue eyes are crinkly at the corners and seem sad and watery, as if tears could tip over the rim at any moment. She is thanking the woman next to me for a little bunch of pink roses and shakes the hands of a couple of other people before turning in the direction of the Café. I have really seen her, at long last, and she is real. I didn't imagine her, she was in front of me. But at the very last moment she stops and turns back, she looks right at me and offers me her hand. The noise and the crowd melts away like the tide, and it is just her and me here. Those beautiful sad blue eyes smile at me. 'Hi, how are you?' she asks. No words come out. I just about manage to lift my lead-heavy hand and it is pressed inside the silky softness of hers. Then her hand slips from mine. She turns away and with a last wave to the cameras, she is gone for ever. The crowds drift away, but I stay for a while, reliving what just happened, treasuring the memory of her warm, soft hand. I'm certain, now more than ever, that Princess Diana would have saved us; she cared about the people that nobody else did.

By the time I return to the nurses' residence I'm exhausted, but happier than I can ever remember. On the whole, I like living here. It's a place for medical people: doctors, nurses and care assistants like me. People don't mix much but it's still nice to hear signs of life. When I first arrived, the only person I spoke to was a gentle little Chinese doctor who lived in the room next to mine. His arms were always folded over his chest as if protecting himself and he kept his head humbly bowed. We both did night duties so we could avoid the human contact we struggled with. Seeing each other as we left for work, rested and ready, we'd wish one another an easy night and go our separate ways. The following morning, tired and messy, we'd stick to the same script. He would ask, 'Did you have a good night?' 'Yes, good thanks,' I'd reply.

But anything can happen behind these thick dark wooden doors. I had been here less than a month when the gentle little Chinese doctor committed suicide. He used his own belt to hang himself on the built-in wardrobe. He must have fallen gently, because I never heard a sound. It turned out I probably knew him better than anyone here, but even I never knew his name. It takes me instantly back to my own suicide attempt and my family's situation, which I know are somehow one and the same. The heartache I have caused flattens me beneath a rock-heavy slab of despair and I envy how he succeeded where I failed.

For a few days after his death, people spoke to one another. It was like they were scared and trying to figure out why he did it, in case it was catching. Was it over-work? Was it lack of pay? Or was he depressed? The possibilities were endless. And then we all started talking about everyday things, like the weather or work, and I sort of liked it for a while; I even made a friend or two. But then I remembered that it's better not to let people get close. I got frightened and wanted to hide back behind my own thick dark door.

When I call Mum for our regular weekly chat from the phone in the corridor, I notice immediately that her voice sounds thick and gluey. 'What is it, Mum, what's wrong?' I ask, concerned.

'They've got Penny and Poppy,' she sobs hysterically.

'What do you mean "got them", who has got them?'

As Mum struggles to calm down, in the background, Mercy, a nurse that I'm friendly with, and a male nurse named Gaz, who looks like Herman Munster, have a disagreement over him using her pans. 'Well there's no harm done is there?' Gaz argues. 'If you leave them in the kitchen, why shouldn't I use them?'

'That's not the point, Gaz! They're my pans. You can't just use other people's stuff! You should at least ask first …'

I watch them, controlling my own urge to cry.

'The Social Work Department,' Mum finally gets out. 'They've managed to force through the adoption and taken them for good. I'll never be able to hold my little girls again, it's all over!'

By this point, Mercy and Gaz have moved off, so I let myself cry for Poppy and Penny, for Mum, and for all of us. Mum explains how Orkney Social Work Department misled us as they must have been planning this for ages. When she's finished, I beg her, 'Mum, just leave Orkney now, please, this is too much. They'll never give you the children back. You have to give up.'

'Don't you think I wish I could? You'll never understand, Esther, not until you have children of your own. Giving up isn't an option!' Mum replies sharply, before continuing, 'Anyway this is pay back for how I let your Dad abuse you all. I deserve this agony. It's all my fault,' she howls.

'No, Mum,' I angrily retort, 'this isn't anyone's fault except Mona Drone's and the Social Work Department up there. She was determined to get the children into care, no matter what you did. You couldn't have stopped them, nobody could.'

Mercy is my best friend here, but when she comes to my room later to bitch about Gaz using her pans, I don't confide that my two youngest sisters have been adopted and I might never see them again. I don't tell anyone – I've learnt my lesson about trusting people. Nobody knows who I was before I came to London, and that's the way I intend to keep it.

But, living at the nurses' residence has made me feel more normal than I ever have before as it seems most people here are running away from something. Gaz, who's in the room just across the corridor from me, is running away from a bitch of an ex-wife. A homosexual Pakistani doctor – my side of the corridor, three doors down – has run away from his hometown of Leeds to escape an arranged marriage. Grace, an Irish nurse and religious fanatic – room next to the main bathroom – is rumoured to have run away from a mental hospital in Ireland from where she apparently stole a nurse's identity that she now uses.

Even Mercy herself, opposite side, four doors down, is on the run from her past. It took a while before Mercy told me the truth about herself. On the outside, Mercy will talk to anyone, whether they like it or not, in her fast, punchy voice. Her round brown eyes glitter cheekily when she's got a bit of juicy gossip. Her long colourful braids will flick through the air, as she throws her head back, releasing bursts of raucous laughter. I had always assumed she was a happy, independent career woman, who had chosen to live at the nurses' residence. So I was shocked when she told me that at 36 she believes she's too old to be here. She angrily spat that she was supposed to be married with children by now and living in a proper house. But here she is, living in a tiny rented room, slogging her guts out trying to build a career out of a job she hates, in a filthy city she can't stand. I was taken aback by her outburst and couldn't think of anything to say, except to limply ask, 'Well, why don't you move back home?'

'It would be too painful!' she replies, her voice faltering.

She'd been living at home with her mum and her dying father for the last four years, and just two days after his funeral, she moved here. She needed to get out. She and her mum have never got on and they couldn't live together, especially once Mercy's dad was dead. He was the cushion between them. She has two sisters, but they didn't help like she thinks they should have. Instead, as a nurse, it fell on her shoulders and she couldn't have a personal life, like they did. And now the best years of her life have passed her by. She's been telling me this turned away from me, seated at my little table, staring out from my window. But now she looks at me, her brown eyes all liquid sad, and softly adds, 'But then I wouldn't have had all that time with my father, and I wouldn't change that for the world.'

I look away, desperate to reach some safe ground – I hate people talking like this.

'I'm sorry, Esther,' Mercy adds, 'I wasn't thinking. Of course you must miss your dad too?'

For a moment it nearly all falls out. How she's wrong. She's been fooled – all dads are evil. There are no nice ones. But I exhale and the moment passes. 'No,' I forcefully reply. 'I've told you before, Mercy, I never knew my dad, he died when I was very little. Anyway, I've got to get a few hours' kip before my night duty,' I add to bring an end to this torturous conversation.

It was a harsh bright September morning when my new life in London ended. Perhaps I had got too comfortable and even bordered on feeling normal. Maybe five months in one place is all I can hope for before being found out for the fraud I am. Returning to my room after an eventless night duty, I discovered a small white card had been posted under my door. That card would change everything.

Turning it over, I feel the blood drain from my face. It's from Marylebone Police Station. It invites 'Esther Black' to 'Come into the station, at your earliest convenience, for a chat regarding a confidential matter. Alternatively, we shall try calling again tomorrow, around 4 p.m.'

I quickly check the corridor, before locking myself in. Was I followed home? Are they watching me now? Dropping to all fours, I crawl to the other side of my room where, reaching up, I yank the cord bringing down the blind to cover my window. Too much breath catches in my throat as I try and work out how many people saw this card being delivered.

The lump in my throat turns to tears, which land and distort the message I'm reading and rereading. What have I done, what have I done, what have I done? How can something this small ruin everything? 'And I'm not Esther Black any more,' I mutter bitterly to myself, ripping the card into the tiniest of pieces. I pull out old milk cartons and cereal packets from my bin and bury the paper flakes beneath all the other rubbish.

The police catch the bad people to protect the good people, don't they? Well then – that makes me bad! My whole life's been about running and hiding; I don't know another way. But I don't want this life any more – I've got nowhere to run to! I was happy in London, I didn't think I'd ever be tracked down here. I thought it was too big and there were too many people. I've had enough of the view from over my shoulder and feeling scared. I'm not going back, I'm never going back – I'd rather be a nobody than be that somebody. But if I'm being chased, what am I supposed to do?

I can't do anything right now – I need to sleep. Peeling off my sweaty care assistant uniform, I slip on a clean T-shirt. Reaching under my mattress, I get my bottle and fill a cup two-thirds full with vodka and top it up with orange – it'll help me sleep. The night shift has tired out my body, but now my mind won't stop racing. I hear footsteps out in the corridor, is that them? Are they out there waiting for me to come out? I gulp the bitter drink in two easy mouthfuls and take an extra nip from the bottle, for luck. I'll probably just lay here like a caged animal, listening and waiting.

Despite everything, I fall into restless slumber and wake with a start on sheets damp from my sweat. It feels like I've only been asleep for minutes, but when I read my watch through blurry eyes, I discover that it's nearly 3 p.m. Scrambling from my bed I know I need to get out of here now! The police are probably already on their way. But when I leave London, where will I go?

Twenty minutes later I'm pushing the exit door from the corridor when I'm startled by a sharp squeak of hinges. 'Esther?'

I spin round to Mercy, leaning from the doorway to her room. She looks me up and down. 'I thought you were on night duties this week, why you going to work now?'

I impatiently explain about promising to go in early, while she stares suspiciously. 'Well, okay,' she says slowly, before excitedly adding, 'but you have remembered our double date tomorrow night, with Steve and Dan, haven't you?'

'Yes of course,' I lie, 'but seriously, Mercy, I've really got to go, I'm already late!'

My life before the little white police card filters back to me. It had got so simple. Outside of work my life revolved around Mercy and her mission to find me a boyfriend. She thinks I should be going on more dates and putting myself 'out there'. Dan is the latest in a long line of potential boyfriends she's set me up with. She's been out with his mate Steve a couple of times and thinks I'll like Dan. 'Esther, he's gorgeous and perfect for you. He's got blond hair, brown eyes and he's so tall!' I'm not worried, Steve and Dan won't last, they're hospital porters and Mercy is after the main prize – a doctor. I've been on a few of her arranged dates, but they all end the same way, me getting drunk and doing things I regret – sleeping with the guy or wanting more than he's willing to give. Anyway, falling in love is for idiots! But how can I explain that to Mercy since she believes falling in love with the right man is the answer to everything.

I take a different route to work but I still expect a tap on my shoulder. Beads of sweat burst and pop on my forehead, making me clammy and prickle. People watch me suspiciously, like I'm strange. They come up too close behind me, almost touching me as they pass. And even from the other side of the street, they eye me warily, whispering about me to one another. 'Calm down!' I order myself. 'They're just ordinary people, they don't know you!' But it's no use, I need to get away from here, because even if they don't know yet, they suspect. But where? I know one thing for certain, it won't be Orkney!

I'm relieved to be doing my last night duty at Wisteria View, with a great old Irish lady, Colleen. She's always keen to point out that at 65 she's 'been doing this job far too long to be following any up-your-arse rules'. So at night, Wisteria View Old People's Home belongs to us, and we smoke inside and each get a three-hour kip. It's during my sleep time, when I'm racking my brains, that my only escape option hits me. I sneak through to the office and lift the handset.

With trembling fingers, I press out a familiar phone number. My guts churn as I pray my call is answered. Eight rings in and I'm about to give up, when a hoarse male voice answers, 'Hello.'

'Adam?' I whisper urgently. 'It's me, Esther.'

'Esther, what's wrong?' he asks worriedly.

'I need to get out of London!' I hear the query in his voice, so I go on, 'I can't explain now Adam, there isn't time. But I must leave by tomorrow! I was wondering, do you still want to move away together?'

I hear the hesitation in his voice, and desperation wells up in me. 'Yes,' he finally answers, and a tidal wave of relief breaks over me.

My voice now choking, I ask, 'Will you meet me and we can move somewhere else – maybe Manchester?'

When he answers, I hear the smile in his voice: 'I've waited so long to hear you say that, Esther. I'm packing already. I can't wait to see you.'

'Me too,' I lie.

CHAPTER EIGHTEEN

Found

I wind my scarf up around my face before pushing open Wisteria View's exit door on a crisp, end-of-summer morning. Thankfully, there are plenty of people to blend into. Bedraggled party people mingle with energetic joggers while most dolefully plod to or, like me, from work. I watch them all to see if they are watching me as I try to control the rising surges of panic in my gut.

By the time I'm running up the steps to the nurses' residence, I've broken out in a cold sweat. I can't wait to get packed and out of here. I realise now that what's happened is probably for the best, I was getting too close to people, especially to Mercy, and you always get hurt in the end. Rushing through the front door, I crash into Philomena, the nosy cleaning lady, who's bent over vacuuming the porch. I rebound off her small but surprisingly solid frame. She glares up at me, her inquisitive brown eyes made larger by thick oversized glasses. 'You in a big hurry?' her high-pitched broken English accuses, over the whirr of the Hoover.

'Yes, I'm tired, I need to get to bed.'

'Mmm,' she murmurs doubtfully, stamping her vacuum cleaner's off switch. 'Police, they lookin' for you,' she says, eyeing me closer.

'Oh right,' I reply in a mildly interested way, while grabbing the door handle, 'well, I'd better get to—'

'What I say if they come back?' she calls after me.

I don't answer, because I won't be here.

I look around the room I've called home for the past year and experience a pang of sadness at having to leave it. Mixed in with the sadness is regret that this life didn't work out, and anxiety for what lies ahead. Pulling my suitcase from the top of the wardrobe, I flip it open and start throwing things in. My clean clothes and night clothes go in before I start sorting my laundry, all the while trying to convince myself that this time with Adam will be different. People change – I've changed! But my thoughts are cut short by a sharp, unfamiliar rap at my door. I drop an armful of clothes and freeze. All I hear is my ragged breath, which to me sounds like a train; surely they must hear it too?

They are back! With my eyes wide and unblinking, I slowly back up to my bed. I can wait this out! But then I hear a voice joining them. 'She no answer?' Philomena's sharp high voice asks.

Interfering bitch, I silently curse.

'No, it's all right, we'll wait. As you said, she's not long come home from night duty, so she'll probably take a minute,' a woman's voice replies.

'You want I open door?' Philomena offers, rattling her keys.

'No, that really isn't necessary,' a man's voice assertively assures her.

My stomach lurches fearfully, they'll have everyone out there with them soon, and then they'll all know. Bounding over, I unlock my door.

'Hello,' I say pointedly to the policeman and policewoman, before glaring at Philomena who continues to watch curiously.

'Good morning,' says a stout red-haired policewoman. 'Are you Miss Esther Black?'

'Yes,' I answer irritably.

'Well, Miss Black, I'm Officer Turner and this is Officer Bryant. May we come in for a little chat?'

'All right,' I agree, reluctantly widening my door.

The policewoman steps in and takes off her hat, releasing a nest of fuzzy ginger hair. She is followed by a long thin streak of a policeman, who stoops to enter my room. There's an uncomfortable silence as I wait for them to speak.

'You might want someone with you, Miss Black,' Officer Turner says eventually. 'This is a very sensitive matter.'

'No, I'm fine!' I reply steadily, trying to keep my nerves under control.

'Miss Black—'

'My surname isn't Black, it's W,' I snap, sick of hearing her repeat it.

'Oh, I'm sorry, that's what we have on our records,' she replies apologetically.

'It hasn't been Black since my dad was jailed. I've changed it!' I reply waspishly, before quietly adding, 'Sorry. I didn't mean to shout, it's just I hate that name.'

'First of all, I don't want you to worry, Miss W. It's nothing you've done wrong. But I suggest you sit down.'

'Oh, okay,' I say, sinking to the edge of my bed to wait for what Officer Turner has to say.

The policewoman moves closer while the policeman stays

by the door. She gives me a little smile. 'Do you recall attending a school for children with special needs by the name of Oakhill House?'

'Yes,' I reply, surprised to hear her mention Oakhill House in the present, when it feels like a lifetime ago.

'Right,' she says, kneeling in front of me. 'Do you recall a member of staff by the name of Adrian Batty?'

'Yes,' I say again, but this time tightly and my breath quickens, so I swallow hard and bite my bottom lip to stop myself shaking.

'Well, as we speak, Mr Batty is in police custody. Several other girls who also attended Oakhill House have come forward and alleged that he sexually abused them.'

I inhale sharply and stare down at my tensed hands. She continues in a gentle voice, 'So, we just need you to write a statement. Then you'll give evidence, and it will all be—'

'NO!' I shout, stepping over to my window. 'I don't want to make a statement or give evidence. I've had enough!'

Her face is shocked, but I can't explain, so I turn away. I need to get away from them, from myself; I'm itchy and restless. I pull up my blind and watch normal people hurrying here and racing there. Busy people, too busy to stop even though my world has. I jump when I feel her hand on my shoulder.

'Look, Esther, Mr Batty has already admitted sexually abusing you. It's just we need your side—'

'Just go away!' I interrupt sharply without turning around.

There's an unbearable silence, while I wait. Eventually she speaks again, 'Esther—'

'What? What do you want?' I demand abruptly, turning on her.

'Why didn't you tell anyone about this before? Keeping this secret must have been an horrendous burden for you, especially with what happened with your father.'

'I SAID GO AWAY! WHY CAN'T YOU PEOPLE EVER LEAVE ME ALONE?' I scream at her, before dropping to my seat and covering my face with my hands.

I'm vaguely aware of the door clicking, but I'm not alone – I'm with my father.

It's been a secret my whole life – our secret – Dad buried it inside me from when I was very small. When he went to jail, I told the police a little of what he did, but they didn't really understand. How could they? It was the only time he ever loved me, because then I was his good little girl.

During those times, he gives me treats, biscuits and sweets. But they are nothing compared with how he strokes my hair, how he smiles at me and tells me how much he loves me, and how he always will, as long as I don't tell. Then, and only then, I'm daddy's little princess.

The flowers are broken, the pink petals split to pieces. But as Dad closes the curtains, he puts them back together again. I know it will happen, but I still watch, a little bit of me always amazed. Then the clinky clunky of his metal buckle like a horse's saddle, they smell the same too, warm leather. He tells me, 'We're going to have some fun together!' The zip cricks down and I still watch the flowers – like they might change. 'What's Daddy got for his little princess?' Then the sharp smell of wee makes my eyes watery. 'Open your mouth, like a good girl,' he says. Then he pushes it in, hard up to the sides, up and in, until I feel sick trying to get out and the back of my throat hurts. 'There, that's it, good girl.' The pink flowers jumble and the petals scatter while he's stroking my hair. 'That's nice, that's it,' he says. Then the hot salty stuff floods into my mouth. 'Ah, lovely,' he groans. I freeze, as he puts his arms around me and I glimpse his gold tooth smiling at me. 'Daddy loves his little princess,' he says, taking a packet of sweets out of his pocket. He gives me three chocolate toffee sweets, like little presents wrapped in glittery red and silver foil. I've done something good: I've made my daddy happy. He turns and opens the curtains and the flowers once more are broken.

My stomach is hurting hollow, like grating metal on concrete. I need to eat. Breathing fast and watching out, I unsteadily climb the drawer handles that lead to the food cupboard. Up and up until I get to the ledge. Checking around again, I listen hard before slowly pulling open the cupboard door. Momentary happiness flickers up in me at the sight of an open packet of digestive biscuits. With trembling hands, I hurriedly push two big biscuits up and out. Pulling open my trousers, I jam them down inside my pants. I can't believe I've nearly done it and my mouth waters as I can almost taste their sweet crumbliness. I jump down to the flagstone floor, all the while checking and listening. Tiptoeing through to the living room, I plan on hiding in a bedroom to eat them. But my stomach drops at the sight of Dad striding past the living-room window on his way to the front door.

My hunger forgotten, I feel the biscuits snap and crumble, as I fall to the floor. My breath catches in my throat. The sofa isn't far away – should I try to crawl behind it? I hear the sharp metal doorknob twisting. I should be taking the biscuits out and hiding them. But I don't – I can't move. I don't do anything. I'm not only trapped inside the house, I'm trapped inside my body. If he catches me I'll get a beating, but it will be ten times worse if I'm caught stealing food. But still I sit, shaking, watching and waiting. Of course he sees me straight away. 'Come 'ere, Esther, help me off with me boots.'

My head is dizzy as robot-like I go to him. Holding on to the doorframe he puts a booted foot up to me. I grip hold of the heel, like I've done so many times before, but never with stolen food in my pants. I tug and tug until his boot slips off, then I do the other one. 'What are you doing lazing about inside?' he growls accusingly.

'I just … I had to … Mum told me to get her a saucepan,' I lie nervously, my fear mounting.

He eyes me suspiciously. 'Well, you're not doing a very good job, are you?'

I try to think what to say but instead I look down, waiting for my punishment. My body is trembling and I'm sure he knows about the biscuits – Dad knows everything. 'Come with me, I've got a surprise for my little girl,' he says in his happy voice and I know what my punishment will be.

Dread covers me as I follow him to his and Mum's bedroom. He sits on the bed and pats his lap. 'Come on up.' Tears well in my eyes as I try to think of a way out, knowing there isn't one. I climb up and sit frozen; waiting. He puts one arm around my waist and with his other hand, he pulls my pants down, revealing the stolen biscuits. I watch the wall, waiting for his anger. 'What have we got here?' he chuckles and I follow his eyes to the biscuit pieces and crumbs. His mouth is smiling, like he's happy to catch me doing something bad and I feel more scared than ever.

'Take your trousers off, Esther, there's a good girl,' he instructs in a high voice.

I climb down slowly, hoping for Mum or someone to come into the house and disturb him. I roll my trousers down, until my bottom half is naked. He has undone his belt and zip, so his white blue willy is near my face. 'Lie down. There's a good girl,' he whispers. I sit on the bed and open my mouth, hoping he will do the putting his willy in my mouth or even getting me to do the shaking his willy thing – I don't want to do the other one.

'No, lie back properly, all the way down.' Tears roll from my eyes as I awkwardly lower myself to my elbows. Why doesn't someone come in and make a noise? I wonder, but as usual, when this happens, the house is empty and quiet. He gets on his knees against the bed and drags me over to him, so he's between my legs. He starts pushing his hard stubby fingers into me. I hear a sharp gasp from far away and see an 11-year-old girl being pushed further backwards, as her father climbs on top of her. I hear her cry out, as his weight squeezes her. She can't breathe and gets so scared she screams. 'Shush, be quiet. There's a good girl,' her father says. She tenses her body hard, but he forces his thingy in her anyway, spreading burning and tearing inside her. She squeezes her eyes, until she sees only black. 'That's it, that's Daddy's good girl.' She can't move, as he stabs and stabs and stabs before he pulls it out and squirts the sticky stuff on her tummy. 'Aaaahhh!' She can smell him, as he breathes hard. 'Go and get yourself cleaned up,' he orders hoarsely.

It's stingy and achy, all inside my body. After I've washed the sticky stuff off and put my trousers and pants back on, he gives me the remains of the biscuits. 'There you go, you've been a good girl. Now get yourself outside and not a word to anyone,' he winks. I want to be happy that I've made Dad happy, but the pain in my tummy hurts when I walk. I go and sit with Tabitha the goat, in her little pen. I stroke her wiry white hair as I eat the biscuits and her marble eyes follow me – sad and knowing.

A knock at my door jolts me back to my room, at the nurses' residence. Blood pounds in my ears. If that's the police again, I'm going to …

I yank the door open. 'Oh, Mercy, sorry I can't talk, I'm—'

'Well, I'm pleased to see you too, love,' Mercy jokily replies, brushing past me, into my room.

'No, it's just not a good time right now,' I stammer.

Mercy looks worried. 'Philomena told me about the police coming to see you. What did they want?'

I look into her big brown caring eyes. She's been such a dependable friend. I should tell her everything. She might even be able to help. She wouldn't judge me, would she? 'Mercy, I've ruined everything,' I cry, my voice cracking, 'it's all my fault.'

Mercy looks confused, 'How have you ruined everything? What do you mean?'

I return to my senses. Of course she would judge me. She would realise what an awful person I've been and she'd hate me for causing everyone so much pain. She's always thought I was a normal person and I don't ever want to see the shadow of disappointing recognition cross her face. 'No, I'm sorry Mercy, it's nothing.'

She looks baffled. 'It doesn't seem like it's nothing. You're as white as a sheet, like you've seen a ghost.'

And she's right; it is a ghost – from my past. Panic builds inside me, I can't handle this. I need to get away. I pick up the clothes I dropped earlier and continue throwing them in the suitcase. 'I'm leaving London, Mercy,' I announce.

'Esther,' Mercy says sternly, 'just calm down. It can't be as bad as that. Tell me what the police wanted you for?'

'It isn't the police Mercy, it's just … I need to get away.'

Mercy looks at me, anxiously. 'Will you go home?'

'No,' I reply defiantly, 'I won't ever be going back there. I want to go somewhere else. I think I just need a fresh start.'

I can't confide in Mercy the shattering realisation that has dawned on me. What everyone else will discover if I testify against Adrian Batty: that I am to blame for it all. My not being able to tell has ruined everything. I have caused other families to have their children taken from them. There would never have been a £6 million inquiry. But, worst of all, it was me that has broken up my family for ever.

There is a tightening in my chest, as I look into Mercy's hurt eyes.

'Right, well …' Mercy's voice trails off before she adds, 'Oh, before I forget, your mum called.'

Mum sounds excited when I ring. 'Are you sitting down, Esther?'

'Yes, why, what's happened?' I reluctantly ask, sure I am about to hear something awful.

'They are letting your brothers Lawrence, Sam and Robin come home! And, it looks as if they might let Holly come home as well!' she replies triumphantly.

'Wow, Mum, that's amazing! But … but I don't understand,' I stutter. 'What … what about Willow and—'

'I know, isn't it incredible?' she laughs.

I should be happy. 'So, so ... how?' I stammer.

The thing that we have all wished for, for so long, is coming true, but it doesn't feel right. The choked-up message coming down a phone doesn't feel big enough. Shouldn't there be some big announcement made somewhere? 'Well,' she explains excitedly, 'Willow is staying put for now, but hopefully that's only a matter of time. It's down to a solicitor from the Child Law Agency. He contacted me and suggested the kids get their own solicitors. Their solicitors appealed on their behalves, and got the supervision orders discharged at their panels. Stupidly simple when it came down to it. After all the wasted years of fighting,' she adds wearily, summing up how I feel.

'But wait a minute Mum, they are all still under 16, aren't they? What about the sibling abuse allegations? How come they are being allowed home now?'

Mum sighs resignedly. 'I don't know. I don't want to look back at what's happened and ask why. I'm just grateful they're letting them come home now.'

Despite the good news, outrage burns inside me at the injustice of it all. I recall Mona Drone's determination to get my brothers and sisters into care, no matter what. I seethe, thinking about how our family has been destroyed for ever by everything Orkney Social Work Department have put my family through. The allegations of abuse used as if they were indisputable evidence. The ridiculous allegations of a satanic sex ring. The other families getting their children back to worldwide fanfare while ours remained lost to us. And then the cherry on the cake: the inquiry that discovered nothing about the real reasons it all happened in the first place.

Now my siblings are creeping home under the cover of darkness, no chartered aircraft, no welcome home bagpipe player or cheering crowds for them, only the echoing squeak of their trainers on shiny airport floors followed by silent cuddles and muffled sobs. 'How dare they?' I storm. 'How can they be allowed to do this and get away with it? This isn't right! No, Mum, you must fight—'

'Esther,' Mum interrupts. She sounds exhausted. 'It's you that's been saying I should just let go of it all and not keep fighting. Besides, I haven't got anything left. Please, let me be happy with this,' she adds pitifully.

'But Mum,' I protest, but then my anger subsides and I see it from her point of view. For the last three years her whole life has been dedicated to fighting Orkney Social Work Department, while everyone else has slowly but surely given up, realising you can't fight a system that plays by its own rules. Part of me is relieved for her that now, maybe, she can start rebuilding her life.

But what I don't confess to Mum is, I more than understand her not wanting to trawl over the past. As I'm not ready to face what Adrian Batty did and more importantly, what I didn't do. It will be over a decade before I'm forced to go back and confront everything.

Afterwards, I ring Adam. I hate how he excitedly says he's been waiting for my call. I squirm further as his happy voice shrinks to wounded bewilderment. I apologise, explaining I couldn't run away with him. I reason to him that it would never have worked out anyway, there is just too much water under the bridge. I need a new start, somewhere with new people – so maybe I, too, can become someone new. He quietly agrees, adding, 'I could never have left Inverness anyway, it's too late for me to start again.'

The following morning Mercy and I share a tearful goodbye at Piccadilly tube station before I board a train to Cardiff. One of my brothers lives there and I'll stay with him while I go to the local college, to finally begin my future.

Part Five

2006–2009

CHAPTER NINETEEN

The baby boy who saved my life

I'm on a night out celebrating my pass marks in five GCSEs when I meet David. I'm not looking for a relationship but this feels different. I'm a 21-year-old girl, desperate to escape my past and unsure where my future is headed. Meeting David, who is 20 years older than me, becomes the best thing in my life. He gives me a stability and security I have never known. In a life where I have never had anyone to depend on, over time he becomes the one person I can trust and turn to in my many times of self doubt.

Because of what happened with Adam when he found out about my past, it takes me three years before I dare confide in David. I reveal everything about my abusive childhood and my father going to jail for it. My time in Oakhill House and Crouchend Alley, and my brothers and sisters being taken into care. And of course I tell him about the infamous satanic sex ring trials. I even tell him about Adrian Batty, although I wasn't able to testify against him, I often wondered whether he got his comeuppance. A couple of years later I'd contacted Eliza, a friend at Oakhill. She told me that she and three other girls had bravely testified against Adrian Batty. He had received five years for child sex abuse offences. Even down the phone it brought back terrifying memories of testifying against my father. It had been one of the most difficult things I had ever done and it had only ever seemed to make my life worse.

In short, I tell David everything, and to my relief he still loves me.

I finally go to university and by the age of 30, I have completed a degree in design. But when it came time for the gown and mortarboard pictures I had dreamed about for so long, I come down with a bad case of flu, so was unable to attend. Ironically, I don't mind as much as I thought I would – I have achieved my degree and that, in itself, is enough for me.

I have only ever wanted two things in life: a degree and a family. So, with my degree in the bag, my attention turns back to having my longed-for baby at last. Ever since my family was ripped apart and I felt I was forced into having an abortion, there has been a hollow ache in the pit of my stomach that I feel can only ever be healed by having a child of my own.

Pregnancy hormones and poisonous fears from my past cast terrifying shadows over the nine months I carry my son. My moods are unpredictable and frightening for me, let alone those around me. I struggle daily, and sometimes hourly, to believe I can do this. And even if I do succeed in having the baby, will the authorities and doctors let me keep him? Or will they try and convince me to have another abortion, or even take him from me after I've given birth?

The baby boy is held up to me by latex-gloved hands. His pink body is bathed in the startling white of the operating theatre. I am surprised how clean he looks. I'd been expecting more blood and gore. His mouth is turned down and his eyes are screwed tight against the blinding light – he isn't happy. He made a sharp squeal when he first came out, but now he seems strangely quiet.

'Here's your boy, he's a big one,' says the man in the surgeon's mask holding him to me.

'I would bet he's over nine pounds,' adds the woman surgeon, who's just cut him from me.

Yes, he is big, much bigger than I thought he'd be. They expect me to say something, something happy I suppose, but I have no words; they are all somewhere else. Somewhere I can't get to. All that's left for me to think is, whose baby is that and where's mine?

David has gone home for the night and I must have been asleep, because the baby boy wakes me up with his whimpering. It's the dead of night, and quiet, with fuzzy soft lights here and there. Somewhere within me I know I must go to him, or be seen to be going to him. I go to get up, but my head and left arm are the only parts that pull forward as the rest of me is still under anaesthetic. My eyes follow a thin tube coming from between my dead-weight legs to a little yellow bag hooked on a pole – when did that happen? I have the 'call nurse' buzzer next to my left hand. I don't want to use it. I don't want to bother them. But what choice do I have? I gently press it and hear it going off urgently and insistently somewhere up the dark hall. After a minute, a nurse jogs through the doors and up to my room. Turning it off, she hurries to the end of my bed. 'Yes, what is it?' she demands, as if I've interrupted her from something much more important.

Doesn't she know? Can't she hear him? He's all unsettled and his whimpering has become crying!

'Should I do something with him, maybe get him out?'

'No, he can wait and you need to sleep,' she retorts abruptly, before disappearing.

But how am I supposed to sleep? His cries are getting louder and I'm churning up inside. I frantically search around for someone to help. He's going to wake everyone up – I must go to him! Using my one feeling arm, I try to hoist my legs towards his cot, but it's no good, I'll have to lay here useless as he suffers.

An agonising wait stretches out before another patient shuffles by. She's all bent over, holding her stomach, obviously in physical discomfort, but I must take my chance.

'Hello, hi, please could you help me? Would you pass me the baby from that cot?' I ask.

'Yes, of course,' she replies helpfully. She dodders over and bends into his cot, struggling to lift him. But somehow between us, we manage to get him to me. 'Are you breastfeeding?' she asks.

I look down. I've got nothing else to give him, so I nod. She helps me put him to my left breast, and we lie there, the baby boy and me – him suckling away and me paralysed until the morning.

As the ward gets lighter, pins and needles spread feelings through my legs and arm. But it's my brain that's gone all cotton woolly and I can't get to my feelings in there, but maybe that's for the best.

The girl in the bed next to me talks at me. Her name is Chloe. She had her baby girl yesterday. She works out there is eight hours' difference between our babies, hers being the older. This baby boy is feeding hungrily. 'He could suck an orange through a straw!' one nurse said and they praise him and me, but Chloe's baby seems too tired to latch on and the nurses are irritated with her. This is Chloe's first baby; at 8 pound 12 she's a good weight. Chloe has been with her partner for over two years and has worked at Barclays Bank longer ... Chloe never stops talking, nothing important, just chatter, but I like how it fills my head and stops me thinking about what's happening or not happening.

I've looked at the baby boy. I didn't mean to. I just found my eyes heading that way. He's got a big forehead and no real chin and without his snubby nose, he'd look just like a red balloon. He opened his eyes this morning; the seals gently cracked and he slowly rolled the balls, left to right, before the lids fell back down – like he was testing them out. Before I forget myself, I must remember the nothing feeling is best. I mustn't get too used to him. For his sake, as much as mine, because I know they won't let me keep him.

I do the practical stuff, feeding, cleaning and dressing him. A nurse shows me how you wash a baby properly, with cotton wool and warm water; he was wobbly on my forearm – like balancing a jelly. When he is dressed and fed, he falls asleep. So I lay him on my bed, side on, like the old lady nurse said. I gather my towel, soap and toothbrush and in agonising slow motion, I hobble over to the bathroom. All the while, holding onto my heavy stinging stomach. The strip of self-supporting bandage covering the Caesarean gash feels too flimsy. With each pain-filled step it feels as if my stomach might splosh out all over this shiny white hospital floor.

Eventually I'm hunched beneath the warm water, having my first shower in three days when I hear a baby cry. Terror rips through me. That will be the baby boy. I must get back to him! Somebody is stealing him! They must have waited for me to go and they're taking him right now! Ignoring the pain, I pull my nightie over my wet body and shuffle back to my bed. It was the baby boy! His face is bunched up and ruby red! Some fucking idiot took him out of my bed and put him in a swaddling blanket. Then they put him in the cot! How dare they? I reach in and lift him out. 'Shh, shhh, it's okay now, it's all right,' I tell him.

I unravel the tight swaddle blanket, while holding the 'call nurse' button down hard, until one appears, her face worried. 'Is everything okay?'

'No,' I say, glaring at her, 'somebody woke the baby up and tied him inside a blanket and they put him in there.' I point accusingly at the plastic cot.

'Oh, I'm sorry. That was me. It just isn't safe to leave babies in beds. Besides, the doctor needed to check him out, before you take him home.'

I continue staring hard at her smug face and I don't know what to say. Did she just say, 'Before you take him home?' Only I'm not sure, because my head popped from my body and floated up to the clouds.

So are they taking him or not? Because if they are, I wish they'd come for him now; it's getting harder to remember that I'm better off without him. When he goes to a real mum and real family they'll be happy I looked after him so well, but what about him and me? I some-times let myself imagine we could be a family, David, me and the baby boy. We're going home like real families do; we have a safe car seat and all the right baby stuff. Might I be allowed this time?

*

When I get him home he hardly sleeps – he just cries. I think he must know something. I cry too. Cry and don't sleep. It's my memories replaying on a great big cinema screen inside my head. I have thoughts, bad thoughts. Dirty black tracks creeping up on me from behind and banging me in the face, then dissolving to nothing. Everyone thinks I know what to do with this baby. They think I'm like a real mum, but I don't know a thing. I wish I could ask someone. Someone who might know. Someone who wouldn't think I'm stupid. They wouldn't laugh at my silly questions, because they would care about me and they might even love me. Maybe someone like a mum!

But my mum? When I got home from the hospital she rang. I froze and stared at her number on the screen, demanding to be answered. But I couldn't because I didn't know what to say. A couple of weeks ago I wouldn't have been off the phone to her. But everything has got mixed up now.

I wish she wouldn't ring. Can't she disappear for a while? Can she see me trembling, hear my breath that's become so shallow I'm dizzy? Six rings then relief, the answering machine clicks in, 'Esther, it's Mum!' Now, the same words in circles, Mum? Mum? Is it fuck, Mum! She was never a mum! She let him hurt me, every day of my childhood. She let it all happen, it's all her fault! I can't speak to her, not now – we would both regret it!

The baby boy watches me watching the phone. He's trying to work me out. He's all soft and new but he's not proper new, he's been here before – or a baby like him. I can't look at him. I mustn't – I will put all this evil shit in him. The fucked-up bitch I am, feeding it to him directly through my milk, fucking him up good. Soon he'll be as fucked up as me. Who said you can break the chain? Mona Drone once said: 'The abused becomes the abuser.' I hate her with everything I have in me, but what if that fucking bitch was right?

Some days I think I can do this. I must be able to do this. I've waited so long for this and everyone says it's natural. I can take him for walks in the fresh air, in his nice pushchair. I can play with his baby toys with him and bath and moisturise him in pretty-smelling baby products. But then I'm changing his nappy and he's lying there, his little legs flopped open, trusting me completely. I'm focusing hard on the blue rabbit on his white baby-gro, with big floppy ears. 'Be here now, Esther,' I tell myself, 'who's a tired bunny rabbit?' I try to sing, but it's coming back, rising up in me like black poisonous bile. Up my stomach it rises. Up into my chest it's filling, 'it's bedtime bunny,' bite my lip until I taste blood, you're not there any more, Esther. But I can't stop it, it's too strong, it's too heavy, too big and BANG!

Dad's big rough hand holding a shiny metal nappy pin points down between the trusting little baby boy's legs and my tummy is flipping over and over and my feet fold and dig into one another, Dad's big hairy face, smiling, then the tiniest prick of red blood, and the sharpest knife-point scream, baby's crooked legs pulled up tight together, screaming right up in my ears, into my head, a million buzzing bees in every hole to me, my chest pressed down, I CAN'T BREATHE! My throat aching, everything hurting! I can't do this! I can never do this!

Mum got away with it. Dad went to jail, but she never did. She's still out there. She could come for this little baby boy. That fucking, evil, whoring bitch got away with it. Why won't this shit stay in the past? I want to be in this moment, I'm supposed to be enjoying this time! I should be meeting the baby boy's eyes when he looks up for mine. I should be holding him close to me. But I have to look anywhere but down and be anywhere but here.

How can I be going through this agony and he still grows? He's so big, he put on over two pounds this week, just from my milk. 'Thriving,' the health visitor called him. When she'd gone, I kept rereading what she wrote in his little red book: 'He's a happy smiley baby.' Me, someone like me, growing a baby like that!

This baby boy is supposed to be a new beginning, but he's brought my past back with him. I hate how he knows me. His clean blue eyes cut straight through me, slice me open and see all the crazy shit that's writ through me. He knows I'm not right, that I'm not a proper mother. He knows I can't do this and I shouldn't be doing this. Women like me shouldn't have children – we're not capable. Other mums know too, that I'm not normal like them, they sense it. They come from nice families and teach their children nice, normal ways, not the crazy abuse I was taught. I know that's not what I'm supposed to teach him, but that's all I've got. How am I supposed to teach him something else, when that's all I know? I've never needed a mother more than I need one now. I need help with practical stuff, like should I change his nappy after a sleep or leave it on until he's had his next feed? Should I carry him everywhere, because he likes it, or should I insist he stays in his pram? Why does he cry so much, is that normal? Instead I've got loads of books, which don't have the answers to any of my problems.

I answer the phone without thinking one day and it's her. 'Hi, Esther.' I panic and throw the phone. It bounces across the room. I sit trembling, watching the phone that has become her weapon in my own home. I replay how she said my name, and realise I don't recognise her voice any more. It was different and distant, like it was coming from another place. I think she knows that I know that the last 20 years since Dad was jailed have been a lie. Even if I talk to her, I wouldn't know what to say, I don't know her any more.

From the moment he wakes he screams and he's angry with me. Well, I'm angry with him too! He depends on me for everything. Sometimes I wonder if I'm his real mum at all – because if I was, would it all feel so wrong and confusing?

Since we've had this baby boy, David and I don't get on at all. David says it's because I won't sleep and I cry too much and get too stressed. I try explaining in words that become screams that not sleeping isn't a choice and crying isn't a pastime. But how can I tell him that I think I'm going mad?

The baby boy smiles at David, his eyes all crinkly. David is happy and gushes, 'I smiled at him, then he smiled back. It was wonderful!' I watch from outside in the cold, like I'm peeping through the curtains of someone else's house. Something inside me yearns to be inside where it looks warm, but I get scared and it's so much easier this way.

I go in sometimes and check him while he sleeps, just to make sure he is still breathing. His soft, pudgy face is smoothed out from the day's grouchiness. His lashes gently rest on his soft pink cheeks, while his little milky lips are all pouchy. I gently caress his fine downy hair, which even in the night light glitters like spun gold. The tiniest part of me considers waking him to hear the lovely little noises he makes. No – he would scream. I know he does things to purposefully wind me up. He knows exactly when to poo at the wrong time, when we're on our way out or when I go to put him down for a nap or at bedtime. And when I try taking him out to baby groups he cries and there's nothing I can say or do to make him stop – so what's the fucking point?

Where do abused children go when they need to report an abuser? Before I can change my mind, I'm speaking to a tired-sounding woman on the phone at Child-line. I tell her what's happened and explain I need advice on what to do about my mum. She questions me on what happened and when. Then she asks my age. When I've answered all her questions, she seems annoyed, as if I'm making a prank call. 'You do realise this is a phone line for abused children, don't you?'

'Yes,' I reply.

'Well, you're an adult,' she says accusingly. 'If you want to report a crime, go to the police!' and the line goes dead.

Funny her saying I'm an adult, just because I'm over 18. But it doesn't make me feel like one. I'm scared and vulnerable – exactly how I felt as a child.

But the Child-line lady is right. I should report Mum to the police, they'll know what to do with her. I want to tell her first. I don't know why. Maybe I'm still hoping she'll say something that will make everything all right, or maybe I want her to beg for my forgiveness. I don't trust myself to know what to say, so I write it down.

Once the phone's ringing my hands feel clammy and my breathing becomes shallow.

'Hello,' she answers and I speak fast. 'Hello, Victoria, it's Esther. I'm ringing to tell you that I'm reporting you to the police because of what you let Dad do to me and how you neglected me the whole of my childhood!'

There's a heavy waiting. The line starts to crackle. Has she put the phone down? But then I hear her exhale, like she's got too much breath.

'You are right, Esther. What I did was unforgivable and I accept whatever you choose to do about it.'

'I need to speak to someone about a child abuser,' I tell the policeman, calmly.

He asks for details. But it's been locked up so long it comes stumbling out in clumsy confused blocky words. How my dad went to jail in 1987 for physical and sexual abuse against me and my siblings. How throughout the whole of my childhood, Mum sat by and let it happen. How when he was jailed, she should have gone too and she's never been punished. How when later we were put in care, she was still never punished and she's got away with it all. I cry and talk until I've told him everything I can think of. I answer all his questions and give him her full name, phone number and address. The policeman says they'll be in touch soon. Somehow, he makes it all sound normal, like I'm making an appointment to have a tooth taken out. But where is the relief? Where is the end?

I can't go on like this, not sleeping and having screaming rows with David. Late one night, after yet another argument, I confess how my past is taking my life over and I can't cope. 'Esther, you must go to the doctor about this.

Please, even if it's only for Oliver!' David begs, his eyes shiny.

'But the reason I'm not going is for him. Don't you get it? They'll take him off me!' I screech, frustrated at how impossible it all feels.

'They won't, because I won't let them!' David reassures me. 'But if you go mad, they'll take him off you anyway!'

I don't look at the doctor. I don't want to see one more judgemental face, telling me what a bad mother I am. Instead I watch my twisting hands as I admit to the doctor how my whole world is a big pointless nothing. I tell her all I do is cry and I can't sleep. I explain that I don't care about anything. But I know enough not to tell her everything. I don't say how I wonder whether I love this baby boy and I don't mention Mum. When I've finished, I realise I'm crying. I look up to check her face, but all she looks is sad.

'First off, you should feel very proud of yourself. You have just taken the hardest step towards getting better, you came here today, so well done,' she smiles. 'From what you've told me, Esther, I suspect you are suffering from severe post-natal depression. Now, we have a couple of options. You can go straight on to antidepressants. They should kick in in about three to four weeks. But you will need to stop breastfeeding.'

I tell her straight away, that isn't an option – as I need to bond with Oliver – and the Health Visitor said breastfeeding is the best thing for that.

'Well then, I'll arrange for you to have counselling sessions.'

There's usually a six-week waiting list, but she makes some enquiries and manages to squeeze me in for next week.

The doctor can say I should feel proud of myself, until she's blue in the face, because nothing will stop me feeling like a failure. My baby is barely four weeks old and I'm going for counselling. Proof, if any were needed, of how fucked up I am.

CHAPTER TWENTY

If only I had told

The following Tuesday I'm at my first counselling session. Bea, my counsellor, is slim and attractive in a posh hippy way. In her mid-forties, she looks sorted, with shiny olive skin, make-up-free brown eyes, and short dark stylishly messy hair. She wears a couple of those chunky silver rings with turquoise stones that I like but never see in the shops. Leaning back, in her oversize soft lamb's wool jumper, she rests one foot on her knee and a Birkenstocked foot peeps out beneath wide linen trousers. She gives me a little smile as if to say, 'Look how approachable I am.'

I point at the normal, come-to-see-the-doctor chair. 'Shall I sit here?'

'Sit where you like or don't sit. You can even lie down if you feel like it, just relax,' she replies in a smoky red wine voice.

I lower myself into the normal, come-to-see-the-doctor chair. I wouldn't be comfortable wandering around and I've lain on a similar blue paper-towelled bench for other reasons. I can't help wondering if that was a test – have I passed?

'Right,' she begins, 'I suggest we start by deciding what you want from your six sessions.'

She waits for me to speak, but instead I feel my eyes prick with tears. I shouldn't be crying, not in front of a stranger. But it feels safe and she can't judge – can she? I let big, fat, angry, frightened tears tip and slip down my cheeks.

'I'm sorry,' I manage to stammer, before a new wave of sobs hit me.

Bea passes me tissues and makes soothing noises. 'You've nothing to be sorry about. I'm sure you have a very good reason to cry, so let yourself.' And she goes on to say something I will hear repeated many times: 'Let the gate open, Esther, and trust the process.'

But I can't help feeling like an idiot, just sitting here sobbing – aware I'm wasting my counselling time. I tell myself off in my head, but it makes no difference. So I try to explain between sobs. But Bea calmly discourages me from speaking. 'Don't try to talk,' she repeats calmly, 'just open the gate and trust the process.'

Glancing at the clock, I realise I've cried for over half the session – what a waste! Nothing is ever going to get better, especially if I don't explain what the problem is. 'I nearly killed him! I nearly killed the baby boy!'

Suddenly, she is pulling my hands from my face and urgently asking, 'Who, Esther, who did you nearly kill? Your baby, did you nearly kill your baby?'

I stop crying for a moment confused. 'No, not my baby!'

'Esther,' she says solemnly, 'I need you to tell me exactly what happened to the baby.'

I don't want to say it. I know she will hate me. But I can't live with this scared feeling that I might do it again. 'It's just I didn't know how to look after babies when I was seven,' I start defensively.

'Of course, you didn't,' she says, looking surprised.

'Dad told me, "Get up to the loft." I was scared as I climbed the thin ladder up to the triangle room, thinking, what will happen now? Then he brought baby Sam up behind me. Sam was crying and I wanted to put my hands over my ears, but Dad handed him to me. Sam isn't much older than zero, because he hasn't been here longer than we've lived in this house and I think that's only four school weeks. "Get him to sleep!" Dad orders, before shutting the trapdoor. Now me and the screaming baby boy are locked up together. I rock him like I think will make him go asleep, but he just wants to scream. It's because he wants milk but I don't have any. If we were in the kitchen, I could get him water in a bottle, then he would stop crying. It's hot up here and this is where the rats live. I think his screaming makes them stay in their holes, but when he stops for breath, I can hear them, scritchy scritchy, then I wish he would scream some more. But it hurts my head inside and makes me want to cry. "Stop crying, please, go to sleep," I say. But he doesn't, he just cries and cries, high and high, his face all red and wet. My arms hurt. "You're too heavy," I tell him. "And I can't rock you for ever," I try explaining, scared because I don't know what else to do. My head burns with his screaming, so we scream together. I lie him on the floor so I can cover my ears, but then he screams new. "BE QUIET!" I scream at him. But he won't. So I push some of his blanket into his black hole mouth, and his voice gets further away and his eyes close. "Good boy, no more crying." I fold my feet under my legs – I don't want them rats chewing my toes. I'm looking round at the darkening triangle when he suddenly wakes up and screams louder and harder. Covering his face in blanket,

I sit on it. His crying gets very far away this time until it stops. I check for rats before I get up and watch birds flying through the clouds, out the little window in the roof.

'When the room got so dark I couldn't see my hands, Dad's head came through the floor. "You can come down now." I take the blanket off Sam and lift his little body. He breathes hard and his shiny wet eyes watch me as I hand him over to Dad. "You're good at looking after babies, Esther. We'll have to give you one of your own," Dad says.'

'Liar!' I cry at Bea. 'Everything he ever said was a lie. I wasn't good at looking after babies, I nearly killed him!'

Bea frowns. 'Esther, you were only seven. You were just a child yourself. Your father was wrong to ever put you in that position. Your mother and father were the parents – not you. Your baby brother was never your responsibility and even if the worst had happened, it still wouldn't have been your fault!'

I wish I could believe her. I desperately want to and if I'm going to get better, I know I need to.

After the session, I'm feeling exhausted, but lighter. I've voiced my worst fears out loud and discovered nothing horrendous happened. I didn't self-combust and as Bea points out – nobody actually died!

I can't sleep. It's the usual poisonous crap, but now Bea's in on it too. Counselling has only made things worse. I've put myself in danger. She'll probably report me to social services. I wish I could phone her and explain. I didn't mean to nearly kill the baby boy and I have got nice feelings for this baby boy of mine. I'd tell her I'm getting to know him and he does seem to have a lovely sweet nature. His eyes are a deep sea blue and his hair is golden fluff, like chick feathers. It's amazing how he's so new – he's milky white. I pressed his foot in a dish of blue paint for a keepsake and he gurgled happily. I stared at the inky map his little foot had made, and realised it proves he's real and he's in the world. He doesn't dirty his nappies on purpose, it's the milk that goes in, and he has no control over when it comes out. He's just a baby and babies don't know anything. I've got to be more careful what I tell Bea from now on. She might be tricking me into telling her things, then she'll have power over me.

I'm wary as I enter Bea's office for my second session. She's leaning back in her chair, acting relaxed and calm. 'Hi, Esther, how's it going?' she asks, smiling.

'Fine,' I reply airily, attempting to match her casual demeanour.

Getting straight to the point, she asks, 'How did you get on with your homework?'

'All right,' I reply lightly. She asked me to write about my flashbacks and do breathing techniques while I was having them.

'Great. So did anything come up? Anything that you'd like to explore?'

'No. I don't want to explore anything. This counselling is just a waste of time!' I snap irritably.

'Well, what are you doing here then?' she replies waspishly, surprising me.

I'm annoyed, but I didn't expect her to be as well. 'I dunno! Mostly just talking about things that I can't ever change while I'm supposed to be trying to be a good mum!'

She stops for a moment, as if thinking. But I want her to fire something at me; I'm ready. Instead she asks another one of her questions: 'What makes you think you aren't already a good mum?'

'Huh!' I retort cynically. 'Of course I'm not a good mum. My mum was a bad mum, and so was I before. So it makes sense that I'll be a bad mum again! Why wouldn't I be?'

'What do you mean "before"? Have you had a child already?'

'Yes, I suppose I have in a way, and I was meant to look after her,' I reply sadly, before explaining, 'In our house the older ones were meant to look after the younger ones and when Holly was born, Dad said she was mine to look after.'

Bea doesn't look like she understands any better and waits for me to continue.

Mum had a baby every year – 15 in all and I was number seven. So every year there was one more screaming black hole. As soon as one got popped out, Mum's belly would start growing big with the next. As we got older, we were supposed to look after the ones younger than us. Dad told me when I was eight I would be looking after the next one. I hoped having my own baby would be the same as having a doll – better even! I've wanted a doll for ages. Tiny Tears is her name and the girl next door has her. She has thick yellow curly hair and round shiny blue eyes that cry real tears, but when you lie her down they click closed. I fantasise about dressing her up in pink outfits and taking her for walks in her pink pram.

Instead, on 9 April 1984, a strange round-faced lady, with a silver upside down watch, pinned to her dress, came to our house. Then the house was hot and smelled strong of metal. Mum did her screaming and crying while the strange lady shouted, 'Push, push!' Big bowls of hot water disappeared into the dark room and came out as bowls of blood. Clean dry sheets and towels went in too and also came out wet and red. And then there was Holly. An angry squashed tomato – I bet she wished she'd stayed inside.

When Holly was born, I had to stay off school for a while and look after her. And now before I leave in the morning, I must make sure to give her a bottle of milk, change her nappy and get her dressed. It makes me tired, but when she looks at me and smiles I don't mind too much. I have to be careful to keep her away from Dad, as sometimes she cries for no reason and he would get angry that I'm not looking after her well enough.

For a while I manage to protect her from Dad. But it's no use; even before she can walk, he starts hurting her.

When I get home from school one day, I hear Holly's terrified screams and my tummy goes twisty. I frantically kick off my school shoes and burst into the kitchen. Usually when Dad is hurting someone else, you stay away. But it's Holly and I can't help it. Hot fire shoots through me at the sight of her bare little body, with a tea towel covering her head. Dad is bent over her, pressing down on her back with one hand and tapping her bottom with the stick, growling 'Stay still!' But she's just a baby and she doesn't understand. She wriggles. She screams and tries to pull away. I hop from one foot to the other in agony, begging her under my breath, 'Stay still, Holly. Please stay still.' If only I could see her face I would tell her, 'If you stay still, it will be over sooner and his anger will finish quicker!'

I shoot desperate looks at Mum, sitting in the corner. But, as usual, she isn't here. She has escaped inside a book, to somewhere where her children's cries don't matter. She isn't like other mums and definitely not like storybook mums – she's a nothing mum. For a moment, I wish for the impossible, that like a plastic mannequin in a shop, she will come to life and stop Dad. 'You're the only one he'll listen to!' I silently beg her. 'Please shout or scream, please just do something. Do anything to protect the baby girl!' But she doesn't, she never does and she never will.

Holly's twisting makes the tea towel fall from her head and suddenly I see her terrified wet red face, crumpled up in pain. 'NO DAD, PLEASE! Please stop hurting Holly!' I hear my voice scream.

Dad turns to me, amazed – he's not used to being interrupted. His lips curl in a jeer. 'Have something to say about it, do you, Esther?'

'I just ...' I falter, the words stuck in me.

I don't know what to say. I just know I need him to stop hurting her. Holly scrambles up from the floor, her eyes wide and terrified, watching Dad as she crawls away and takes cover behind the couch. Dad doesn't try to stop her. He's looking at me. 'Not so brave now, are you, Esther? What you going to do?'

Trembling and with my head lowered the carpet patterns blur. My armpits sting savagely at me and there's a fearful stabbing in my stomach. My body isn't my own, as I take off my clothes and lower myself to the ground in front of Dad. Shakily pulling the tea towel up over my head, I try to allow myself a little gap down the side, small enough that he doesn't see it, to help me guess when the pain is coming. My body tenses and I just want to cry out. But no tears, not now, I need to see. My skin prickles all over, as I hear the thin stick whip the air so fast it whistles, before Dad stops it right at the last second, and taps it lightly on the backs of my legs. A little scream escapes my throat and I hear him laugh, before suddenly shouting, 'Feet to the floor!' He whacks the bottoms of my feet hard, which had sprung up by themselves. Stupid feet, I silently curse, why doesn't my horrible body do as it's told? Dad does his pretending and laughing for a while longer. When he's had enough playing, he hits me everywhere, my bum and my back, over and over and over, hard stinging whips, until he gets tired out.

My face is wet and my throat aching and scratchy from quiet crying. The pain on my back and legs is stingy and numb for now, but I know it will get worse. Where he's hit me will be almost white, with little pink lines before they become long, swollen, reddish-purple lumps that will eventually go to dark grey-green bruises. But for now I must stay still, until Dad gives me permission to move. This might be straight away, if he wants me to do something. Or, like today, I have to lie and wait, while everybody goes on around me. I hate this most, my bare painful back and legs can be trodden on, or knocked into and I don't know where it's coming from. While I lie here, I pray Dad isn't watching and dare to slowly cross my feet and push my fists up under my chin. Maybe he will just forget about me, or I could have to wait, until he moves on to hurting one of my brothers or sisters, then I can get up.

Back in Bea's office tears fall from my chin, as I recall the pain of the abuse. But worse than that was Mum not giving a shit. 'See, she didn't give a toss about any of us. She was a shit mum. She just fucked off into books! We couldn't do that, we could never escape him!'

Bea wears her mild concerned expression. 'But why aren't you angrier with your dad?' she asks.

'Because he was a nutcase!' I retort, 'but Mum, she was a normal person from a normal background. She would have known it was wrong and she could have stopped him!'

'Could she?' Bea asks.

For a moment I'm too stunned to reply. But when I do, I feel annoyed at Bea's on-the-fence attitude. Even over the most obvious things. 'What do you mean, "could she"? Of course she could,' I angrily snap.

To Victoria,

I'm writing to you because my counsellor told me to. She said write to your mum about how you feel. But I'm not sure how I feel. She says I have to 'open the gate and trust the process' – whatever that means!

I'm angry mostly! I'm sure of that and I've got lots of questions I want to ask you. Did you never realise I'd grow up? Did you think I would be a defenceless child for ever? Didn't you think I would one day find out how wrong it all was? I want to know about when I was a baby. I know you didn't love me enough to look after me, but did you ever love me, even at the start, just a little? Was I a wanted child? Do you remember me as a little girl? Was I cute? Did passing strangers comment on me? Why did you never protect me? Why did you let him hurt me all the time? Why did you let me starve? Why didn't you love me? WHY DID YOU GIVE BIRTH TO ME?

You don't know Oliver. You'll never know him and what a wonderful little baby he is. I do everything I can with him, including taking him to massage classes. This morning we had the third one. It's quite an expensive course, £65 for five sessions. They say it's one of the best things you can do for bonding with your baby. But Oliver hates it. From the minute we walk into the room and find the other mums cross-legged, in a peaceful semi-circle, Oliver howls. I have to wrestle the clothes from his tense little body while the other babies are gently slipped from theirs. He cries harder – as if he knows what's coming. Sometimes I even get to pour out the oil and rub it in my hands to warm it. I am just about to put it on him, when he ups the volume and screeches ferociously until his little face is a purple scrunchie. So, as usual, with my eyes filled with tears of frustration, I have to pick him up and spend yet another session pacing the dismal community centre. While the normal mothers contentedly massage their perfect babies.

'Don't worry,' teacher coos, 'it will be better when it's part of his routine,' then I imagine blowing her away by roaring 'ROUTINE? WHAT FUCKING ROUTINE?'

I nearly left the baby the other day. He cried so long, I got scared he'd never stop. David was in the living room, so I laid the baby in his cot, like an angry red star. It was raining, but I didn't care, I just knew I had to be away from him.

I walked up around the houses at the back of ours and ended up sitting on the wet muddy earth by the duck pond. I stayed so long the ducks got brave enough to flock at my feet, demanding bread I hadn't got. I just kept thinking the baby boy is better off without me. It's better I go now, so he won't remember me. He's six weeks old and all I bring him is shit. But who will feed him? Who will look after him? And what if he's sent to a place where they don't love him?

I unlocked the front door and I paused on the threshold for a moment. How can there be only a few small steps, between such a giant decision?

Inside Oliver had gone to sleep, and everything was peaceful at last. 'Where have you been?' David asked.

'Just for a walk,' I mumbled.

Esther

'Please help me stop the flashbacks?' I beg Bea at our third session. 'They're so real, it's like I'm reliving the abuse over and over again!'

She explains it's because I've never dealt with the trauma of the abuse before, so the memories got suspended. Having Oliver has triggered them back to life. She tells me the medical term is post-traumatic stress disorder. 'If you want to get better, Esther, sooner or later you will have to deal with these memories properly,' she warns. 'You will have to learn to open the gate within yourself and let them come out.'

She then teaches me some meditation techniques so I can explore the abuse without getting overwhelmed by it.

Talking me down into what she calls a relaxed hypnotic state, Bea gently whispers, 'Imagine a big strong oak tree that's been growing for hundreds of years. To that tree we will attach an unbreakable metal rope. We are going to tie this rope around your waist and around the thickest part of the oak tree. When you feel secure enough, we are going to explore your past. Do you understand?'

'Yes,' I whisper, and in my mind, I examine the rope, pulling it, to test it.

When I feel secure, she asks, 'Esther, what does your past look like?'

I look at it from a distance. 'It's in a forest and it's huge and black. Like a very big lake, that goes down for ever,' I dully reply.

'Right. What we will do now is talk about your memories before we properly contextualise them. So they can be put in your past, where they belong. Okay?'

I agree, feeling myself slowly nod.

'All right,' Bea continues, 'as we do this, you must always keep in mind the most important part,' and even though I'm under hypnosis, I know what she's going to say and mouth it with her, 'Let the gate open and trust the process.'

When she brings me round after hypnosis, there's a few minutes of the session left and Bea casually asks, 'How's it going with Oliver?'

'Well,' I start, 'he's making such leaps in his development. Far ahead of the markers,' I gush. 'And his eyes follow you around the room,' I say, demonstrating with my own, before remembering something else. 'Oh and he's reaching for things too, like his toy giraffe the other day, he reached up and tried to bat it! He really is amazing, you wouldn't believe it!' I finish, grinning.

Bea smiles. 'But, you know what this means, don't you, Esther?'

I'd got carried away talking and forgotten there'd be questions. With Bea there are always questions. 'Um ...' I say, trying to figure out its relevance.

'It means,' Bea interrupts, 'that you must be amazing, because you made someone like him.'

'Thank you,' I say, blushing.

'No,' she replies firmly, 'I'm not saying it as a compliment, it's true.'

I walk out of her office on air.

When I'm playing with Oliver later, a little bit of me dares to hope she might be right.

I'm tense and fidgety as I arrive for my fourth session and when Bea asks, 'How are you feeling today, Esther?' I don't try to hide. 'I'm nervous. I can't do this any more. I'll have to stop coming!'

'Why are you nervous?' she asks.

'I've had to leave Oliver with a friend. I didn't want to, but David's at work!'

'Well, you could have brought him with you,' Bea offers, simply.

'What, to counselling?' I say, shocked at her even suggesting it. 'I can't bring him here! I'm a bad enough mother as it is. I don't want all his earliest memories being fucked up!' I snap.

'Esther, I'm sure he won't remember a—'

'No!' I interrupt, 'I'm fucking him up enough by dragging up all this crap and I don't want to do it any more!'

'How are you fucking him up, as you put it? By having counselling and trying to get better?'

'It's not just that. It's that I'm always unhappy. I can't sleep and I'm stressed. He's picking up on it all and it's probably damaging him for life!'

Bea considers what I've said for a moment. 'Esther, he's only a matter of weeks old. I'm quite certain he won't remember any of this. And, by the time he does have permanent memory, you're going to be much better. Then you'll be able to create wonderful life-long memories together! Isn't that something worth aiming for?'

As usual Bea makes perfect sense out of something that, only a few moments ago, seemed completely tangled up. I reluctantly nod my agreement.

'Talking of earliest memories, what's yours?'

'Being hungry,' I reply immediately.

'Hungry for what?'

'Everything,' I reply blankly. 'I thought the pain in my tummy was normal, until the day I learned it felt better if I ate something.'

I'm alone and I'm crying, my throat hurts, but mostly my tummy hurts. The good thing about getting older is I can get myself food. But first you must make sure Dad isn't home. There's goat feed in that big black bin, I've seen my older brothers and sisters eating it. Copying their example, I gather a couple of plastic crates and pile them against the bin. Unsteadily climbing onto the crates, I reach up and knock the lid off. Gripping the top of the barrel, I pull myself up to see my prize; crispy, delicious yellow flakes of corn and black chewy bits of black liquorice glint up at me, hidden among foul-tasting, dry green grass pellets.

But first the tricky bit, turning myself upside down, without toppling in. With one hand, I get a good hold of the inside of the barrel and I use the other to grab greedy handfuls of the feed. I fill the curled hem of my top, before carefully climbing backwards and dropping myself to the ground. I run and hide in the grass where, separating the feed, I scoff the flakes and liquorice.

When I get back to the house, I immediately sense something is wrong. Dad's home and he's on the warpath. I hear the older ones asking each other, 'Who did it? Who took the goat bin lid off and let the goats get in, so they could eat all the feed?' I'm cold and shaky and try to stay out of the way. But nobody considers it might be me anyway; I'm too young and small to do something like that, aren't I? I don't even go to school yet. But I couldn't help it – I was so hungry.

Dad lines up my older brothers and sisters and hits them over and over again until someone confesses. I guiltily watch from a distance, learning a valuable lesson – always replace the bin lid!

'I'll never let Oliver know hunger like that,' I promise myself aloud.

'I'm sure you won't,' Bea reassures me.

I look at her uncertainly. 'So do you think they'll give me a chance? You know, a chance to prove myself, before they take him?'

Bea looks confused. 'Before who takes him?'

Does she really not know? It feels so obvious, like I'm a blue alien sat here and Bea is pretending not to notice. 'The social workers!' I reply irritably.

I watch her response carefully to see if she's in with them. 'Esther, whatever makes you think they would just take your baby from you?'

Feeling weak under the pressure of holding in my fears, I dissolve into tears. I tell her how my father was jailed for the abuse he'd done to me and my brothers and sisters. But then I was put in care, where I attempted suicide. Then Orkney Social Work Department snatched my younger siblings and put them into care as well. I sob bitter tears about the forced adoption of my two youngest sisters and Adam's and my baby that never was. I finish by crying, 'Of course they could take him. They could come for him today, or just take him whenever they feel like it!'

Bea looks horrified. 'Well, I can certainly see why you would think they could, but believe me, nowadays they can't. We live in a civilised society and there are laws against that kind of thing!'

I nod, but I don't believe her. 'Maybe down here there are, but it could still happen in Orkney,' I protest, 'it's an evil place. Anything can happen there, it's got no laws.'

Bea leans back, steepling her fingers, as if deep in thought. 'It is never the place, Esther, it's the people. And you never know, one day you might even consider going back there. It sounds like it could help with your healing process.'

'Go back to Orkney?' I retort in disgust. 'Why would I ever do that?'

She looks at me in her usual serene way. 'Esther, if something feels that painful and you have such strong, negative feelings about it, it is always worth exploring.'

I look at her doubtfully, dismissing the idea immediately as Bea's therapy mumbo jumbo.

'Hello, little boy, have you been good?' I ask Oliver, when I pick him up from my friend's house. I'm sure there was a flicker of recognition in his deep blue eyes. It made me think that maybe all along all we had to do was get to know each other. And now he's beginning to learn that I'm his real mother – the same way I'm getting to know him as my baby.

Later that day after his bath, I laid him on the bed to dry him. He started giggling, like being dried was the funniest thing. I laughed back and started doing silly noises and making funny faces. He laughed even more. It sounded wonderful – fast, then slow and high and squeaky – it was the loveliest noise I ever heard.

'Esther, would you mind if we continued exploring where we finished last week?' Bea asks at the beginning of my fifth session.

My stomach flips nervously. 'What about it?'

'Well, there's a couple of things I don't understand,' she says, eyeing me suspiciously.

I feel my body tighten. I have to clench my fists to stop my hands from shaking. 'What don't you understand?' I ask, trying to hold her gaze.

She drops her head to one side inquiringly. 'Well, why did you attempt suicide? And why would that make the social workers take your siblings?'

There is a buzzing inside me, as if she's talking from very far away. The heavy black shadow that's been bearing down on me for so many years is pulling me under. I'm slipping and I must gasp for air. Tiny cracks splinter the walls and they become oozing wounds. The bricks and mortar melt and I feel myself burst, 'IF ONLY I HAD TOLD! It's all my fault! I destroyed my family, because I couldn't tell!' I rage, collapsing over her desk.

Bea silently passes me the tissues and waits a heartbeat, before she coaxes, 'Come on, Esther, trust the process. Open the gate and let it all come out. What couldn't you tell? What is it you've been hiding?'

Without meeting her gaze, I tearfully explain. 'When Dad went to jail, I couldn't tell the police about the sexual abuse. And when I went to Oakhill, a care worker called Adrian Batty started raping me and I couldn't tell then either. I tried talking to my best friend, Eliza, but I couldn't say it. It was like it was locked inside me or something. I didn't know what to do about it, I was desperate. So I tried to kill myself. I thought it would solve everything – but I fucked that up as well.

'Then they wouldn't send me home and they put me in a high security children's home. Ever since my dad was jailed, my family's social worker, Mona Drone, wanted to put my younger brothers and sisters into care. So when I couldn't tell, she said one of my older brothers must have raped me. I said it wasn't true, but they wouldn't believe me. They took my siblings into care because they said there was a chance they'd get abused. I tried really hard to tell someone, I really did, but the words wouldn't come out. If only I could have told about him, everything would have been so different! Why couldn't I tell, Bea, what's wrong with me?' I tearfully demand.

Bea's hand is on my arm. 'Esther, there is nothing wrong with you. You have been very badly betrayed and let down and I am so sorry,' she gently replies.

I inhale sharply, I'd been expecting recriminations, accusations and even insults, but instead she repeats herself, while wiping tears from her eyes.

'What do you mean?' I ask unsteadily.

'Can't you see? None of this is your fault! But I don't think it's the fault of the people you've been blaming all these years, either! Because of your past, your wiring has got twisted and if there's any hope of you ever recovering, we've got to straighten it out,' she explains. 'It seems to me that you and your family were victims of a very corrupt system up there, and it was the social workers' handling of the situation that enabled a certain someone to abuse it, or more accurately, abuse you.'

I go to interrupt, but Bea cuts me off. 'If that person hadn't done what he did to you, then nothing else could have happened. After your father's imprisonment, everything you and your family have been put through, and that goes for the other four families, is a direct result of one person's actions!'

My mind is buzzing as I try to figure out who Bea is talking about. She continues, 'If this was a triangle, there is one point you are missing. You have your own guilt well covered and you've pinpointed the Social Work Department up in Orkney, but who is at the third point?' she asks earnestly.

I return her stare, feeling confused – does she mean Mum or Dad?

'Okay,' she goes on, 'it's very important you get this, Esther, so let's look at it from their perspective. You were an incredibly vulnerable 14-year-old girl whose father had recently been jailed for physically and sexually abusing you. This person had access to your files, so they knew your history well. They could predict what you would and, more importantly, what you wouldn't do – tell!'

'ADRIAN BATTY!' I gasp.

'You've got it!' Bea breathes. 'He knew exactly what he was doing, right from the start. It was a well-planned predatory attack, over and over again. And he let you down so badly, not just as a man, but as an authority figure. He is the cause of all of this, not you.'

I listen in stunned silence as she explains further. 'He would have known from your file how much you struggled to tell about the abuse your dad had done to you. You had been trained not to tell your whole life, and he took advantage of that in the most depraved way possible. You were his victim, the perfect victim – a locked box!'

By the time she's finished my back is pressed against my chair, while my hands fiercely wipe away the tears that course down my cheeks – I don't want to miss a word!

It hits me like a thunderbolt. For all these years, the closest thing to my heart has been the secrets from my past. I claimed victory every time I stopped someone from getting to know me, or anything about me. Thinking the further people were from me was a measure of how clever I was. Always holding back, never opening up, laying false trails and, if all else failed, running away. I had created my own prison built from abuse, fear and anger. It kept others out, but ultimately it locked me in. The precious treasures I so desperately gripped onto and defended weren't gold but poison. That poison was preventing me from opening up and living my life. I had become the living dead, a ghost floating on the edge of the world. The scars and pain from the abusers, who were supposed to love me and look after me, had shut me down. So while I wouldn't feel hurt any more, neither would I feel love or happiness.

I had obliterated potential relationships before they ever had a chance to begin. But now it endangered the most important relationship of my life: the one between my son and me! I have to change and I have to change now!

I feel the poison flaking from me like dry sand, and with it years of crippling guilt and knife-sharp pain begin to lift. But Bea hasn't quite finished. 'Adrian made you a victim then, Esther, but it's up to you, whether you continue being one!' she warns.

'Well, they aren't going to prosecute Mum!' I announce, slumping into the chair beside Bea's desk, at our sixth and final session.

Bea eyes me calmly. 'Aren't they?' she asks lightly.

'No,' I say shortly, folding my arms.

'And why do you think that might be?' Bea asks, leaning back.

I feel myself twitching in irritation. I was expecting some surprise, maybe even shock. Not the same silly questions upon questions. 'Well, the Criminal Prosecution Service's reason,' I reply exasperatedly, 'is she hasn't abused any children in the 20 years since Dad was jailed. So, they say, there isn't enough danger to the public to justify prosecuting her!'

I wait – hoping maybe for a little outrage. But none is forthcoming. Bea is her same, annoyingly calm self. So I resign myself to the question I know will follow.

'And has she abused any children in the last 20 years?'

I know the answer, but I don't want to say.

Bea studies me for a moment. 'When your father went to jail, what did she do? Did she continue to abuse you?'

'No,' I reply, 'but ...'

'Well, what did she do?' Bea interrupts. 'Did someone have to stop her?'

'No, they didn't,' I reply, remembering. 'She got tablets from the doctor, but that's not the—'

'What was she like after she'd taken the tablets, Esther?'

I think back. 'It was like she woke up,' I whisper, 'like she'd been in a dream and came back to life as a different person,' I add quietly. I feel my eyes watering, as I recall how Dad going to prison was the key to Mum's release.

Bea passes the tissues and waits for a moment. 'Do you think it's possible that she was in fact a different person? That the shadow of a mother you grew up with was someone else? Perhaps an abused woman in a deep depression?'

'I'm not sure what you mean,' I reply, only half getting it.

'Well, are you the same person who first walked through that door?'

'No, I'm not,' I say, recalling the journey I've been on this last couple of months.

'Do you think that if your mum could have got help earlier, she would have changed sooner? That maybe if she had been lucky enough to have been born in a different time, her life might have been different?'

Then it all becomes clear. If I had been born in Mum's time, I wouldn't have been able to get help either. I remember how she got better and she was a good mum. But after only a couple of years ... and I cry out, horrified at the memory. She was made brutally childless. I'd been seeing it from my point of view. I'd been so full of my own fear of them taking Oliver from me, I had forgotten that for one mother, that nightmare had been a reality.

'Mum, what happened?'

She knows what I'm talking about and it's as if she's been waiting for my call. In a voice not much louder than a whisper, she asks, 'Where would you like me to start?'

'At the beginning,' I reply, 'when you had your first baby, like me.'

Her voice cracks with pain as she confesses, 'When I met your father I told him I didn't want children and he seemed okay with it. But then I got pregnant. I begged him to let me have her adopted and he agreed. But when I had her, he wouldn't let me, he forced me to keep her. I couldn't believe such hate was possible for something so helpless, an angry alien suckling on me, clenched to me ...'

I can't listen to her talking about my oldest sister this way. I interrupt, 'All the years of my childhood, you seemed dead. Do you remember any of those times?'

She sounds sad. 'They are only grey fuzzy shapeless memories. It's as if they happened in someone else's life, not mine,' she admits.

'But,' I continue, 'when Dad went to jail what changed? How come you seemed so different?'

'I don't know,' she confesses weakly. 'I went to the doctor and he put me on tablets. It took a few weeks before one day I woke up and realised that he wouldn't be coming back from jail. I'd escaped. But then I looked around and I had all these children. Children I'd given birth to in a far-away place and I started getting to know them and their personalities ...'

I am reminded of Oliver and me and how we're getting to know one another and how our relationship is growing stronger day by day.

Mum goes on. 'Then one day I realised I loved you all, deeper than life itself. And when they took the younger ones, I knew all I could do was fight. It was my job to look after them, for good or bad – because I was their mother!' she says, breaking into a whimper.

As she continues talking, I see her as the young girl she was – barely 20, struggling with her first baby in the 1960s. She explains how nobody talked about post-natal depression then. 'I was scared I'd be thrown into a mental hospital,' she admits. So, instead, with the birth of every child, the bottled-up feelings got worse. They turned septic and slowly but surely killed all of her emotions, until she became the empty shell of a mother from my childhood.

Suddenly I'm filled with deep burning compassion and sadness for her. She had 15 babies, but she never knew baby love. And when she realised the preciousness of what she had, it was all too late – her arms were made brutally empty. What had she become? A child is an orphan when it loses its parents, but what is a parent when it loses its children? Maybe, as her relentless fighting proved, they are always a mother, wherever their children are. I feel desperately sad that her time has gone, and it wasn't how it should have been for her or any of us. When Dad went to jail, it wasn't a new start – it was the beginning of a new nightmare. It's as if through Mum I have glimpsed a ghost from my possible future. And I can't help feeling grateful that I have been given the chance to mother the best way I can. She can't change her past, but because of her I can choose my future.

I phone Mum every couple of days and at first our conversations are stilted and awkward, as if we are two strangers getting to know one another, which in lots of ways we are. She asks me about my life and Oliver, and I tell her and we build from there.

*

Four months later I'm sitting on the couch with Oliver when I realise I'm at a place I never dared imagine I would get to – I'm in the moment, with my seven-month-old baby boy. At first, I hated how he took me back to the past, but now I know I needed to go there. And with his new eyes he has brought me back into the present with him. It is only now, that I am still and I hear my breath, I realise how long and hard I've been running.

Oliver reaches his chubby little arms up to me, open and waiting, his sparkly blue eyes full of recognition. It is up to me. I fill my arms with him. 'I love you, Oliver,' I whisper, 'I love you with all of my heart. You are my son and I am your mother.'

EPILOGUE

Return to Devil's Island

It is 2010, Oliver is four years old and we are travelling up to Orkney. We are joined by his little brother Max, who has just turned one. My heart races as I scan the other passengers' faces while boarding the ferry at John O'Groats. But Bea's words drive me on: 'If something is that painful it has got to be worth exploring.'

I had been expecting the wild angry waves and overwhelming sickness of my childhood, but today the Atlantic Ocean is calm and serene and she sparkles lazily in the August sun. My stomach plunges at a 'Welcome to Orkney' sign as we drive in from the pier. Looking round I gasp – there it is – my childhood home! Only two fields away. Crook Farm – three little rectangles in the distance.

Today is the best of my childhood summer memories. Under vast blue Viking skies on a landscape of soft yellows and heathery mauves, the warm sun is on my skin and the slightest of breezes carry the scent of wild Scottish flowers. In the distance a farmer's tractor trundles amid a storm of diving seagulls that pluck fat worms from freshly turned soil. David, my sons and I wander along the stony beach – the one I raced to with my sister Bella and played often, with my siblings, as a girl. Sometimes I will momentarily forget how time has left my childhood family behind. I turn, expecting to see Bella at my side. When I find she is not there, I want to cry out, 'Stop, we can't leave my sister. She needs me! We must stay here in case she comes back!' But, instead there is David and my two boys – my future happiness, forever intertwined with my bitterly painful past.

Leaving the beach behind we drive towards Crook Farm. I need to get a closer look. When we are parked outside the gate at the end of the drive my chest tightens and tears well in my eyes. I get out and sit alone for a few minutes to remember. Climbing into the car, Oliver's voice brings me back from the dark place I've been. 'But Mummy, you haven't opened the gate!' he says in surprise.

'No, we're not going to the house,' I reply, trying to adopt a cheerful tone.

'Well,' David starts, 'will you ever come here again?'

Oliver joins in. 'Yes, Mummy, open the gate.'

Despite my emotional rawness, I feel a glimmer of excitement at the thought of seeing Crook Farm again. Bea's words ring in my ears: 'Trust the process and open the gate.' I push the gate – relishing the metal's force against gravel and stone – wide open, feeling the memories behind it flood into me.

Two collie dogs leap up at the car and bound about us excitedly as we get out. A man with a thick dark beard wearing blue overalls ambles over, his cheery round face smiling, 'How do?'

'Hi,' I nervously reply, uncertain of the reception I'll get when I admit who I am. 'I used to live here. I was one of the W children,' I explain. Did I see him flinch?

'Well, I expect you'd like to have a look around,' he offers warmly, gesturing to the house.

His children come out to see who's here – as I did myself when a child. They look like happy, loved children and Crook Farm feels light and hopeful. But nothing can stop pain-filled stabs of nostalgia swirling up around me as the salty sea air takes me straight back – reminding me all at once of everything. The farmer shows me round. And to the smell and sounds of my past, I politely nod and smile at all the changes he's made to the ruins of my childhood. Of course I can't look properly, because all I want to say is, 'Would you mind leaving now, this is my family's home.'

But they are just an ordinary family, mother, father and three children. And it suddenly hits me why my family were doomed from the moment we set foot here. Dad was already on the run from the authorities. Orkney was never a satanic island – it was my father who was the devil.

'What was that place?' asks Oliver, as I'm buckling him into his car seat.

'That's where I used to live with my family.'

'But Mummy, we're your family.'

'Yes, Oliver,' I smile. 'You are my family!'

Afterword

I have needed to write *If Only I Had Told* since I was 17, so it has taken me 20 years.

Other books have been written about Orkney's satanic sex scandal. A few documentaries have been made, countless articles have been penned and even a play was staged. All were searching for one thing: the truth.

Although none of them would ever find it, because they never asked the right people. For the first time, as heartbreaking as it has been, I have dared to tell my story. I have attempted to answer why those children were taken and why my own siblings were snatched and ultimately what it took to bring down a whole community, pitting them against the state.

But it would take giving birth to my son in 2006, a full 14 years later, for me to dare start writing my story. I picture my sons reading it one day and exclaiming, 'Ah, now it all makes sense. Now we understand why you struggled so much to be a mother.'

I am not saying all parents from abusive backgrounds will mess it up. But having a baby doesn't magically transform anyone into a good parent. Also it is a sad fact of life that what you are taught as a child, good or bad, is incredibly difficult not to replicate yourself when you become a parent. Initially, I found trying to be a good mother comparable to being thrown into a foreign country where I didn't understand the accent or the customs. But while it has been the most challenging journey I have ever been on, it has also been the most rewarding.

The last 20 years of my life have been riddled with guilty questions. Why didn't I tell the secrets I knew earlier? If I had told, would it have changed anything? Would my siblings still have been taken into care? Would the other families' children have been snatched? Would there have ever been a £6 million inquiry? And would the child care system in Scotland have needed overhauling? It seems almost inconceivable that one wrong turn in life can change everything, forever.

As I write this, child abuse allegations are coming to light involving a television star of my youth, Jimmy Savile. This man was highly respected, especially with regard to the charity work he did and the millions he raised. But sadly, it appears his professional life was nothing more than an elaborate deception, concealing his depraved appetite for abusing children. In the early stages of the revelations, a lot of criticism was aimed at the victims. Why had they waited until he had died before they had said anything? If the abuse was that bad, why hadn't they come forward sooner?

First of all, and perhaps most importantly, abusers have a victim-radar. They know which children to target. Whether this is due to a child's innate vulnerability or signs that show they have suffered from previous abuse, abusers make it their business to be able to tell who will be a silent victim. Once the child has been abused, the perpetrator will know their victim is likely to believe they have caused the abuse.

Then, due to low self-esteem, the victim will struggle with the confidence needed to tell, fearing they won't be believed. To report sexual abuse to adults is perhaps the hardest thing for a vulnerable child to do.

In order to tell, the victim needs to reach a point in their lives where they have high enough self-esteem to believe that they do not deserve the abuse they have suffered. Then a good support network is needed, including someone they can trust enough to confide in. But when you have been abused, high self-worth and trust are the areas you struggle with most.

Social workers are the adults children are supposed to be able to confide in. I now realise that social workers have a difficult job to do. They walk the thin line between 'Why didn't you do something?' and 'Why don't you stop interfering in other people's business?' However, I must speak from the point of view of a child who had a social worker at ten years of age. Despite this, it was another four years before my father was imprisoned for the abuse of my siblings and me.

Through my extensive childhood contact with social workers, both in and out of the care system, I recall two distinct types. The social worker my siblings and I had, who clocked in, shut his eyes to anything that would cause him hassle or paperwork, and those who are doing the job because they genuinely care about young people and want to help.

Unfortunately, even if I had told the social workers in my life at that time, I don't believe they would have listened. In a minefield of a job, where decisions sometimes have tragic consequences, I believe social workers should aim to keep an open mind and never judge: the abused does not always become the abuser. But above everything else, children need them to listen, listen and listen again.

During my siblings' so-called disclosure therapy sessions, the social workers did not appear to have given any consideration to the fact that they were dealing with children who had been emotionally, physically and sexually abused by their father before he was jailed. Instead they made massive assumptions in the interests of creating a picture of a satanic sex ring, involving many other families, to fit in with what they already believed. Throughout their interviews, my siblings made the connections for them, but the social workers did not hear them: they were too busy listening to each other.

But the job of safeguarding children does not solely rest on the shoulders of social workers. I recall the police being called to my childhood home on several occasions. Between our early social worker and the police, my siblings and I suffered years of unnecessary abuse. I can't help feeling bitter that their inaction not only prolonged our suffering but also, in turning a blind eye, sanctioned it.

I don't believe a person ever truly recovers from child abuse but, like the grief you feel after the death of a loved one, it is something you learn to live with. Challenges come up often and without warning. This might be during interactions with ordinary people, or with those in authority, or like me, everything hitting you all at once, when you give birth to your children.

On the positive side, I believe being abused has made me a more compassionate and caring person, with a desire to help others who have suffered.

When I was pregnant I often wished there was someone or somewhere I could turn to for help and advice on issues that were pertinent for me, due to my past. Unfortunately there wasn't, so I have since set up Survivormum.com. Survivormum.com is aimed at reaching out to parents like myself, who want to not only survive abuse, but thrive.

Through writing this book, I have realised I would never have been able to tell before now. I had been raised from a baby to hide secrets and keep them away, becoming the perfect victim – a locked box.

So today I tell. I tell for my sons, so one day they will know the truth. I tell for other victims of abuse, because I know that the hardest thing to ever do is tell, and I hope that, in so doing, one day they can find a way to tell their own story. But I tell mostly for the little girl I was, the one who never could.

Questions I continue to search for answers to:

1. Why was my sister Bella's testimony allowed to stand following her psychiatric assessment?
2. Why were no allegations of sibling abuse ever tried in legal court?
3. Did the Orkney Social Work Department lie about my family, conceal evidence and, when their backs were against the wall, did they steal evidence? If so, why?
4. Did the council and the Social Work Department make life so difficult for Judith Hope after her reinstatement? Why wouldn't they let her do her job?
5. What did Orkney Social Work Department have to gain, or more importantly lose, by behaving the way they did?

6. Why didn't the remit of the inquiry into satanic abuse cover my family?

7. Why weren't experts who would have been able to advise the Orkney inquiry on my family's plight given a voice at the inquiry?

8. Why did the social work system keep my siblings in care for so long?

9. How did Orkney Social Work Department get away with having my two youngest sisters adopted?

10. Why have my family never received an apology for all the needless anguish and suffering we have been through?

Acknowledgements

Thank you to my siblings Eddy, Stella, John, May and Bill.

Thank you to my friends Helen, Jen, James, Sarah, Vera and Rob. With a special thank you to Brian for allowing me the time and space to write this.

And another very special thank you to Charlotte Cole at Ebury for making editing this book so much less painful than it otherwise could have been.

About the author

Esther W spent much of her childhood growing up on South Ronaldsay in Orkney, where her father was convicted of physical and sexual abuse. Today, Esther has a BA in design and lives in the West Midlands. Her website and blog is survivormum.com, where she charts the day-to-day demands of being a mother to two wonderful and very active boys while breaking the chains of her past.